Helmut Schmidt and British–German Relations

The former West German chancellor Helmut Schmidt grew up as a devout Anglophile, yet he clashed heavily and repeatedly with his British counterparts Harold Wilson, James Callaghan and Margaret Thatcher during his time in office. *Helmut Schmidt and British–German Relations* looks at Schmidt's personal experience to explore how and why Britain and Germany rarely saw eye-to-eye over European integration, uncovering the two countries' deeply competing visions and incompatible strategies for post-war Europe. But it also zooms out to reveal the remarkable extent of simultaneous British–German cooperation in fostering joint European interests on the wider international stage, not least within the transatlantic alliance against the background of a worsening superpower relationship. By connecting these two key areas of bilateral cooperation, Mathias Haeussler offers a major reinterpretation of the bilateral relationship under Schmidt, relevant to anybody interested in British-German relations, European integration and the Cold War.

MATHIAS HAEUSSLER is Assistant Professor (*Akademischer Rat a.Z.*) at Regensburg University in Germany, having previously been Lumley Research Fellow at Magdalene College, Cambridge. He has held fellowships at Bonn University and the Library of Congress.

Helmut Schmidt and British–German Relations

A European Misunderstanding

MATHIAS HAEUSSLER
University of Regensburg, Germany

CAMBRIDGE
UNIVERSITY PRESS

University Printing House, Cambridge CB2 8BS, United Kingdom

One Liberty Plaza, 20th Floor, New York, NY 10006, USA

477 Williamstown Road, Port Melbourne, VIC 3207, Australia

314–321, 3rd Floor, Plot 3, Splendor Forum, Jasola District Centre,
New Delhi – 110025, India

79 Anson Road, #06–04/06, Singapore 079906

Cambridge University Press is part of the University of Cambridge.

It furthers the University's mission by disseminating knowledge in the pursuit of
education, learning, and research at the highest international levels of excellence.

www.cambridge.org
Information on this title: www.cambridge.org/9781108482639
DOI: 10.1017/9781108697132

© Mathias Haeussler 2019

This publication is in copyright. Subject to statutory exception
and to the provisions of relevant collective licensing agreements,
no reproduction of any part may take place without the written
permission of Cambridge University Press.

First published 2019

Printed in the United Kingdom by TJ International Ltd, Padstow Cornwall

A catalogue record for this publication is available from the British Library.

Library of Congress Cataloging-in-Publication Data
Names: Haeussler, Mathias, 1988– author.
Title: Helmut Schmidt and British-German relations : a European
misunderstanding / Mathias Haeussler.
Description: Cambridge, United Kingdom ; New York, NY : Cambridge University
Press, 2019. | Includes bibliographical references and index.
Identifiers: LCCN 2018061320 | ISBN 9781108482639 (alk. paper)
Subjects: LCSH: Schmidt, Helmut, 1918–2015. | Prime ministers – Germany (West) –
Biography. | Great Britain – Relations – Germany (West) | Germany (West) –
Relations – Great Britain. | Europe – Economic integration.
Classification: LCC DD260.85 .H34 2019 | DDC 327.4104309/045–dc23
LC record available at https://lccn.loc.gov/2018061320

ISBN 978-1-108-48263-9 Hardback

Cambridge University Press has no responsibility for the persistence or accuracy of
URLs for external or third-party internet websites referred to in this publication
and does not guarantee that any content on such websites is, or will remain,
accurate or appropriate.

Contents

List of Illustrations	*page*	vi
Acknowledgements		viii
List of Abbreviations		xii
Introduction		1
1 The Young Helmut Schmidt and British–German Relations, 1945–1974		21
2 Harold Wilson, 1974–1976		54
3 James Callaghan, 1976–1979		100
4 Margaret Thatcher, 1979–1982		149
Conclusions		208
Bibliography		222
Index		246

Illustrations

1.1 Helmut Schmidt during a three-week school exchange to Manchester at the age of thirteen, July 1932. Source: Bundeskanzler-Helmut-Schmidt-Stiftung Archiv. *page* 25

1.2 As Minister of Defence, Helmut Schmidt established a close partnership with his British counterpart Denis Healey, pictured here in October 1969. Source: Bundeskanzler-Helmut-Schmidt-Stiftung Archiv. 45

2.1 Helmut Schmidt speaking to the Labour Party Conference on Europe, 30 November 1974. Source: Photo by Roger Jackson & Peter Cade/Central Press/Hulton Archive/Getty Images. 71

2.2 French President Giscard D' Estaing invites Prime Minister Harold Wilson to move in closer for 'La Photo de Famille' at the first world economic summit at Rambouillet, 17 November 1975. Source: Bettmann/Getty Images. 91

3.1 James Callaghan enjoyed excellent personal relationships with his European partner Helmut Schmidt, 1977. Source: Photo by Roger Jackson & Peter Cade/Central Press/Hulton Archive/Getty Images. 105

3.2 James Callaghan (left) frequently had to mediate the strained relationship between the American President Jimmy Carter (centre) and Helmut Schmidt (right). Source: Photo by Evening Standard/Hulton Archive/Getty Images. 135

4.1 The row over Britain's contributions to the European Commission budget dominated the complicated relationship between Helmut Schmidt (right) and Margaret Thatcher (left). Source: Photo by Régis BOSSU/Sygma via Getty Images. 176

List of Illustrations vii

4.2 In spite of their regular fallouts over the European
Community budget, Helmut Schmidt (left) and Margaret
Thatcher (centre) cooperated closely in trying to mediate
US Cold War policies under Jimmy Carter and Ronald
Reagan, 11 May 1981. Source: Bettmann/Getty Images.   203

Acknowledgements

Helmut Schmidt's former secretary once claimed that the biggest sign of gratitude she could ever hope to receive from her boss was one of silent approval.[1] Trying to avoid overidentification with my book's key protagonist, I would instead like to express my deep appreciation to the many people and institutions without whom this project would never have been possible. First and foremost, my doctoral supervisor David Reynolds has my gratitude for many more reasons than I am able to mention here. His detailed and extensive comments on my work at all stages of the research and writing process have been of enormous help and encouragement. He has also offered invaluable personal support at crucial stages. I would also like to thank my adviser, Sir Richard J. Evans, as well as my examiners Anne Deighton and Kristina Spohr, whose incisive feedback and support offered invaluable help and inspiration at various stages of the project. I am also grateful to the British Arts and Humanities Research Council (AHRC) for providing me with a full doctoral grant (Grant number: AH/J500094/1) that enabled me to concentrate fully on my research without having to worry about finances. Finally, I am extremely fortunate to complete the book as Lumley Research Fellow at Magdalene College Cambridge, and I am deeply grateful to the Master and Fellows for their generosity as well as for providing a most inspiring and friendly intellectual home over the past three years.

My research has greatly benefited from numerous stays abroad, which exposed me to different academic cultures and helped me approach my topic from new perspectives. In 2012–13, I spent one academic year as a DAAD scholar (*Forschungsstipendiat*) at the Rheinische Friedrich-Wilhelms-Universität Bonn, where Dominik Geppert has proved a most supportive mentor and welcoming host. I would also like to thank Jessica Gienow-Hecht (now at the Freie

---

[1] *Die Zeit*, 11 December 2008.

Acknowledgements ix

Universität Berlin) for integrating me so well into the academic life at the 'neighbouring' University of Cologne. In 2014, I benefited enormously from a four-month research stay at the John W. Kluge Center at the Library of Congress in Washington DC, which offers the most stimulating and vibrant research environment one can imagine. The Annual Thesis Prize of the British International History Group was a crucial display of confidence in my work during the very final stages of the writing process, and I am very honoured to have received the award. Finally, the staff at Cambridge University Press, particularly my editor Liz Friend-Smith, have been consistently brilliant in guiding me through the complicated process of writing my first-ever book, and I am also very grateful to the three anonymous readers for their incredibly supportive and insightful comments on the manuscript.

Historical research inevitably depends on the quality of available sources, and this book would not have been possible without the generous help and assistance of countless archivists and librarians. Heike Lemke at the Privates-Helmut-Schmidt-Archiv (Hamburg; now the Bundeskanzler-Helmut-Schmidt-Stiftung Archiv) deserves to be singled out for tirelessly browsing through the incredibly rich and extensive files preserved at the archive. I would also like to thank the staff at the Bundesarchiv (Koblenz), the Friedrich-Ebert-Stiftung (Bonn), the Gerald Ford Presidential Library (Ann Arbor, MI), the Jimmy Carter Presidential Library (Atlanta, GA), the Library of Congress (Washington DC), the Politisches Archiv des Auswärtigen Amts (Berlin), the Ronald Reagan Presidential Library (Simi Valley, CA), and The National Archives (Kew) for all their help and support. Finally, I would like to thank the late Helmut Schmidt for granting access to his political and private archives, as well as for conducting an extensive interview in September 2013.

Over the years, I have benefitted enormously from inspiring and stimulating exchanges with many friends and colleagues in the academy, many of whom have also read and commented on various parts of my work. I would particularly like to thank Martin Albers, Edoardo Andreoni, Lindsay Aqui, Susan Colbourn, Christopher Cotton, Ruud van Dijk, Catherine Evans, Michael Gehler, Florian Greiner, Jonathan Hunt, Haakon Ikonomou, Piers Ludlow, Hannah Malone, Emmanuel Mourlon-Druol, Glen O'Hara, Martin Herzer, Eirini Karamouzi, Jens Kreutzfeldt, Andreas Lutsch, Gottfried Niedhart, Helen Parr, Alexander Reinfeldt, Angela Romano, Robert

Saunders, Padraic Scanlan, Thomas Schwartz, Marius Strubenhoff, Henning Türk, and Jonathan Wright. Mechthild Roos deserves to be singled out for having read and commented on countless drafts of the manuscript, and her always incisive and good-humoured feedback – as well as her singularly scrupulous attention to detail – have made the final book a much better one. I am also deeply grateful for the congenial friendship that has developed in our daily 'virtual office' over the past few years.

The reason I decided to embark upon doctoral research in history in the first place is due not least to the incredibly stimulating intellectual environment I have experienced during my undergraduate studies at the Department of History at Queen Mary University of London, as well as during my MPhil in Modern European History at the University of Cambridge, and I would particularly like to thank James Ellison, Christina von Hodenberg, Joel Isaac, Jon Lawrence, Helen McCarthy, and the late Professor John Ramsden for their inspiration and encouragement at the earliest stages of my academic career. James Ellison in particular has played a crucial role in sparking my interest in 'Britain and Europe' in the first place and continues to be a most supportive mentor to this day, whereas John Ramsden not only convinced me of the merits of studying history in the first place, but also managed to drag me into the Queen Mary Players! Given his own significant work on British-German relations, I am saddened that he did not live to see this book published.

Research and writing can be a lonely and rather isolating experience at times, I therefore count myself extremely lucky to be surrounded by a close circle of wonderful friends who have kept me focused on what is really important in life. Particular mention deserve Florian Bruns; Phillip Feier; Anja Fricke; Patrick Igoe; Alexa Kornau; Paul, Katharina, and Mathilda Langfermann; Jasmin Lörchner; Hannah Malone; Wanda Martini; Thomas McCall; Maximilian and Katrin Meckes; Lizzie Norton-Henry; Anna Ross; Matthias Scherer; Manuel Wagner; Maximilian Westphal and Katharina Zech. Quite a few have provided a physical as well as an emotional 'home away from home' at times, and I will always cherish the many memories of my stays in Cologne, Galveston, Hamburg, Hanover, Leipzig, London, Munich or San Francisco. Most importantly, Maria-Theresa has been an unfailing 'rock' of stability, as well as the most supportive and loving partner I could ever have dreamed of. I cannot put in words how much I am

Acknowledgements xi

looking forward to the new adventures and experiences we are about to embark upon.

Finally, the biggest thanks are due to my family. During my time in the United States, I was extraordinarily fortunate to regularly escape the 'DC smoke' to visit the American part of my family in Boston. I will always treasure the many memories of that period, and I will always look back fondly on the great hospitality of the McLaughlin family, and in particular my late great-aunt Annmarie McLaughlin. I would also like to thank Marian and Fred Brown, who might well be considered my 'unofficial' family in the United Kingdom. Most gratitude, however, is due to my 'official' family. My grandmothers Betty Häußler and the late Helene Kristen, as well as my parents, Astrid and Gerhard Häußler, have offered unfailing encouragement and support over the past few years in many more ways than I can ever hope to repay. In fact, the very reason that I live and breathe my subject perhaps even more than many others is due to my parents' rather bold decision in August 2002 to move from the small Bavarian town of Dorfen to the rather more cosmopolitan city of London. Little did I know at the time what a profound impact this decision would have on my future life and work.

Cambridge and Munich, 13 June 2018.

Abbreviations

BAOR	British Army of the Rhine
BBC	British Broadcasting Cooperation
BK	*Bundeskanzler* (Federal Chancellor)
BKA	*Bundeskanzleramt* (Federal Chancellery)
BMWi	*Bundesministerium für Wirtschaft und Energie* (Federal Ministry for Economic Affairs and Energy)
BPA	*Bundespresseamt* (Federal Press Office)
CAP	Common Agricultural Policy
CDU	Christian Democratic Union of Germany (*Christlich Demokratische Union Deutschlands*)
COCOM	Coordinating Committee on Multilateral Export Controls
CSCE	Conference on Security and Co-operation in Europe
CSU	Christian Social Union in Bavaria (*Christlich-Soziale Union in Bayern*)
DM	Deutsche Mark
EC	European Communities (sometimes also: European Community); included ECSC, Euratom and EEC
ECSC	European Coal and Steal Community
EEC	European Economic Community
EG	*Europäische Gemeinschaft/Europäische Gemeinschaften* (see EC)
EMS	European Monetary System
EMU	Economic and Monetary Union
EP	European Parliament
EPC	European Political Cooperation
ERW	Enhanced Radiation Warhead
EUA	European Unit of Account

List of Abbreviations   xiii

FBS	Forward-Based Systems
FCO	Foreign and Commonwealth Office
FDP	Free Democratic Party (*Freie Demokratische Partei*)
FRG	Federal Republic of Germany (*Bundesrepublik Deutschland*)
GDR	German Democratic Republic (*Deutsche Demokratische Republik*)
GLCM	Ground-Launched Cruise Missile
GNP	Gross National Product
HPG	High Level Planning Group (of NATO)
IISS	International Institute for Strategic Studies, London
IMF	International Monetary Fund
INF	Intermediate-Range Nuclear Force
ITN	Independent Television Network
JET	Joint European Torus
LRTNF	Long-Range Theatre Nuclear Forces
MAD	Mutually Assured Destruction
MBFR	Mutual and Balanced Force Reductions
MCA	Monetary Compensatory Amounts
MLF	Multilateral Force
MEP	Member of the European Parliament
MP	Member of Parliament
NATO	North Atlantic Treaty Organization
NEC	National Executive Council (of the British Labour Party)
NPG	Nuclear Planning Group (of NATO)
NSC	National Security Council
OECD	Organisation for Economic Co-operation and Development
OPEC	Organization of the Petroleum Exporting Countries
PDRY	People's Democratic Republic of Yemen
PM	Prime Minister
POW	Prisoner of War
PREM	Prime Minister's Office
QMV	Qualified Majority Voting
SALT I and II	Strategic Arms Limitation Talks I and II

SAS	Special Air Service
SPD	Social Democratic Party of Germany (*Sozialdemokratische Partei Deutschlands*)
TNF	Theatre Nuclear Forces
TUC	Trade Union Congress
VAT	Value-Added Tax
WEU	Western European Union

Introduction

> Almost thirty years ago, in 1957, when the Treaty of Rome that set up the European Economic Community was before the German parliament for ratification, I abstained from voting because I then thought – much as I was convinced of the necessity of European integration – that the EEC could never be successful in the absence of British experience and pragmatism. In the intervening thirty years I have had a lot of disappointments as well as positive experiences. One of the former has been to learn that almost no woman or man in England's political class, whether belonging to the right wing or the left wing of the political spectrum, and almost no woman or man in office in Whitehall, thinks that the Atlantic Ocean between England and America is broader than the channel between England and continental Europe. ... On balance, I have come to think that General De Gaulle was right in his belief that the British are not really prepared to cast their lot with the rest of European nations.
>
> Helmut Schmidt, 1985.[1]

In light of Britain's impending departure from the European Union (EU), Helmut Schmidt's damning verdict on British attitudes towards post-war Europe seems as potent today as when the former West German Chancellor first uttered these words in a public lecture at Yale more than thirty years ago. Ever since the late 1940s, tensions over European integration have overshadowed an otherwise flourishing post-war relationship between Britain and the Federal Republic of Germany (FRG).[2] After

---

[1] H. Schmidt, *A Grand Strategy for the West: The Anachronism of National Strategies in an Interdependent World* (New Haven, CT: Yale University Press, 1985), 52–3.

[2] A note on terminology: for better readability, 'Germany' always refers to the Federal Republic of Germany (FRG), i.e. West Germany, unless specifically indicated otherwise. Similarly, the 'European Communities' (EC), which were sometimes also referred to as the 'European Community', included the European Coal and Steel Community (ECSC), the European Atomic Energy Community (Euratom), and the European Economic Community (EEC) from the Merger Treaty in 1967 until the founding of the European Union in 1993. In practice,

2   *Introduction*

Britain's initial refusal in the 1950s to join the emerging European institutions such as the European Coal and Steel Community (ECSC) or the European Economic Community (EEC) from the outset, Germany's subsequent reluctance to back Britain's two membership applications in 1961–3 and 1967 against French resistance foreshadowed many of the dynamics that cloud the bilateral relationship to this day. Though Britain eventually did join the European Communities (EC) in 1973, its open scepticism towards new European initiatives such as direct elections to the European Parliament (EP) or the European Monetary System (EMS) continued to compromise British–German relations during much of Schmidt's chancellorship in the 1970s; developments that were not helped by Britain's attempts to renegotiate its terms of membership in 1974–5, or by its fight to reduce its EC budget contributions from the late 1970s onwards. The 1990s then saw British–German tensions over Europe reach new heights. Whereas France and Germany sought to counter widespread fears over German reunification by embedding the reunified country tightly in ever closer European structures through the Maastricht Treaty, the British government instead regarded such attempts at greater integration as potential vehicles for German political and economic domination: Margaret Thatcher's notorious weekend seminar on the 'German national character' in March 1990, and her Trade Secretary Nicholas Ridley's anti-German *Spectator* interview in July that same year, have long since entered the cannon of British–German folklore.[3] It is thus of little surprise that, to many German commentators at least, the eventual result of the 2016 'Brexit' referendum seemed to mark an almost logical culmination of more than seventy years in which Britain had always been a problematic and at times even hostile partner inside the EC/EU. 'Never wholeheartedly with the European cause', the journalist Theo Sommer wrote in the German weekly *Die Zeit* in April 2017, offering a damning verdict on Britain's allegedly destructive role in the European integration process since the 1950s.[4]

---

however, the vast majority of everyday references to the 'EC' during the 1970s referred to the EEC rather than the ECSC or Euratom. This practice is also adopted in the book, again unless specifically indicated otherwise.

[3] 'Appendix: The Prime Minister's Seminar on Germany', 24 March 1990, in Her Majesty's Stationary Office (ed.), *Documents on British Policy Overseas, Series III Vol. VII: German Unification 1989–1990* (London: Routledge, 2010), 502–9; *The Spectator*, 14 July 1990.

[4] *Die Zeit*, 4 April 2017.

Introduction 3

Helmut Schmidt, Chancellor of West Germany from 1974 to 1982, did not live to see the result of the 2016 referendum, but it is likely that he would have agreed with such *longue durée* interpretations of the post-war relationship. Indeed, his personal experiences with Britain closely mirror those of many post-war German politicians who became disillusioned with British attitudes towards European integration during the course of their careers. Born in December 1918, the young Schmidt grew up in a world where Britain occupied a central role in his worldview; perceptions that were strengthened by his heavy exposure to British politics and culture in the notoriously 'Anglophile' North German port-city of Hamburg. After serving as soldier on the Eastern front during the Second World War, Schmidt's political socialisation in the late 1940s then took place within the British occupation zone of Germany. This meant that the energetic young politician regarded Britain self-evidently as part of any future European order, leading not least to his refusal to vote on the Treaties of Rome in 1957. According to Schmidt, it was only during his time in government from the late 1960s onwards that he became disappointed by Britain's sceptical attitude towards European integration. As German Chancellor, he clashed repeatedly with his British counterparts Harold Wilson and particularly Margaret Thatcher; apparently an experience so traumatic that, when writing his memoirs in 1990, he decided to open his chapter on Britain by graphically recounting how the British Prime Minister swung her handbag and demanded 'her money back' at the Dublin European Council in 1979.[5] As a result of these first-hand experiences, Schmidt eventually came to believe in his later years that Britain's half-hearted attitude towards European integration reflected merely one symptom of a much more general British aloofness and detachment from its European neighbours. 'The Queen, the Commonwealth and the special relationship with the US is much more important than Europe', he asserted in one of his last interviews to the British newspaper the *Guardian* in December 2013, exclaiming at the height of the Eurozone crisis that Britain was 'less European-minded than Greece'.[6]

---

[5] H. Schmidt, *Die Deutschen und ihre Nachbarn: Menschen und Mächte II* (Berlin: Siedler, 1990), 91.
[6] *Guardian*, 22 December 2013.

Schmidt's cliché-laden narrative mirrors more general perceptions of British–German relations after 1945, where the two countries' very different attitudes towards European integration are frequently depicted as major obstacles in what is otherwise seen as a constructive, if somewhat unremarkable, bilateral relationship. 'For neither country was the other the most important', the historian Anne Deighton remarked on post-war British–German relations, 'nor yet so unimportant as to be safely ignored'; and it is a judgement that can be found in many other general surveys of the period as well.[7] The few more specialised studies of 1970s British–German relations similarly reveal the picture of generally cordial and well-functioning bilateral cooperation which was nonetheless compromised significantly by tensions over European integration. Klaus Larres, for example, contends that 1970s British–German relations were 'dominated by problems and complications caused by Britain's lukewarm attitude to the EC'; William Wallace agrees that 'the problems of Britain's position within the European Community [were] hanging over the whole relationship, despite the firmness of Britain's military commitment and despite, from the early 1970s, shared enthusiasms for European Political cooperation'.[8] These interpretations mirror a more general and somewhat teleological tendency in the historiography of European integration to depict Britain as the EC's eternal outsider or 'awkward partner', whose allegedly 'abnormal' attitudes towards the integration process are frequently contrasted with the allegedly 'normal' behaviour of other EC member-states.[9] Desmond

---

[7] A. Deighton, 'British–West German Relations, 1945–1972', in K. Larres and E. Meehan (eds.), *Uneasy Allies: British–German Relations and European Integration Since 1945* (Oxford: Oxford University Press, 2000), 43–4. Major general surveys are S. Lee, *Victory in Europe: Britain and Germany Since 1945* (Harlow: Longman, 2001); J. Noakes, P. Wende, and J. Wright (eds.), *Britain and Germany in Europe 1949–1990* (Oxford: Oxford University Press, 2002); R. Morgan and C. Bray (eds.), *Partners and Rivals in Western Europe: Britain, France and Germany* (Aldershot: Gower, 1987).

[8] K. Larres, 'Introduction: Uneasy Allies or Genuine Partners? Britain, Germany, and European Integration', in Larres and Meehan, *Uneasy Allies*, 16; W. Wallace, *Britain's Bilateral Links with Western Europe* (London: Routledge & Kegan Paul, 1984), 29–30.

[9] A term famously coined by S. George, *An Awkward Partner: Britain in the European Community* (Oxford: Oxford University Press, 1990). For a recent critical engagement with George's thesis from an interdisciplinary angle, see O. Daddow and T. Oliver, 'A not so awkward partner: the UK has been champion of many causes in the EU', *LSE Brexit Blog*, 15 April 2016: http://blogs.lse.ac.uk/brexit/2016/04/15/a-not-so-awkward-partner-the-uk-has-been-a-champion-of-many-causes-in-the-eu/ [accessed on 17 November 2016].

Introduction 5

Dinan's major history of post-war European integration, for example, lists both 'the significance of Franco–German leadership' and 'British detachment' as some of the key enduring features of the integration process; his chapter on the 1970s even contrasts the 'close Franco–German relations' at the time explicitly with the corresponding 'sorry state of Anglo–French and British–German relations'.[10] Most other histories of 1970s European integration similarly place great emphasis on the renewal of the so-called 'Franco–German axis' under Schmidt and the French President Giscard d'Estaing, interpretations that are often linked to implicit or explicit criticisms of British aloofness.[11] This ties neatly into a wealth of literature trying to identify some deeper root causes behind Britain's alleged semi-detachment from the European integration process.[12] Whatever the

[10] D. Dinan, *Europe Recast: A History of European Union*, 2nd Edition (Basingstoke: Macmillan, 2014), 9, 150.

[11] The classic works on the Franco–German relationship during the 1970s are H. Simonian, *The Privileged Partnership: Franco–German Relations in the European Community 1969–1984* (Oxford: Clarendon Press, 1985); H. Miard-Delacroix, *Partenaires de choix? Le chancelier Helmut Schmidt et la France, 1974–82* (Frankfurt am Main: P. Lang, 1993); M. Waechter, *Helmut Schmidt und Valéry Giscard d'Estaing. Auf der Suche nach Stabilität in der Krise der 70er Jahre* (Bremen: Edition Temmen, 2011). As regards more general histories, see J. Elvert, *Die europäische Integration* (Darmstadt: Wissenschaftliche Buchgesellschaft, 2006), 101–3; W. Loth, *Building Europe: A History of European Unification* (Berlin and Boston: De Gruyter Oldenbourg, 2015), 213–42, 439–40; D. Dinan, *Ever Closer Union: An Introduction to European Integration* (Basingstoke: Macmillan, 1999), 57–93. More nuanced is Mark Gilbert, who deliberately refrains from explicit criticism of Britain's role even though he agrees with the main interpretation of the 1970s as a period of the revitalization of Franco–German collaboration; M. Gilbert, *European Integration: A Concise History* (Lanham, MD: Rowan & Littlefield Publishers, 2012).

[12] To name just a few examples, D. Gowland and A. Turner, *Reluctant Europeans: Britain and European Integration, 1945–1998* (Harlow: Longman, 2000); H. Young, *This Blessed Plot: Britain and Europe from Churchill to Blair* (London: Macmillan, 1999); S. Greenwood, *Britain and European Integration Since the Second World War* (Manchester: Manchester University Press, 1996); B. Grob-Fitzgibbon, *Continental Drift: Britain and Europe from the End of Empire to the Rise of Euroscepticism* (Cambridge: Cambridge University Press, 2016); E. Dell, *The Schuman Plan and the British Abdication of Leadership in Europe* (Oxford: Oxford University Press, 1995); M. Beloff, *Britain and the European Union: Dialogue of the Deaf* (Basingstoke: Macmillan, 1996); R. Denman, *Missed Chances: Britain and Europe in the Twentieth Century* (London: Cassell, 1996). For an excellent revisionist take on much of this literature, see J. W. Young, *Britain and European Unity, 1945–1999* (Basingstoke: Macmillan, 2000).

6   *Introduction*

quality of British–German relations in other areas, so the narrative goes, Britain's unilateral refusal to embrace the higher ideals of European integration meant that the post-war relationship between Britain and Germany could never reach the lofty heights of the Franco–German relationship, which stood at the very heart of the European project. By contrast, evidence of strong British–German cooperation within the wider realm of European security and defence is usually side-lined and confined to more specialised studies, which correspondingly often talk about a 'hidden dimension' or even 'silent alliance' of the post-war relationship between the two countries.[13]

This book offers a new and different interpretation of 1970s British–German relations, asking why the European integration dimension has come to dominate perceptions of the bilateral relationship and thus overshadow the many other areas of bilateral collaboration to such a large extent. More precisely, it argues that Schmidt's damning verdict on Britain's role in Europe is part of a bigger West German perspective on post-war international relations in which European integration came to occupy a strategic centrality in ways that – for various reasons – were not replicated in Britain. As a result, Schmidt came to interpret Britain's scepticism towards the EC as a sign of a more general British scepticism or aversion against cooperation with its European partners, in spite of the fact that the two countries cooperated exceptionally closely in various multilateral frameworks to further what both perceived as shared West European interests on the global stage. This applies in particular to the remarkably intense bilateral cooperation inside the transatlantic alliance during the so-called 'second' Cold War in the late 1970s and early 1980s. Yet, whereas British policy-makers were frequently able to isolate intra-EC tensions from other areas of close West European cooperation, their German counterparts – and Schmidt in particular – tended to regard such intra-EC clashes as more general threats to European stability and international effectiveness. The consequence was that the intense bilateral cooperation in non-EC areas was little-noticed outside a small circle of policy-makers and experts, and that perceptions of the British–German relationship have

---

[13] K. Kaiser and J. Roper (eds.), *Die Stille Allianz. Deutsch-Britische Sicherheitskooperation* (Bonn: Europa Union, 1987); C. Bluth, *Britain, Germany, and Western Nuclear Strategy* (Oxford: Clarendon Press, 1995); B. Heuser, 'Britain and the Federal Republic of Germany in NATO, 1955–1990', in Noakes et al., Britain and Germany in Europe, 141–62.

Introduction 7

become overshadowed by a disproportionate preoccupation with intra-EC tensions both at the time and in subsequent historical writing. By embedding the 'European integration' story firmly within the wider picture of 1970s West European cooperation, the book therefore argues that at the heart of British–German relations under Schmidt lay deeply competing visions and clashing designs for post-war West European cooperation: incompatible strategies and mutual misperceptions, rather than simply one-sided British obstructionism. This is the big 'misunderstanding' that lies at the heart of 1970s British–German relations.

The book's analytical focus on Helmut Schmidt, without doubt one of post-war Germany's most influential strategic thinkers, reveals these interconnections between intra-EC and non-EC areas of cooperation far more clearly than a conventional bilateral study could have done.[14] While British–German relations during Schmidt's chancellorship were obviously shaped by an intricate web of multiple-level interactions and highly complex bureaucratic entanglements, it is nonetheless the case that the key patterns and major decisions of the bilateral relationship during the 1970s emerged primarily on the highest political level.[15] As Daniel Sargent put it in his recent study of 1970s US foreign policy, it is only 'at the very highest level that policies cohere and overarching strategic purposes emerge. Strategy ... is what holds the policymaking enterprise together, imbuing disconnected actions (and inactions) with coherence, direction, and purpose'.[16] Approaching the British–German relationship through the prism of Schmidt's interactions with his British counterparts thus reveals the often highly divergent British and German national strategies and wider worldviews at the heart of many bilateral

---

[14] For a recent study of Schmidt's strategic thought and foreign policy, see K. Spohr, *The Global Chancellor: Helmut Schmidt and the Reshaping of the International Order* (Oxford: Oxford University Press, 2016).

[15] For the structures of 1970s British–German relations, as well as of the bilateral and multilateral relationships between Britain, France, and Germany, see first and foremost H. Wallace, 'The Conduct of Bilateral Relationships by Governments', in Morgan and Bray, *Partners and Rivals*, 136–55; as well as H. Wallace, 'Bilateral, Trilateral and Multilateral Negotiations in the European Community', in ibid., 156–74.

[16] D. Sargent, *A Superpower Transformed: The Remaking of American Foreign Relations in the 1970s* (New York, NY and Oxford: Oxford University Press, 2015), 8.

8   *Introduction*

tensions during the 1970s.[17] It also serves to uncover the many intellectual linkages between European integration and non-EC areas of bilateral cooperation in the eyes of many policy-makers, two areas that have thus far been studied largely in isolation.[18] At the same time, the focus on high-level policy-making also re-introduces elements of human agency and chance into the study of international politics, showing how the holistic way in which national leaders like Schmidt and his British counterparts approached foreign policy also made them susceptible to at times significant misperceptions and distortions. Indeed, one of the central findings of the book is that Schmidt's personal preoccupation with intra-EC politics was one of the main reasons behind his more general disappointment with Britain during his time in office, a preoccupation that eventually came to cloud his judgement and compromise British–German cooperation in other areas as well.

This approach is all the more relevant since Schmidt was not only a shrewd observer of 1970s international politics, but also an active shaper of its course. As is well known, Schmidt's time as German Chancellor from 1974 to 1982 coincided with profound shifts in both the global economy and the East–West conflict, as well as with Britain's troubled first years inside the EC after its belated membership in 1973. In trying to cope with these new challenges, Western leaders embarked upon cautious but sustained attempts at global governance, triggering a proliferation of personal summitry on the highest level which found its institutional expressions in the creation of the

---

[17] In so doing, it builds on a growing literature in International History that focuses on the perceptions and mindsets of key actors. See, for example, S. Casey and J. Wright, *Mental Maps in the Early Cold War Era, 1945–68* (London: Macmillan, 2011); S. Casey and J. Wright (eds.), *Mental Maps in the Era of Détente and the End of the Cold War 1968–91* (London: Macmillan, 2015). More generally on the themes of 'political leadership', see R. A. W. Rhodes and P. Hart (eds.), *The Oxford Handbook of Political Leadership* (Oxford: Oxford University Press, 2014) or A. Brown, *The Myth of the Strong Leader: Political Leadership in the Modern Age* (London: Bodley Head, 2014). I have also used similar approaches in my studies of Schmidt's attitudes towards European integration. See M. Haeussler, 'A "Cold War European"? Helmut Schmidt and European Integration, c. 1945–1982', Cold War History 15/4 (2015), 427–47; and M. Haeussler, 'The Convictions of a Realist: Concepts of "Solidarity" in Helmut Schmidt's European Thought, 1945–82', *European Review of History: Revue Européenne d'histoire* 24/6 (2017), 955–72.

[18] Thereby mirroring a more general historiographical tendency that will be discussed in later parts of the chapter.

Introduction 9

European Council (1974) and the world economic summits (1975).[19] These wider transformations of the international system also had a marked impact on the British–German relationship, where a similar trend towards the personalisation of bilateral diplomacy can be observed – not least in the institutionalisation of biannual British–German consultations in1976. Schmidt, a recognised expert on financial-economic as well as military-strategic matters, clearly benefitted from these new fora of international politics, in that they enabled the self-confident and rhetorically gifted Chancellor to pursue his policies in a highly personal style that often circumvented lower diplomatic levels and channels of communication.[20] As the book shows, such high-level diplomacy between Schmidt and his respective counterparts could at times have a considerable effect on the quality and effectiveness of 1970s British–German relations. At best, a close and confidential personal relationship between Schmidt and his respective British counterparts, such as during James Callaghan's premiership from 1976 to 1979, served as a bridge to alleviate misunderstandings and increase mutual trust, sometimes even ensuring that intra-EC tensions did not spill over into other areas of bilateral cooperation. At other times, however, failures in high-level communication exacerbated more general bilateral tensions, triggering erosions of trust that extended far beyond the concrete issues at stake. The focus on Schmidt therefore reveals how the growing importance of multi- and bilateral high-level summitry during the 1970s played a key part in shaping the short-term course of the British–German relationship, even though it did not change the deeper underlying divergences in British and German national strategies, particularly as regards European integration.

[19] For an excellent introduction to the growing literature on the phenomenon, see E. Mourlon-Druol and F. Romero (eds.), *International Summitry and Global Governance: The Rise of the G7 and the European Council, 1974–1991* (London and New York, NY: Routledge, 2014). With a tighter focus on the Cold War, see D. Reynolds and K. Spohr (eds.), *Transcending the Cold War: Summits, Statecraft, and the Dissolution of Bipolarity in Europe, 1970–1990* (Oxford: Oxford University Press, 2016).

[20] For Schmidt's handling of summitry, see J. von Karczewski, *Weltwirtschaft ist unser Schicksal: Helmut Schmidt und die Schaffung der Weltwirtschaftsgipfel* (Bonn: Dietz, 2008); for case studies, K. Spohr, 'Helmut Schmidt and the Shaping of Western Security in the Late 1970s: The Guadeloupe Summit of 1979', *The International History Review* 37/1 (2015), 167–92; Spohr, *Global Chancellor*, 10–32.

10   *Introduction*

Although the book's main focus is on the high-level interactions between Schmidt and his British counterparts during his chancellorship, it also contributes to three broader and interlinked areas of historical investigation: British–German relations, British attitudes towards post-war Europe, and the more general history of European integration. As regards the bilateral relationship, the book's new empirical findings largely confirm previous judgements that British–German relations under Schmidt were generally benevolent and constructive yet compromised unnecessarily by tensions over European integration.[21] Where it differs from most previous studies, however, is in its interpretation of the causes behind these tensions. Writing largely without the availability of primary sources, historians have thus far tended to mirror Schmidt's own judgement that it was primarily Britain's destructive role inside the EC that was to blame for bilateral tensions. Julie Smith and Geoffrey Edwards, for example, claim that Britain 'rarely took the lead' inside the EC and 'on many occasions seemed unnecessarily bellicose, in marked contrast to the Germans'; Klaus Larres agrees that Britain 'continued to be a most awkward ally' during the 1970s.[22] Sabine Lee, though offering an overall more positive picture of 1970s British–German relations, similarly suggests that 1970s Britain eventually came to supersede France 'as the *bête noir* of European integration in spirit, word and sporadically in deed'.[23] By contrast, this book pays equal attention to the German role during the many intra-EC disputes at the time, interpreting such differences as mutual misunderstandings based on incompatible national strategies and clashing visions, rather than blaming them simply on one-sided British obstructionism. It also offers a more comprehensive picture of the bilateral relationship by highlighting the many non-EC areas of

[21] The only study based on primary-source research focuses exclusively on the European dimension, and largely echoing Schmidt's own interpretation of one-sided British obstructionism. T. Birkner, *Comrades for Europe?: Die 'Europarede' Helmut Schmidts 1974* (Bremen: Edition Temmen, 2005). For early studies of British–German relations under Schmidt written largely without access to primary sources, see J. Smith and G. Edwards, 'British–West German Relations, 1973–1989', in Larres and Meehan, *Uneasy Allies*, 45–62; Lee, *Victory in Europe*, 148–78; P. E. An, 'Anglo–German Relations in the EC/EU 1979–1997' (unpublished PhD thesis, University of Cambridge, May 2006), 83–126.

[22] Smith and Edwards, 'British–West German Relations, 1973–1989', 61–2; Larres, 'Introduction', in ibid., 13.

[23] Lee, *Victory in Europe*, 233–4.

Introduction   11

bilateral cooperation, where Britain and Germany frequently collaborated closely and effectively, and which leads to a significantly more positive judgement on the overall state of 1970s British–German relations than the one that can be found in most previous studies.

This approach also challenges the way we think more specifically about British attitudes towards Europe during the 1970s. Whilst the historiography on Britain's changing attitudes towards the integration process in the 1950s and 1960s has undergone some significant historical revisionism,[24] the image of its role once EC membership had been achieved in 1973 is still dominated by the popular notion of Britain being Europe's 'awkward partner'; an image prominently ingrained in the title of Stephen George's influential study from the 1990s.[25] This is partly due to a lack of original historical research on the topic. The few studies that are available commonly show the picture of a Britain struggling to come to terms with the complexities of EC membership, frequently obstructing the Community's internal workings and evolution as a result.[26] Such analyses can also be found in more specialised studies investigating major events of 1970s European integration, most importantly as regards Britain's refusal to join the EMS in 1978–9.[27] Yet, although the book does not seek to deny

---

[24] The evolution of the literature is captured well in J. Ellison, 'Britain and Europe', in P. Addison and H. Jones (eds.), *A Companion to Contemporary Britain 1939–2000* (Oxford: Blackwell, 2007), 517–38. See also O. J. Daddow, *Britain and Europe Since 1945: Historiographical Perspectives on Integration* (Manchester: Manchester University Press, 2004).

[25] George, *Awkward Partner*.

[26] S. Wall, *The Official History of Britain and the European Community, vol. 2: From Rejection to Referendum, 1963–1975* (Abingdon: Routledge, 2012) remains the most extensive work, but only runs up to 1975. The surprising lack of historical research on 'Britain and Europe' in the 1970s is also discussed in N. P. Ludlow, *Roy Jenkins and the European Commission Presidency, 1976–1980: At the Heart of Europe* (London: Palgrave, 2016), 11–13. There are also two new major studies for the 1974–5 renegotiation and referendum period: R. Saunders, *Yes to Europe! The 1975 Referendum and Seventies Britain* (Cambridge: Cambridge University Press, 2018), and L. Aqui, 'An Exceptional Case: Britain, Renegotiation, Referendum and the European Community', unpublished PhD thesis (Queen Mary University of London, 2018). See also J. W. Young, 'Europe', in A. Seldon and K. Hickson (eds.), *New Labour, Old Labour: The Wilson and Callaghan Governments, 1974–1979* (London: Routledge, 2004), 139–53.

[27] Peter Ludlow's classic work on the creation of the EMS, for example, claims that Britain's 'ambivalent and unhelpful attitude' towards the scheme was only part of 'an increasingly tedious story of misunderstanding and non-cooperation between London and the rest of the EEC'. See P. Ludlow, *The Making of the*

12   *Introduction*

the existence of bilateral tensions within the narrowly defined realm of intra-EC politics, its decision to move beyond purely intra-Community matters reveals significantly more positive and proactive British attitudes towards cooperation with its European partners during Schmidt's chancellorship. Particularly within the transatlantic alliance, Britain – freed from domestic pressures and its structural disadvantages within the EC – in fact played a remarkably constructive and proactive role in fostering joint European responses to the manifold global challenges of the 1970s.[28] By revealing the extent of British–German collaboration in these non-EC areas of 1970s West European cooperation, the book thus contributes significantly to a more nuanced and positive interpretation of Britain's role in 1970s European politics than the ones available to date.

More generally, the book therefore speaks to two broader trends in European integration historiography over recent years: attempts to deconstruct some of the progressivist narratives underlying our understanding of the integration process, and the analytical widening of the historiography by moving beyond the narrow analytical confines of internal EC/EU politics. As regards the former, Mark Gilbert's

European Monetary System: A Case Study in the Politics of the European Community (London: Butterworths, 1982), 245, 296. Mourlon-Druol's more recent work similarly claims that the episode marked the beginning of 'British self-exclusion from the advancement of EEC cooperation' – in contrast to Ludlow, however, he is careful to point out that this does not necessarily imply a negative judgement of Britain's decision. E. Mourlon-Druol, *A Europe Made of Money: The Emergence of the European Monetary System* (Ithaca, NY and London: Cornell University Press, 2012), 276.

[28] For studies stressing Britain's very proactive role in European cooperation over foreign policy and security and defence issues during the 1970s and beyond, see T. Oliver and D. Allen, 'Foreign Policy', in I. Bache and A. Jordan (eds.), *The Europeanization of British Politics* (Basingstoke: Macmillan, 2006), 187–200; G. Clemens, 'Der Beitritt Großbritanniens zu den Europäischen Gemeinschaften', in F. Knipping and M. Schönwald (eds.), *Aufbruch zum Europa der zweiten Generation: Die europäische Einigung 1969–1984* (Trier: Wissenschaftlicher Verlag, 2006), 306–28; J. Kreutzfeldt, *'Point of Return': Großbritannien und die Politische Union Europas 1969–1975* (Stuttgart: Steiner Verlag, 2010). Recent specialised studies of 1970s multilateral cooperation in the realm of security and defence issues have further substantiated the extent of British–German collaboration. See K. Spohr, 'Conflict and Cooperation in Intra-Alliance Nuclear Politics: Western Europe, the United States, and the Genesis of NATO's Dual-Track Decision, 1977–1979', *Journal of Cold War Studies* 13/2 (2011), 43, 88; Y. Okamoto, 'Britain, European Security and the Cold War, 1976–9', unpublished PhD thesis (Queen Mary University of London, 2014).

Introduction 13

impassionate rejection of the teleological tendencies still evident in much EC/EU historiography has clearly acquired new urgency in light of current political developments, with historians now increasingly ready to question the allegedly inherently progressive nature of the EU's evolution.[29] Here, the book's analytical sensitivity towards the competing narratives of European integration in 1970s Britain and Germany clearly builds on Gilbert's agenda by precisely reconstructing how such competing narratives stood at the very heart of many British–German tensions over European integration at the time. Rather than depicting Wilson or Thatcher as the 'villains' to be contrasted with the 'saints' Schmidt and Giscard, the book instead seeks to historicise such notions by analysing *how* and *why* these actors came to reflect such different attitudes towards the integration process at the time.[30] In similar vein, the book also builds on recent attempts to embed studies of the integration process much more firmly within the wider evolution of the international system during the 1970s.[31] In contrast to previously dominant interpretations of the 1970s as a decade of stagnation and 'Eurosclerosis', these new works have presented markedly more

[29] M. Gilbert, 'Narrating the Process: Questioning the Progressive Story of European Integration', *Journal of Common Market Studies* 46/3 (2008), 641–62. For recent studies building on these insights, see H. A. Ikonomou, A. Andry, and R. Byberg (eds.), *European Enlargement Across Rounds and Beyond Borders* (London: Routledge, 2017); as well as a recent special issue of the European Review of History: F. Greiner, 'Introduction: Writing the Contemporary History of European Solidarity', *European Review of History: Revue européenne d'histoire* 24/6 (2017), 837–53; V. Conze, *Das Europa der Deutschen: Ideen von Europa in Deutschland zwischen Reichstradition und Westorientierung* (Munich: De Gruyter, 2005), part 2–5. See also as most of the works listed in footnotes 31 and 32 below.

[30] For the notion of saints and villains, see also Gilbert, *European integration*, 7.

[31] A trend that is reflected even in some of the titles of recent scholarship on 1970s European integration. See G. Migani and A. Varsori (eds.), *Europe in the International Arena During the 1970s: Entering a Different World* (Brussels: P. Lang, 2011); C. Hiepel (ed.), *Europe in a Globalising World: Global Challenges and European Responses in the 'long' 1970s* (Baden-Baden: Nomos, 2014); J. Laursen (ed.), *The Institutions and Dynamics of the European Community, 1973–83* (Baden-Baden: Nomos, 2014). For overviews of this historiographical trend, see K. K. Patel, 'Provincialising European Union: Co-operation and Integration in Europe in a Historical Perspective', *Contemporary European History* 22/4 (2013), 649–73; F. Romero (ed.), 'The International History of European Integration in the Long 1970s: A Roundtable Discussion on Research Issues, Methodologies, and Directions', *Journal of European Integration History* 17/2 (2011), 331–60.

14   *Introduction*

positive assessments of 1970s European integration, revealing how the West Europeans managed to carve themselves a distinct niche in international politics and thereby planted the seeds of many subsequent developments during the 1980s.[32] Again, the book's findings add significant empirical substance to this emerging consensus, showing how British–German cooperation played a key part in the emergence of an identifiable European position within the wider international arena, particularly as regards the transformation of the transatlantic alliance during the so-called 'second' Cold War from the late 1970s onwards.[33]

Yet, while the deconstruction of progressivist narratives and the analytical opening up of European integration historiography have undoubtedly furthered our understanding of the process, these developments have at times come at the expense of conceptual precisions, triggering bigger questions of how the history of European integration can be connected with the wider history of post-war Europe without losing sight of its specifics and distinctiveness.[34] Over recent years, historians

---

[32] In addition to the works listed above, see also some more specific case studies such as E. Mourlon-Druol, 'Filling the EEC Leadership Vacuum? The Creation of the European Council at the December 1974 Paris Summit', *Cold War History* 10/3 (2010), 315–39; E. Karamouzi, *Greece, the EEC and the Cold War, 1974–1979. The Second Enlargement* (Basingstoke: Macmillan, 2014); A. Romano, *From Détente in Europe to European Détente. How the West Shaped the Helsinki CSCE* (Brussels: Peter Lang, 2009); A. Romano, 'Untying Cold War Knots: The European Community and Eastern Europe in the Long 1970s', *Cold War History* 14/2 (2014), 153–73. The transatlantic tensions between the EC and the US following Henry Kissinger's call for a 'Year of Europe' in 1973 have aroused particular historical interest; see D. Möckli, *European Foreign Policy During the Cold War: Heath, Brandt, Pompidou and the Dream of Political Unity* (London: I.B. Tauris, 2009), and A. E. Gfeller, *Building a European Identity: France, the United States, and the Oil Shock, 1973–1974* (New York, NY and Oxford: Berghahn, 2012).

[33] The historiographies on European integration and the Cold War still seem to move largely in isolation from one another, in spite of their numerous interconnections. For recent attempts to rectify this, see N. P. Ludlow, 'European integration and the Cold War', in M. P. Leffler and O. A. Westad (eds.), *The Cambridge History of the Cold War, Vol. II: Crises and Détente* (Cambridge: Cambridge University Press, 2010), 179–97; N. P. Ludlow (ed.), *European Integration and the Cold War: Ostpolitik-Westpolitik, 1965–1973* (Abingdon: Routledge, 2007); K. K. Patel and K. Weisbrode (eds.), *European Integration and the Atlantic Community in the 1980s* (Cambridge: Cambridge University Press, 2014); Loth, *Building Europe*, 251–61.

[34] For an intriguing recent discussion of these problems, see M. Gehler, 'Internationale Geschichte und ihre europäischen Zugänge', in B. Haider-Wilson, W. D. Godsey, and W. Mueller (eds.), *Internationale Geschichte in*

Introduction 15

have started to scrutinise the alleged uniqueness and originality of the post-1945 European integration process, challenging not least the novelty of supranationalism and highlighting the EC/EU's similarities with earlier forms of international governance.[35] Following from this, Kiran Klaus Patel has suggested that the EC/EU's historical novelty may not necessarily lie in its institutional originality, but rather in the ways in which it 'self-fashioned' itself as a new and revolutionary approach to international cooperation in order to overcome centuries-old antagonisms between European nation-states.[36] The historical importance and political function of the integrationist project might therefore be seen not primarily in its concrete institutions or every-day technical mechanisms, but rather in its political symbolisms and self-conscious political and cultural representations.[37] Such self-affirmative narratives of European integration as the main and only model of post-war European cooperation, however, were of course not universally accepted, but acquired very different degrees of political legitimisation in different European countries and societies.

It is here that the book's key contribution to the literature can be found. Not only does the book reveal how the different legitimacy of such self-affirmative narratives in 1970s Britain and Germany stood at the very heart of many of their intra-EC tensions, but it also analyses how such conflicting political narratives then impacted and shaped concrete attitudes and policies of key decision-makers on the highest level. The book's focus on Schmidt's high-level interactions with his British counterparts offers a unique window into these bigger questions, in that it explains why the EC came to form the key reference point for any type of European cooperation in the concepts and worldviews of German policy-makers like Schmidt, as well as why it never managed to acquire a similarly central role in British mind-sets and strategies at the

---

Theorie und Praxis / International History in Theory and Practice (Vienna: Verlag der österreichischen Akademie der Wissenschaften, 2017), 165–206.

[35] Ibid.; U. Lappenküper and G. Thiemeyer (eds.), *Europäische Einigung im 19. und 20. Jahrhundert: Akteure und Antriebskräfte*(Paderborn: F. Schöningh, 2013); K. K. Patel, 'Europäische Integration', in J. Dülffer and W. Loth (eds.), *Dimensionen Internationaler Geschichte* (Munich: De Gruyter, 2012), 353–72.

[36] Patel, 'Provincialising European Union', 649.

[37] W. Schmale, *Geschichte und Zukunft der Europäischen Identität* (Stuttgart: Kohlhammer, 2008); G. Morgan, *The Idea of a European Superstate: Public Justification and European Integration* (Princeton, NJ and Oxford: Princeton University Press, 2005).

time.[38] By exposing these intellectual, ideological, and emotive interconnections (or indeed lack thereof) between European integration and other areas of European cooperation, the book thus shows why the story of intra-EC tensions has come to occupy such a central role in our perceptions of 1970s British–German relations, thereby also shedding fresh light on the relationship between the integrationist project and the more general history of post-war European cooperation.

Given the centrality of Schmidt's personal experience of British–German relations to the book, I was extremely fortunate to be granted access to Schmidt's extensive personal collection of primary source materials, allowing me to closely trace and reconstruct the evolution of Schmidt's attitudes towards Britain from as early as the late 1940s. In total, I spent over two months at Schmidt's private archive in Hamburg, dwelling on materials as diverse as essays from his student days to handwritten notes taken on the menu cards at European Council dinners. These findings have been supplemented by in-depth research in Schmidt's political archive at the Friedrich-Ebert-Stiftung in Bonn, which offers copies of important memoranda, records of meetings, briefings, interdepartmental communications, and so on. I also conducted an interview with the late Helmut Schmidt on 23 September 2013.

Further, the book dwells on extensive research in the governmental records of Germany and Britain. For the period of Schmidt's chancellorship, I have utilized the records of the German Chancellery Office (*Bundeskanzleramt*) at the German national archive (*Bundesarchiv*) in Koblenz, as well as the extensive files of the German foreign ministry (*Auswärtiges Amt*) preserved at its archive in Berlin (*Politisches Archiv des Auswärtigen Amts*). For the British side, research has been based primarily on the materials preserved at the National Archives in Kew, where I have accessed materials from the Prime Minister's Office, the Cabinet Office, and the Foreign Office. This sample has been significantly widened at key moments of the British–German relationship to include the viewpoints of other departments, as well as key memoirs and parliamentary and press opinion.

---

[38] For the benefits of such comparative biographical approaches to the European integration historiography, see also Gehler, 'Internationale Geschichte und ihre europäischen Zugänge', 199–201.

Introduction 17

Since one of the book's main objectives is to show how British–German cooperation played a crucial part in the emergence of a more coherent West European role in 1970s international politics, I have also made extensive use of American sources in order to provide an external perspective on intra-European relations, as well as to bring out more clearly the complex web of transatlantic cooperation in which the bilateral relationship was operating during the final decades of the Cold War. I have accessed records of three Presidential Libraries: Gerald Ford (Ann Arbor, Michigan), Jimmy Carter (Atlanta, Georgia), and Ronald Reagan (Simi Valley, California). These libraries generally do not only host the President's files, but they also contain extensive records from other key figures of the respective administrations, most importantly the respective National Security Advisers. Additionally, I have made use of the rich volumes on the *Foreign Relations of the United States* (FRUS) published by the US Department of State, as well as of various private papers located at the Library of Congress (Washington, DC) including the files of Paul Nitze, Elliot Richardson, and Henry Brandon.

The book is structured chronologically, divided into four main chapters stretching from Schmidt's earliest years in politics after 1945 to the end of his chancellorship in October 1982. Following the first chapter which traces the evolution of Schmidt's attitudes towards Britain in the context of the more general developments of British–German relations from 1945 to 1974, the next chapters then assess the bilateral relationship under Schmidt during the respective premierships of Harold Wilson (1974–6), James Callaghan (1976–9), and Margaret Thatcher (1979–82). This structure not only serves to illuminate the different approaches towards European and British–German cooperation by Schmidt's different British counterparts, but it also highlights the importance of high-level diplomacy in either mediating or exacerbating the underlying structural dynamics of 1970s British–German relations.

The first chapter utilises rare materials from Schmidt's private archive to trace the evolution of his changing attitudes towards Britain in the context of his more general political maturation in the 1950s and 1960s. It reveals how Schmidt's post-war socialisation in the British occupation zone crucially influenced his views on Britain in the late 1940s and 1950s, demonstrating the extent of British 'soft power' on Continental Europe in the immediate post-war years. Yet, the chapter then moves on to analyse how Schmidt's attitudes from the late 1950s onwards underwent drastic changes, triggered by his evolving geostrategic thought and changing perceptions of West Germany's national interests in light of the rapidly shifting power balance between Britain and Germany during the period. By the late 1960s, Schmidt had come to prioritise West Germany's bilateral relationships with France and the United States over the British–German relationship, something that is evident not least in his rather muted support of Britain's second application to join the EC in 1967, and in his actions as Minister of Defence (1969–72) and Minister of Finance (1972–4).

With Britain's belated entry into the EC in January 1973 and Schmidt's election as Chancellor in May 1974, the scene seemed set for a strengthening of British–German relations. The second chapter investigates why such initial hopes led nowhere, placing particular emphasis on the very different attitudes of Schmidt and his British counterpart Harold Wilson towards the EC. Whereas Schmidt actively sought to reform and revitalise the EC to tackle the manifold political and economic crises of the early 1970s, Wilson instead embarked upon a controversial and highly divisive 'renegotiation' of Britain's EC membership which soured bilateral relations and led to an erosion of trust between Schmidt and Wilson that extended far beyond intra-EC politics. Contrasting Schmidt's and Wilson's very different approaches towards European integration during and after the renegotiations, the chapter analyses how the EC had by the 1970s become the central cornerstone of West Germany's foreign policy, whereas British European policy was still shaped primarily by domestic and party-political pressures. As a result, Wilson's 'renegotiation&referendum' exercise triggered a certain British self-marginalisation inside the EC while at the same time strengthening the Franco–German axis between Schmidt and the newly elected French President Giscard d'Estaing. These developments also had a markedly negative impact on British–German cooperation outside the formal EC framework, particularly in the global debates over energy and the proposed North-South conference.

Though James Callaghan was four years older than his predecessor Wilson, his election as PM injected a new sense of energy and vitality into the bilateral relationship, as the third chapter shows. Sharing Schmidt's preference for high-level personal diplomacy and displaying a more realistic sense of Britain's post-imperial power and capabilities,

Introduction 19

Callaghan soon managed to strike up a strong personal relationship with his German counterpart Schmidt, in which the two leaders were guided by their mutual belief in the necessity of West European cooperation in an increasingly interdependent world. Not only did Schmidt's and Callaghan's close high-level cooperation prove remarkably effective in solving many long-standing bilateral disputes, but it also eased tensions in areas where interests continued to diverge, not least inside the EC. Most importantly, close British–German relations under Schmidt and Callaghan played a crucial part in strengthening the West European pillar inside the transatlantic alliance, particularly after the election of Jimmy Carter in November 1976 had led to a serious deterioration of US–West German relations. Therefore, the chapter shows how Callaghan's high-level diplomacy with Schmidt was of crucial importance in repairing and strengthening the bilateral relationship after Wilson as well as in fostering common West European positions inside the transatlantic alliance, even though it could not bridge the wider conceptual gulf separating Britain and Germany over European integration.

If Callaghan's close relationship with Schmidt constituted an important mediating factor in British–German relations, then Margaret Thatcher's personal diplomacy had the exact opposite effect. The fourth chapter shows how Thatcher's aggressive and highly personalised agenda to reduce Britain's contributions to the EC budget led to lasting deteriorations in British–German relations, particularly since Schmidt yet again proved unwilling to jeopardise Franco–German relations by siding openly with the British. At the same time, however, Schmidt and Thatcher collaborated closely inside the transatlantic alliance, taking the European lead in implementing NATO's dual-track decision and shaping the alliance's response to major international crises such as the Soviet Union's invasion of Afghanistan or the declaration of martial law in Poland. Yet, whereas Thatcher was able to compartmentalise intra-EC tensions and frequently sought to isolate them from other areas of bilateral cooperation, Schmidt instead believed that the public fallouts over the EC budget compromised Western Europe's more general political cohesion and thus jeopardised Western unity at a time of resurgent global crises. Therefore, the chapter reveals the many interconnections between European integration and the wider pattern of West European cooperation in the minds of key German policy-makers like Schmidt; interconnections that go a long way in explaining the tensions and virulence triggered by the British budgetary question.

The concluding chapter then returns to Schmidt's personal narrative sketched out above, embedding his story within the wider pattern of post-war British–German relations. It argues that Schmidt's disillusionment with Britain's European policies is ultimately an expression of the different role of the EC in the foreign policies of Britain and Germany, but that it does not adequately describe the nature and extent of British–German cooperation during his chancellorship. Schmidt's frequent clashes over Europe with his British counterparts thus reflect the different perceptions and narratives of European integration in post-war Britain and Germany. Following from this, the book stresses the need to take into account more fully the role of narratives and ideas in the study of international history, and suggests how an analytical focus on key actors like Schmidt might help reconnect the history of European integration with the wider international history of Western Europe during the Cold War. The chapter also reflects on what Schmidt's story might be able to tell us about British–German tensions over European integration today, particularly in light of Britain's 'Brexit' vote of June 2016.

1 | The Young Helmut Schmidt and British–German Relations, 1945–1974

The almost thirty years between the end of the Second World War in 1945 and Helmut Schmidt's election as West German Chancellor in 1974 saw profound shifts in the relative power balance between Britain and Germany. In 1945, Britain was a victorious power with still global reach; its dominions and colonial possessions stretched across Africa, Asia, and Australia, and it still counted over 700 million people as citizens of the British Empire and Commonwealth.[1] The scope of Britain's geostrategic reach was matched by its financial and economic dominance: in 1950, Britain produced almost a third of Western Europe's industrial output, and half of the world's trade was conducted in Pound Sterling.[2] Germany, by contrast, was a comprehensively defeated, divided and occupied country, shouldering the unique historical burden of the Holocaust and the Second World War.[3] Less than thirty years later, however, the situation looked very different indeed. By 1970, the FRG had become Western Europe's undisputed economic powerhouse, with its share of world exports of manufactures amounting to almost 20 per cent.[4] The FRG's economic power had also become increasingly reflected in the political realm, with the country taking on prominent roles inside the multilateral alliances of the EC and NATO. Britain, by contrast, was suffering from a profound loss of military, political and economic strength caused by its transition to a medium-sized post-imperial power. By the mid-1960s, Britain's share

---

[1] A. Deighton, 'Britain and the Cold War, 1945–1955', in M. P. Leffler and O. A. Westad (eds.), *The Cambridge History of the Cold War, Vol. I: Origins* (Cambridge: Cambridge University Press, 2010), 112–32; R. Self, *British Foreign and Defence Policy Since 1945: Challenges and Dilemmas in a Changing World* (Basingstoke: Macmillan, 2010), 31.

[2] Self, *British Foreign and Defence Policy*, 2.

[3] H. P. Schwarz, 'The Division of Germany, 1945–1949', in Leffler and Westad, *CHCW, Vol. I*, 133–53.

[4] D. Reynolds, *Britannia Overruled: British Policy and World Power in the Twentieth Century* (Harlow: Longman, 2000), 225.

of the world's exports had fallen to around 14 per cent, and the population of what little remained of the fading British Empire amounted to less than five million, including four million citizens of Hong Kong.[5] To many contemporary observers, it seemed like Germany may have 'lost the war' but 'won the peace', a debate that has since become notorious in British political discourse.[6]

As this chapter shows, it is only in this wider context that the young Helmut Schmidt's changing attitudes towards Britain prior to his chancellorship can be understood, since they were shaped first and foremost by his changing perceptions of West Germany's national interests and role in the post-war world. While his views in the early 1940s and 1950s were still influenced by his strong personal affinity to the Anglo-Saxon world and British soft power at the time, by the 1960s, Schmidt's focus had already shifted towards the United States and France as West Germany's two main partners in international politics: France as the indispensable partner for bilateral reconciliation as well as international rehabilitation through the European integration process, and the United States as the only guarantor of military and economic security in the Cold War. These two main pillars would remain at the heart of Schmidt's conceptions of West German foreign policy thought throughout his active political life.[7] Britain, by contrast, became the sorry third, which reflected the country's more general decline in international influence during the 1950s and 1960s. Though Schmidt remained supportive of strong British–German relations and endorsed Britain's eventual EC membership, he had clearly come to regard the bilateral relationship with Britain as subordinate to West Germany's pivotal relationships with France and the United

---

[5] Self, *British Foreign and Defence Policy*, 31, 70.

[6] C. Barnett, *The Audit of War: The Illusion and Reality of Britain as a Great Nation* (Basingstoke: Macmillan, 1986) remains the classic example. For a historical reading of contemporary 'declinism' debates, see J. Tomlinson, *The Politics of Decline: Understanding Post-War Britain* (Harlow: Longman, 2000); R. English and M. Kenny (eds.), *Rethinking British Decline* (Basingstoke: Macmillan, 1999). For a striking contemporary example of how 'declinism' influenced the British debate over EC membership amongst policy-making elites, see the interviews with prime ministers, foreign secretaries, and high-ranking officials collected in M. Charlton, *The Price of Victory* (London: BBC Publications, 1983).

[7] I argue this more comprehensively in M. Haeussler, 'A "Cold War European"? Helmut Schmidt and European Integration, c. 1945–1982', *Cold War History* 15/4 (2015), 427–47.

States in the wider context of European integration and the Cold War. The evolution of the early Schmidt's attitudes towards Britain can thus be seen to illustrate the country's more general diminishing importance to West Germany during the 1950s and 1960s; a period that marked both the FRG's resurgence as a major international player through pronounced multilateralism and Britain's contrasting reduction into a post-imperial, medium-sized European power.[8] These wider developments created powerful path dependencies that would shape British–German relations far into Schmidt's chancellorship and beyond.

Helmut Schmidt's Early Anglophilia and British Soft Power in the Late 1940s

As a young boy growing up in inter-war Hamburg, Schmidt was probably bound to develop a certain affinity to the Anglo-Saxon world. Hamburg, still the world's third largest trading port in 1912, had consciously fostered strong commercial and cultural links with Britain for many centuries, with historical evidence of bilateral contacts dating back to at least 1266.[9] The historically close relationship between Hamburg and Britain left a marked cultural imprint that clearly shaped the young Schmidt's upbringing and early education. In his memoirs, Schmidt dwells at length on the alleged influence of British literature and music on his early education, recalling having read works by Oscar Wilde or George Bernhard Shaw as a young boy.[10] Yet, British–German links in Hamburg also manifested themselves in more tangible ways through personal contacts and strong networks in trade and education. Indeed, Schmidt's only travel abroad prior to the Second World War had been a three-week school exchange to Manchester in 1932, during which he was interviewed by the local newspaper, the *Manchester Evening Chronicle*. In a series of short interviews, the thirteen-year-old Schmidt reported amongst other things that Germans 'eat more sausages than here', and that Sundays were 'foolish in England' given that all sports and cultural activities

[8] Reynolds, *Britannia Overruled*.
[9] T. Drössel, *Die Engländer in Hamburg 1914 bis 1945* (Göttingen: Cuvillier, 2008), 2; A. D. Petersen, *Die Engländer in Hamburg, 1814 bis 1914: ein Beitrag zur hamburgischen Geschichte* (Hamburg: Bockel, 1993).
[10] H. Schmidt, *Die Deutschen und Ihre Nachbarn* (Berlin: Siedler, 1992) 100–1.

were 'forbidden'.[11] While it is important not to read too much into such early exposures, these childhood experiences seem to have left a marked impression on Schmidt, and he frequently referred to his self-proclaimed 'Anglophilia' in many of his later writings and speeches.[12] When I interviewed him towards the end of his life in September 2013, more than eighty years after the school exchange, he still managed to recall the exact address of his host family and readily shared memories of the host mother, Mrs Bake: 'whenever I went to school – I had to attend the English school, – she kissed me goodbye. And I found that quite annoying, I remember that'.[13]

Such historically close ties were surely part of the reason why British politics and culture exercised such a strong ideological pull on many young Germans in post-war Hamburg. Like many of his generation, Schmidt, who had been born just after the First World War in December 1918, had never experienced democratic rule as an adult, and was thus hungry for intellectual influences from abroad after 1945.[14] The cooperative and relatively informal way in which the British administered the occupation of Hamburg also offered a largely benevolent environment for Schmidt's post-war political education.[15] In this regard, a particularly important figure was the

---

[11] *Manchester Evening Chronicle*, 15 July 1932; *Manchester Evening Chronicle*, 18 July 1932; *Manchester Evening Chronicle*, 19 July 1932. Schmidt also recalled these interviews in conversation with *The Times* journalist Patricia Clough in 1981. See Privates Helmut-Schmidt-Archiv (Hamburg), Eigene Arbeiten (henceforward: PHSA/EA), BPA, Niederschrift des Gesprächs/ Interviews BK Schmidt mit Mrs. Patricia Clough (*The Times*), 14 Uhr im Bundeskanzleramt, 13 November 1981.

[12] See, for example, Schmidt, *Die Deutschen und ihre Nachbarn*, 99–101; PHSA, EA, Juli–Oktober 1983, H. Schmidt, II. Hamburgische Anglophilie, 1 August 1983; H. Schmidt, Mein Hamburg, *Die Zeit*, 1 October 2005; and the relevant parts of his film documentary H. Schmidt, *Ein Mann und seine Stadt: Der Hanseat über seine Heimat Hamburg* (NDR, 1986).

[13] Interview with Helmut Schmidt, 23 September 2013.

[14] H. Schmidt, 'Politischer Rückblick auf eine unpolitische Jugend', in H. Schmidt and L. Schmidt (eds.), *Kindheit und Jugend unter Hitler* (Berlin: Siedler, 1992), 213–54; for an account of the 1945ers general generational experience, or an excellent account of Schmidt's generational experience, see M. Roseman, 'Generation Conflict and German History, 1770–1968', in M. Roseman (ed.), *Generations in Conflict: Youth Revolt and Generation Formation in Germany 1770–1968* (Cambridge: Cambridge University Press, 1995), 32.

[15] C. Knowles, 'Winning the peace: the British in occupied Germany, 1945–1948', unpublished PhD dissertation (London: King's College London, 2014); F. Rosenfeld, 'The Anglo-German Encounter in Occupied Hamburg, 1945–50',

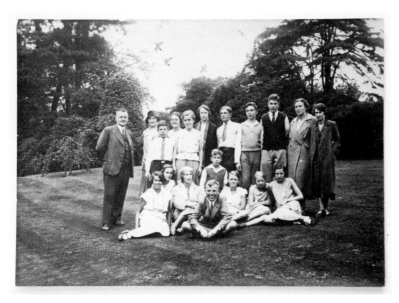

1.1 Helmut Schmidt during a three-week school exchange to Manchester at the age of thirteen, July 1932. Source: Bundeskanzler-Helmut-Schmidt-Stiftung Archiv.

British Regional Commissioner Sir Vaughan Berry, whose liberal governing style helped foster a cooperative and relatively friendly climate between Britons and Germans.[16] Though not acting in an overtly political function, Berry was a long-standing Labour activist with strong personal relationships with Herbert Morrison and Hugh Dalton,[17] and soon turned out to be an active political re-educator by setting up informal British–German tea parties and discussion groups for politically interested Germans. Amongst the most eager participants was the young Helmut Schmidt, who decades later would still recall the liberal atmosphere of these meetings and the feeling of being

unpublished PhD dissertation (New York, NY: Columbia University, 2006); M. Ahrens, *Die Briten in Hamburg: Besatzerleben 1945–1958* (Munich and Hamburg: Dölling und Galitz, 2011); I. D. Turner (ed.), *Reconstruction in Post-War Germany: British Occupation Policy and the Western Zones 1945–1955* (Oxford: Berg, 1989).

[16] For a fascinating case study of Berry's role and impact, see Knowles, 'Winning the Peace', 163–87.
[17] Ibid., 164.

treated like an equal by the British.[18] When Berry died in 1979, Schmidt even rang the British PM James Callaghan asking him to convey his personal grief to Berry's widow.[19]

Schmidt's personal experience of the British occupation also shaped his first active steps in German politics. As early as 1946, Schmidt became a member of the Social Democratic Party (SPD) in Hamburg, a local branch that was considerably less dogmatic than the SPD's national executive and tried to attract a bourgeois, middle-class electorate as well as its traditional working-class base.[20] In so doing, the SPD's Hamburg branch largely mirrored the British Labour government under Clement Attlee at the time, and Schmidt's close engagement with British policies was a key factor in the evolution of his early political views.[21] As part of his economics degree at the University of Hamburg, for example, Schmidt wrote an extensive essay on the 'Basic Lines of Socialization in England' in 1947, stressing Labour's pragmatic, flexible approach to economic policy-making and using amongst other sources Evan Durbin's *Politics of Democratic Socialism* and Hugh Dalton's *Practical Socialism For Britain*.[22] During a speech at a local SPD meeting in July 1948, he similarly praised the Labour government as the only successful European socialist force in Western Europe, suggesting that its strength came from the undogmatic attempt to integrate elements from all social classes rather than remaining stuck in class-based rhetoric.[23] Consciously or not, Schmidt therefore established a close intellectual link between the British Labour Party and the Hamburg SPD's own distinct regional identity in the wider social democratic movement in post-war Germany.

Partly as a result of his exposure to British thinking, the young Schmidt soon developed political ideas that ran contrary to the SPD's official party

---

[18] Interview with Helmut Schmidt, 23 September 2013; also, Schmidt, *Die Deutschen und ihre Nachbarn*, 101.

[19] Politisches Helmut-Schmidt-Archiv, Friedrich-Ebert-Stiftung (Bonn) [henceforward:1/HSAA] 006593, Vermerk über Telefongespräch BK mit PM Callaghan, 7 March 1979.

[20] H. Christier, *Sozialdemokratie und Kommunismus: Die Politik der SPD und der KPD in Hamburg 1945–59* (Hamburg: Leibniz-Verlag, 1975).

[21] For the historic links between the British Labour Party and the German Social Democrats, see S. Berger, *The British Labour Party and the German Social Democrats, 1900–1931* (Oxford: Oxford University Press, 1994).

[22] PHSA/EA, Band 1, Grundlagen der Sozialisierung in England, 25 January 1947.

[23] PHSA/EA, Band 1, Eröffnungsansprache durch Helmut Schmidt, Eddigehausen, 23 July 1948.

line. At the time, Schmidt's opposition to the SPD leadership around Kurt Schumacher centred primarily on his different perceptions of post-war Germany's future international role, resulting out of Schmidt's rather different generational experience from the great majority of the SPD's executive. Party leader Schumacher, for example, was first and foremost a political child of Weimar Germany. Having aggressively opposed the rise of the Nazis during the 1920s and then spent ten years imprisoned in various concentration camps, he regarded the Allied victory not as defeat but as liberation of the German people and therefore believed that any future European order would have to start with a unified and democratic Germany embedded in a socialist Europe of self-determined and equal nation-states.[24] The young Schmidt, by contrast, approached foreign policy from a more pragmatic viewpoint. As leader of the German Socialist Student Movement (SDS) in the late 1940s, he was keen to reconnect the German Social Democrats to their international counterparts, for example by organising an international conference of Socialist youth organisations with seventy participants from fifteen different countries in April 1948.[25] These international contacts made the young Schmidt aware of the profound distrust and suspicion that existed against Germany all across Europe. Therefore, Schmidt soon became convinced that any future German policy would have to be conducted in full cooperation and harmony with its European neighbours in order to stand any chance of success. Already in June 1948, for example, Schmidt warned in a local SPD publication that the SPD's nationalist stance over the *Ruhrstatut* would only isolate it internationally,[26] even forwarding his article to a British Labour Party MP to show 'the English comrades that there are factors in the German socialism which have other ideas than the official party line'.[27] He also attacked Schumacher openly in the SPD's party magazine a few months later, writing that the party leader's opposition to the *Ruhrstatut* was 'wrong and dangerous ... because it may well compromise future possibilities for cooperation in Western Europe'.[28]

---

[24] P. Merseburger, *Der Schwierige Deutsche: Kurt Schumacher* (Stuttgart: DVA, 1995), 7–8.

[25] 1/HSAA005004, Conference Report, 8–15 April 1948; Barsbüttel, 19 May 1948.

[26] 1/HSAA005006, Eine Chance für Europa, SDS Gruppe Hamburg: Rundbrief, June 1948.

[27] 1/HSAA005003, Schmidt to Eady, 28 June 1948.

[28] H. Schmidt, 'Das Ruhrstatut – drei Wochen später', in *Der Sozialist: Mitteilungsblatt der Landesorganisation Hamburg* 4/2, 1 February 1949.

28   *The Young Helmut Schmidt, 1945–1974*

Thus, partly as a result of his political education in the post-war years and his exposure to British ideas, Schmidt was at the forefront of a new generation of SPD politicians who advocated a more Westernised and internationalist foreign policy during the late 1940s; a policy that frequently stood at odds with the party leadership's dogmatic insistence on socialism and German unity. It is noteworthy that another key member of this new generation was Schmidt's fellow North German Willy Brandt, whose twelve years in Scandinavian exile and subsequent political maturation in Cold War Berlin had instilled in him similarly strong internationalist convictions.[29] In May 1950, Schmidt and Brandt were part of the tiny minority of SPD politicians who spoke out openly in favour of the Schuman Plan, being among the only eleven delegates who defied the negative party-line at the decisive party convention in 1951.[30] In due course, however, Brandt's and Schmidt's views would become commonly accepted wisdom within the SPD, as the party moved towards the centre and embraced a more pragmatic foreign policy culminating in the famous Godesberg Programme of 1959.[31] It was a change that reflected much bigger shifts in the international politics of the late 1940s and 1950s, which were decisive not only for the evolution of Schmidt's personal views but also for the wider pattern of post-war British–German relations.

Britain, Germany, and the Emerging Post-War European Order in the 1950s

In the late 1940s, the German question stood at the very heart of European politics. Although the country had been comprehensively defeated in the Second World War and was now occupied by the four wartime allies France, the United Kingdom, the Soviet Union, and the United States, a more permanent solution to its future proved difficult to achieve. The Allied wartime summits at Yalta and Potsdam had

[29] S. H. Krause, 'Neue Westpolitik: The Clandestine Campaign to Westernize the SPD in Cold War Berlin, 1948–1958', *Central European History* 48 (2015), 79–99; A. Wilkens, 'Willy Brandt und die europäische Einigung', in M. König and M. Schulz (eds.), *Die Bundesrepublik Deutschland und die europäische Einigung 1949–2000: Politische Akteure, gesellschaftliche Kräfte und internationale Erfahrungen* (Stuttgart: Steiner, 2004), 168–71.
[30] Merseburger, *Schumacher*, 470.
[31] B. Faulenbach, *Geschichte der SPD: Von den Anfängen bis zur Gegenwart* (Munich: Beck, 2012), 72–82.

Britain, Germany, and the Post-War order 29

revealed profound disagreements between the victorious powers: whereas the Soviet Union insisted on substantial reparations and territorial demands, the United States aimed for an economically and politically revitalised Germany kept in check by international peace-keeping organisations and reintegration into a liberal post-war economic order.[32] The British eventually fell behind the American line, keen to reduce the considerable economic costs of administrating the British occupation zone and anxious not to repeat the situation following the First World War. The worsening East–West relationship contributed to these dynamics, as the British increasingly feared an eventual infiltration of Germany with Communist ideology and hoped to revive the German economy in light of the emerging Soviet threat. Thus, Britain's overarching objective became to commit the United States permanently to the defence of Western Europe, a strategy that eventually resulted in the founding of the NATO in 1949.[33] A few years later, Britain also orchestrated the creation of the Western European Union (WEU), the scheme that eventually settled the question of German rearmament under NATO and permanently committed British troops to the defence of Europe.[34] In so doing, Britain carved itself a niche as one of the United States' most important West European allies in the realm of security and defence; a position it continued to inhabit for much of the Cold War.

Such close Anglo–American cooperation put France on its back foot. Having suffered from three German invasions in less than a century, it was understandably less keen for a revival of German power, initially advocating an uncompromising and far-reaching programme of deindustrialisation, reparations, and even the eventual dismemberment of

---

[32] D. J. Reynolds (ed.), *The Origins of the Cold War in Europe: International Perspectives* (New Haven, CT and London: Yale University Press, 1994).

[33] Deighton, 'Britain and the Cold War', 112–32; A. Deighton, *The Impossible Peace: Britain, the Division of Germany and the Origins of the Cold War* (Oxford: Oxford University Press, 1990).

[34] A. Deighton, 'The Last Piece of the Jigsaw: Britain and the Creation of the Western European Union, 1954', *Contemporary European History* 7/2 (July 1998), 181–96; J. W. Young, 'German Rearmament and the European Defence Community', in J. W. Young and M. Dockrill (eds.), *The Foreign Policy of Churchill's Peacetime Administration, 1951–55* (Leicester: Leicester University Press, 1988), 81–109. More generally, also S. Dockrill, *Britain's Policy for West German Rearmament, 1950–1955* (Cambridge: Cambridge University Press, 1991); S. Mawby, *Containing Germany: Britain and the Arming of the Federal Republic* (Basingstoke: Macmillan, 1999).

Germany. Yet, France – like most other European powers – was also highly dependent on the German economy and its resources, not least in light of its own reconstruction and modernisation programme.[35] To overcome this dilemma, the French government thus unveiled the so-called Schuman Plan for a European Coal and Steel Community on 9 May 1950: by pooling French and German coal and steel resources under a shared supranational authority, the ECSC offered a scheme for the revitalisation of the German economy which did not pose the simultaneous threat of a revival of German power.[36] As such, the French proposal was also highly attractive to the Germans themselves: not only did it offer the opportunity to revitalise its economy in a way that was acceptable to its European neighbours, but it also offered a potential route to international rehabilitation and reacceptance in the international community. Through its bold proposal for the ECSC, France had regained the initiative for the design of post-war Europe, at least in the economic field.[37] It also provided the impetus for the much more ambitious EEC founded on 1 January 1958, which set up a customs union with an explicit political goal towards an 'ever closer union' between the six founding members France, West Germany, Italy, and the Benelux countries.[38]

Britain might have taken the lead in the construction of Europe' post-war security system, but it largely stood aside from such attempts at economic integration, in spite of having been invited to take part in both the ECSC and EEC negotiations. In 1950, the Attlee government seriously discussed participation in the ECSC, but eventually declined to take part largely because of its unwillingness to pool British sovereignty over its coal and steel industries in the supranational institution of the High Authority.[39] More significant, however, was the British refusal to

---

[35] For a recent study that embeds French attitudes towards post-war Europe in a more long-term context of France's economic strategy, see L. A. Brunet, *Forging Europe: Industrial Organisation in France, 1940–1952* (Basingstoke: Macmillan, 2017).

[36] 'The Schuman Declaration', 9 May 1950: https://europa.eu/european-union/about-eu/symbols/europe-day/schuman-declaration_en [accessed on 13 June 2018].

[37] W. Hitchcock, 'France, the Western Alliance and the Origins of the Schuman Plan 1948–1950', *Diplomatic History* 21/4 (1997), 603–30.

[38] For an authoritative recent overview of the EC's founding years, see Loth, *Building Europe*, 20–74.

[39] J. W. Young, *Britain, France and the Unity of Europe 1945–51* (Leicester: Leicester University Press, 1984); C. Lord, *Absent at the Creation: Britain and*

take part in the proposed EEC in 1955–8, even though potential advantages of membership were again discussed seriously. Yet, British policy-makers saw little economic attraction in the proposed European customs union with a common external tariff, given Britain's significant extra-European trade; politically, they also remained sceptical over the concept of supranationalism as a prerequisite for closer West European integration. Above all, however, it was widely believed amongst British elites that the proposed scheme was simply too ambitious and thus unlikely to succeed.[40] When it did succeed, however, the negative consequences for Britain soon became evident. Not only did the EEC member-states' unexpectedly quick economic progress contrast with the comparatively sluggish performance of Britain, but there were also frequent signs that the EEC's economic strength would eventually translate into political power. 'For the first time since the Napoleonic era', PM Harold Macmillan wrote as early as October 1959, major European powers were 'united in a positive grouping, with considerable political aspects, which … may have the effect of excluding us both from European markets and from consultation in European policy'.[41] This soon resulted in a profound shift of British policy. After a singularly unsuccessful last-minute attempt to jeopardize the EEC's creation through the counter-proposal of a European Free Trade Area (FTA), Britain eventually applied for EC membership in July 1961.[42] But it was a decision that was motivated almost exclusively by defensive considerations, driven by fears of being excluded from a politically and economically powerful trading bloc on the Continent.

Britain's eventual EEC application in the early 1960s put the Germans into a formidable dilemma, feeding into much wider debates

----

    the Formation of the European Community, 1950–2 (Aldershot: Dartmouth, 1996); Dell, *British Abdication of Leadership*.

[40] There is now a wealth of literature on Britain's approach towards European integration in the 1950s and 1960s. The most authoritative overviews are A. S. Milward, *The United Kingdom and the European Community, Vol. I: The Rise and Fall of a National Strategy, 1945–1963* (London: Cass, 2002), and, for the bigger context, Young, *Britain and European Unity*.

[41] Macmillan to Selwyn Lloyd, 22 October 1959. As quoted in J. Ellison, 'Accepting the Inevitable: Britain and European Integration', in W. Kaiser and G. Staerck (eds.), *British Foreign Policy, 1955–64: Contracting Options* (Basingstoke: Macmillan, 2000), 179.

[42] On the doomed FTA proposal, see in particular J. Ellison, *Threatening Europe: Britain and the Creation of the European Community, 1955–58* (Basingstoke: Macmillan, 2000).

over the FRG's basic foreign policy orientation. To be sure, the vast majority of the German political elite at the time strongly supported British membership for both economic and political reasons, hoping that Britain might serve as a political counterweight to France and transform the nascent EEC into a more liberal and outward-looking community.[43] There were also hopes that British membership would lead to a more united and coherent Western Europe on the international stage, rather than one split between EEC and non-EEC members.[44] The key obstacle, however, was the strong French opposition to British membership, with President Charles de Gaulle in particular fearing that Britain would irrevocably change the EEC's economic character and thereby also undermine French leadership of the Community.[45] France's eventual decision to veto the British application in January 1963 thus exposed a key strategic dilemma of the FRG's foreign policy throughout the Cold War, namely whether to prioritise Franco–German cooperation or Germany's wider Anglo–American links and the transatlantic alliance.

The majority of German public opinion may have tended to favour the transatlantic course, but Chancellor Konrad Adenauer thought otherwise and made a conscious strategic decision to acquiesce in the French veto. Less than two weeks after the French veto, he travelled to Paris to sign the Franco–German Friendship Treaty (Élysée Treaty) on 22 January 1963. This effectively sealed the fate of Britain's first EEC application, even though the German *Bundestag* later added a preamble to the Treaty that reaffirmed the FRG's commitment to the transatlantic

---

[43]   E. Conze, 'Staatsräson und nationale Interessen: Die "Atlantiker-Gaullisten"-Debatte in der westdeutschen Politik- und Gesellschaftsgeschichte der 1960er Jahre', in C. A. Wurm, U. Lehmkuhl, and H. Zimmerman (eds.), *Deutschland, Großbritannien, Amerika: Politik, Gesellschaft und Internationale Geschichte im 20. Jahrhundert, Festschrift für Gustav Schmidt zum 65. Geburtstag* (Stuttgart: Steiner, 2003), 213.

[44]   These were not least the views of the then German Foreign Minister Gerhard Schröder. T. Oppelland, 'Gerhard Schröder: Protagonist des atlantischen Europas', in König and Schulz, *Deutschland und die europäische Einigung*, 129–46.

[45]   For the first application, see N. P. Ludlow, *Dealing with Britain: The Six and the First UK Application to the EEC* (Cambridge: Cambridge University Press, 1997). Also A. Deighton and N. P. Ludlow, 'A Conditional Application: British Management of the First Attempt to Seek Membership of the EEC, 1961–3', in A. Deighton and A. S. Milward (eds.), *Building Postwar Europe: National Decision-Makers and European Institutions, 1948–63* (Basingstoke: Macmillan, 1995), 107–22.

alliance.[46] But the damage in the British–German relationship was done. 'French duplicity has defeated us all', Macmillan wrote in his diary after the final breakdown of the negotiations; yet, he also complained bitterly about the lack of German support due to 'the fatal survival of Dr Adenauer (The Pétain of Germany)'.[47] Such singling-out of Adenauer was misguided, however, as subsequent events would prove: the episode was only the first of many instances where Germany would eventually decide to prioritise the long-term preservation of Franco–German relations and consolidation of the EEC over its short-term relations with Britain.[48] By the early 1960s, the nascent European integration process had already triggered a profound – and lasting – shift in the triangular relationship between France, Germany, and Britain.

Prioritising France and the United States: Helmut Schmidt's Changing Attitudes Towards Britain in the 1960s

In terms of personal backgrounds and political worldviews, the young Schmidt could hardly have been more different to Adenauer at the time. Born in 1876, Adenauer's life had been shaped primarily by his background as a Catholic Rhinelander in Imperial and Weimar Germany, as well as by his subsequent political persecution by the Nazis. After 1945, Adenauer deeply believed that Prussian militarism and subordination to the nation-state had been at the very heart of National Socialism, and he retained a certain distrust in the German nation and people throughout his life. Thus, he regarded European integration not only as a vehicle for Franco–German reconciliation, but also as an indispensable reassurance against the internal revival of Prussian nationalism.[49]

---

[46] O. Bange, *The EEC Crisis of 1963 – Kennedy, Macmillan, De Gaulle and Adenauer in Conflict* (Basingstoke: Macmillan, 2000).

[47] Diary Entries for 4 February 1963 and 28 January 1963, in P. Catterall (ed.), *The Macmillan Diaries, Vol. II: Prime Minister and After, 1957–1966* (London: Macmillan, 2011), 536, 539.

[48] N. P. Ludlow, 'Constancy and Flirtation: Germany, Britain, and the EEC, 1956-1972', in Noakes et al, *Britain and Germany in Europe*, 105–7. For literature on British–German relations over European integration in the 1950s and early 1960s, see S. Lee, *An Uneasy Partnership: British–German Relations Between 1955 and 1961* (Bochum: Brockmeyer, 1996); M. P. C. Schaad, *Bullying Bonn: Anglo-German Diplomacy on European Integration, 1955–61* (Basingstoke: Macmillan, 2000).

[49] W. Loth, 'Konrad Adenauer und die europäische Einigung', in König and Schulz, *Die Bundesrepublik Deutschland und die europäische Einigung*, 39–60;

His attitudes towards the United States and Britain, by contrast, lacked such emotional attachment, even though his staunch anti-Communism meant that he strongly supported Anglo–American military involvement in Western Europe. He had also been deeply disappointed by the British PM Macmillan's somewhat conciliatory behaviour during the second Berlin crisis from 1958 to 1961, something from which their personal relationship never recovered.[50]

The young Schmidt, by contrast, belonged firmly into the so-called *Atlanticist* camp of German politics. After an early interest in economic and transport policies, he started to make his name as an expert on security and defence issues in the early 1960s, publishing a widely-noticed book on nuclear strategy in 1961.[51] Schmidt's views were shaped significantly by his largely autodidactic study of Anglo–American literature on the subject, as well as by his intense involvement in various transatlantic networks including the London International Institute of Strategic Studies (IISS), the *Atlantikbrücke*, and the annual British–German *Königswinter* conferences.[52] In the foreword of his first

H. P. Schwarz, 'Adenauer und Europa', *Vierteljahreshefte für Zeitgeschichte* 27 (1979), 471–523.

[50] Lee, *Uneasy Partnership*.

[51] H. Schmidt, *Verteidigung oder Vergeltung: Ein deutscher Beitrag zum strategischen Problem der Nato* (Stuttgart: Seewald, 1961). Also translated into English the following year, H. Schmidt, *Defence or Retaliation: A German Contribution to the Consideration of Nato's Strategic Problem* (Edinburgh: Oliver and Boyd, 1962). For the book's impact, Spohr, *Global Chancellor*, 39–40.

[52] For Schmidt's intense involvement in the IISS and his close relationship with its founding director Alaistar Buchan, see the correspondence in 1/ HSAA005591, starting with Schmidt to Buchan, 2 May 1959; 1/ HSAA005591, Buchan to Schmidt, 16 March 1961; Buchan to Schmidt, 11 October 1961. For his role in the Atlantik-Brücke, of whose executive committee he became a member in 1967, see the correspondence in 1/ HSAA005529. More generally on the role of transatlantic networks in post-war Europe, T. Gijswijt, 'Uniting the West: The Bilderberg Group, the Cold War and European Integration, 1952–1966', unpublished PhD thesis (Heidelberg: Ruprecht-Karls-Universität, 2007); V. Aubourg, 'Organizing Atlanticism: The Bilderberg Group and the Atlantic Institute, 1952–1963', *Intelligence and National Security* 18/2 (2003), 92–105; and most recently A. Zetsche, 'The Quest for Atlanticism: German-American Elite Networking, the Atlantik-Brücke and the American Council on Germany, 1952–1974', unpublished PhD thesis (Newcastle upon Tyne: Northumbria University, 2016). For the role of informal networks in the shaping of the British–German relationship, C. Haase, 'The Hidden Hand of British Foreign Policy? The British-German Koenigswinter Conferences in the Cold War', in C. Haase (ed.), *Debating Foreign Affairs:*

book, for example, Schmidt lists Denis Healey, Alastair Buchan, Henry Kissinger, and Basil Liddell Hart as key influences.[53] French voices, by contrast, were remarkable mainly because of their absence, as Schmidt himself admitted in a speech to the IISS around the time.[54] While this reflected the comparative aloofness of French thinkers from many such transatlantic networks, there may also have been some personal reasons behind Schmidt's comparative lack of early interest in France: he could not speak French himself, and, as a North German Protestant, he also did not like the distinctively Catholic overtones of a lot of the integrationist rhetoric surrounding the nascent European Communities in the 1950s.[55]

As a result, Schmidt perceived Britain's first EC application from a distinctively Anglo–American viewpoint. Already in 1957, Schmidt had abstained from voting on the Treaties of Rome in the German Bundestag because he believed that only a bigger Europe, including Britain as well as the Scandinavian countries, had any realistic chance to succeed in the long run.[56] His focus on security and defence issues reinforced these beliefs, as he increasingly feared that an economically divided Europe between EC and non-EC countries could undermine West European unity in the Cold War. 'How does Europe actually intend to fight and win the economic competition with the Soviet Union,' Schmidt wrote to a fellow German parliamentarian in December 1959, 'if it splits up economically?'[57] During a little-noticed stint at the European Parliament from 1959 to 1962, he

---

The Public and British Foreign Policy Since 1867 (Berlin: Philo, 2003), 96–133. More generally, C. Haase, *Pragmatic Peacemakers: Institutes of International Affairs and the Liberalization of West Germany, 1945–73* (Augsburg: Wissner, 2007). For Schmidt's records on the Königswinter conferences, see the extensive files in 1/HSAA005537.

[53] Schmidt, *Verteidigung oder Vergeltung*, 9–10.

[54] PHSA/EA, Band 11, Handwritten notes on 'NATO and the Defence of Europe: Vortrag bei IISS', 6 June 1961. Schmidt's experience undoubtedly reflects a more general trend in post-war transatlantic networks, as numerous people have commented on France's self-exclusion from such circles. See, for example, D. Healey, *The Time of My Life* (London: Michael Joseph, 1989), 247; or Morgan, 'Preface', xiv.

[55] Haeussler, 'Convictions of a Realist', 964–6.

[56] Unfortunately, no contemporary records from the 1950s could be found, even though Schmidt later traced his voting record on the matter for a publication. See the correspondence and annotated draft PHSA/EA, Juli-Okt. 1983, 'II. Hamburgische Anglophilie', 1 August 1983.

[57] 1/HSAA005132, Schmidt to Dr Schmidt, 11 December 1959.

similarly argued that the intensification of the European integration process without Britain would only sharpen economic divisions in Western Europe, leading to potentially disastrous consequences for Western Europe's political unity.[58] Schmidt's main argument for British EC membership was therefore political: the FRG's very survival depended on the cohesion of both Western Europe and the transatlantic alliance, yet Britain's exclusion from the EC fatally undermined such cohesion, not least in light of Britain's military importance to the defence of Western Europe.[59] In April 1960, Schmidt even published a highly polemical newspaper article under the heading 'Hitler also underestimated England' in which he warned against any steps towards further European integration without Britain:

Already before 1914 and again under Hitler, German foreign policy has steered into catastrophes not least because of its false estimation of England's importance, English power and perseverance, and German presumptuousness vis-à-vis the British nation, which is proud to have proved itself in all wars for centuries.[60]

The key reason why Schmidt appeared so passionate about British EC membership was because it tied into much bigger questions about Western Europe's future position in the transatlantic alliance. Whilst the United States and Western Europe had moved largely in synch during the late 1940s and 1950s, the change in the superpower relationship between the United States and Soviet Union during the early 1960s now raised concerns about the future of the transatlantic partnership. In light of the emerging nuclear parity between the United States and the Soviet Union, the West Europeans increasingly questioned the credibility of the American security guarantee for Western Europe, fearing that the United States would ultimately be likely to shy away from a nuclear confrontation with the Soviet Union at a time of emerging nuclear parity.[61] In his first book, Schmidt summed up the emerging West European dilemma quite succinctly: 'if the USA reacts in

---

[58] PHSA/EA, Band 10, Verhandlungen des Europäischen Parlaments, No. 5A, 31 March 1960.
[59] See ibid.; *Echo*, 2 April 1960; *Echo*, 9 April 1960. [60] *Echo*, 9 April 1960.
[61] W. Burr and D. A. Rosenberg, 'Nuclear Competition in an Era of Stalemate, 1963–1975', in Leffler and Westad, *CHCW Vol. II*, 88–111. For US–European relations during the 1960s more generally, see T. A. Schwartz, *Lyndon Johnson and Europe: In the Shadow of Vietnam* (Cambridge, MA: Harvard University Press, 2003).

a determined and powerful way to Soviet threats of aggression, then the Europeans will immediately fear to be dragged into an "unnecessary" war. If, on the other hand, the United States shows itself ready to negotiate, then the Europeans will fear that the US leadership sacrifices European interests because of their own nuclear-strategic vulnerability'.[62]

Amongst the Europeans, the issue provoked heated debates whether Western Europe should strive to maintain the closest possible link with the United States, or instead work towards a more independent role on the international stage. The French President Charles de Gaulle was the most prominent proponent of the latter view. After his return to power in 1958, he worked consistently towards a more independent foreign policy, famously calling for a pan-European system stretching from the Atlantic to the Urals. After the Cuban Missile crisis of 1962, de Gaulle's calls for greater European autonomy intensified, culminating in France's withdrawal from NATO's military command in 1966–7.[63] While the so-called 'Gaullist challenge' triggered divisions amongst all NATO members, tensions were felt most strongly in West Germany, the country at the very heart of both the EC and the transatlantic alliance.[64] Whereas German supporters of de Gaulle, mainly found amongst South German Catholics such as Franz-Josef Strauss, believed that a more independent European role based on a strong Franco–German axis would increase their leverage with the United States, the so-called German 'Atlanticists' maintained that the defence of Western Europe was unthinkable without the closest involvement of the United States.[65]

For the evolution of Schmidt's attitudes towards Britain, these wider changes in mid-1960s international politics had two slightly contra-dictory consequences. First, the French withdrawal from NATO's

---

[62] Schmidt, *Verteidigung oder Vergeltung*, 70.

[63] F. Bozo, 'France, "Gaullism," and the Cold War', in Leffler and Westad, *CHCW Vol. II*, 158–78; G. H. Soutou, 'The Linkage Between European Integration and Détente: The Contrasting Approaches of de Gaulle and Pompidou, 1965 to 1974', Ludlow, *European Integration and the Cold War*, 12.

[64] For the German debate, see T. Geiger, *Atlantiker gegen Gaullisten: Außenpolitischer Konflikt und innerparteilicher Machtkampf in der CDU/CSU 1958–1969* (Munich: Oldenbourg, 2008), and Conze, 'Atlantiker-Gaullisten Debatte', 197–226.

[65] Though it should be noted, as Geiger does, that neither side thought it could break ranks with one or the other completely.

military wing inevitably reinforced the importance of Britain and Germany as Western Europe's two most important members of the transatlantic alliance. As such, the two countries shared roughly similar strategic goals, particularly after Britain's retreat from many of its global responsibilities and its reduction to a largely European power during the 1960s. Given that they both relied heavily on NATO and the US security commitment to the defence of Western Europe, they were particularly concerned about the continuing credibility of NATO's defence strategy in light of nuclear parity between the superpowers, and therefore started to work closely together to shape NATO strategy according to West European interests.[66] In spite of some remaining tensions over nuclear sharing, Britain and Germany thus soon emerged as the major European driving forces behind the shift of NATO's doctrine from 'deterrence' to 'flexible response' in the 1960s.[67] Such British–German cooperation eventually found its institutional expressions in the establishment of the Nuclear Planning Group (NPG) in December 1966, and the Harmel Report of January 1967 which enshrined the dual-track approach of deterrence and détente in the alliance's doctrine.[68] Partly as a result of the Gaullist challenge, then, Britain and Germany came to form the West European nucleus within the wider transatlantic alliance in security and defence issues from the mid-1960s onwards.

Second, however, the Gaullist challenge also illustrated the FRG's strategic dependence on Franco–German cooperation to Schmidt, particularly once his rise to the SPD's first rank of politicians in the 1960s forced him to acquire a more comprehensive understanding of West German foreign policy. As a result, Schmidt developed the firm strategic conviction that the EC with the Franco–German relationship at its core provided an indispensable framework for post-war Germany to anchor its foreign policy safely and permanently in a multilateral setting. To Schmidt, this was important not only because of Germany's recent history and exposed geopolitical position, but also because of

[66] T. Macintyre, *Anglo-German Relations During the Labour Governments 1964–70: NATO Strategy, Détente and European Integration* (Manchester: Manchester University Press, 2007), 122–46; Bluth, *Western Nuclear Strategy*, 179–200.

[67] For the bilateral tensions over nuclear sharing, see J. W. Young, 'Killing the MLF? The Wilson Government and Nuclear Sharing in Europe, 1964–66', *Diplomacy and Statecraft* 14/2 (2003), 295–324.

[68] Bluth, *Western Nuclear Strategy*, 179–200.

France's role as one of the four powers responsible for the protection of Berlin. At the height of the Gaullist challenge, Schmidt therefore spoke out strongly and repeatedly against an escalation of Franco–German tensions. The FRG should never 'become the leading voice of the anti-French position', he wrote in a newspaper article in January 1966, given that it 'was much more dependent on Paris in the conduct of its foreign policy than the other four [EC] member-states'.[69] At the same time, however, he was ardent that any independent European policy without or against the United States remained unthinkable, thereby shedding light on the FRG's key strategic dilemma of being dependent on both France and the United States. The Germans had to 'avoid a final confrontation between Paris and Washington' at all costs, Schmidt accordingly claimed a few weeks later, since 'neither Berlin nor the Federal Republic' could be protected 'without closest cooperation with the United States'.[70] This almost equal emphasis on both France and the United States in Schmidt's conceptions of German foreign policy would remain a constant thread in Schmidt's thought throughout his active political life and beyond.[71] Britain, by contrast, came to play an increasingly subordinate role in Schmidt's eyes, which to some extent mirrored the country's more general international and economic decline during the 1960. 'Bonn cannot hope for British help in solving the short-term problems', he wrote in a major newspaper article in *Die Zeit* in September 1966, since 'London will be preoccupied by its East-of-Suez problems, and its economic and foreign trade problems, for the foreseeable future'. In his eyes, any British–German relationship going beyond 'reserved cordiality' thus seemed unlikely – a striking reversal of the views he had articulated during Britain's first EEC application only a few years earlier.[72]

The change in Schmidt's views became evident in his rather half-hearted attitude towards Britain's second application for EC membership in 1967, where he made clear that there was little perspective of Germany supporting the British cause against continuing resistance by the French.[73] Interestingly, Schmidt justified this position primarily by

---

[69] *Hamburger Sonntagsblatt*, 30 January 1966.
[70] *Abendzeitung*, 29 March 1966. [71] Haeussler, 'Cold War European', 433–6.
[72] *Die Zeit*, 16 September 1966.
[73] For British–German relations over Britain's second application, see H. Philippe, *'The Germans Hold the Key': Anglo-German Relations and the Second British Approach to Europe* (Augsburg: Wissner, 2007); K. Böhmer, '"We Too Mean

the FRG's overriding national interest in the stability of the Franco–German relationship; a key long-term strategic consideration to which the question of British EC membership now seemed subordinate to Schmidt. When the British PM Harold Wilson toured EC capitals in February 1967 to gather support for the British application, for example, Schmidt claimed in one of his regular newspaper columns that British hopes for strong German backing were misplaced. 'Given its particular interests and its resulting tight bonds to France', he wrote, 'the Federal Republic cannot . . . act as a battering ram and immediately open up the door to the EEC for the English by exercising pressure on Paris'.[74] At the annual *Königswinter* Conference in 1967, Schmidt even attacked some British delegates directly for taking German support for granted: 'they expect substantial help from us and forget that we have no lever in our hands as regards Paris'.[75] Yet again, the profound change in Schmidt's attitudes reflected more general changes in the power balance between West Germany and the United Kingdom. Ultimately, the FRG government under Chancellor Kiesinger proved as unwilling as Adenauer had been a few years earlier to prevent de Gaulle's second veto of British EC membership in November 1967, clearly prioritising the preservation of the Franco–German relationship and the EC over British membership.[76] It was only de Gaulle's departure in 1969 that altered the context of the British–German relationship once again.

British European Community Membership, German Ostpolitik, and Helmut Schmidt as Minister of Defence, 1969–1972

On 21 October 1969, Willy Brandt was elected German Chancellor, becoming the first Social Democratic leader of the young Federal Republic. Brandt's election triggered profound changes in the FRG's

---

Business": Germany and the Second British Application to the EEC, 1966–67', in O. Daddow (ed.), *Harold Wilson and European Integration: Britain's Second Application to Join the EEC* (London: Cass, 2003), 211–26.

[74] *Abendzeitung*, 21 February 1967. See also H. Schmidt, 'Deutschland und das europäische Sicherheitssystem der Zukunft', *Wehrkunde* XVI/3 (March 1967), 118.

[75] H. Schmidt, 'The Shaping of Europe and the Role of Nations', in Deutsch-Englische Gesellschaft e.V., *Europe's Role in a Changing World: Deutsch-Englisches Gespräch, Königswinter, 10.-12. März 1967* (Düsseldorf, 1967), 21.

[76] Philippe, 'The Germans Hold the Key'; Böhmer, 'We Too Mean Business'.

British European Community Membership 41

domestic and foreign policy orientation. Domestically, Brandt embarked upon an ambitious programme of social reform and political liberalisation; in the realm of foreign policy, he set into action his ideas for *Ostpolitik*, the process of peaceful reconciliation and cooperation with the GDR and Eastern Europe. Whereas the FRG's previous governments had insisted at least in public on their sole right to represent the German people ('Alleinvertretungsanspruch') and that German reunification had to precede any attempt at East–West détente, the Brandt government now publicly reversed this logic: it argued that any successful West German foreign policy had to first accept the realities of the post-war settlement by starting a dialogue between East and West, and that the division of Germany could only be overcome if the bigger division of Europe was overcome too.[77] The most important achievements of Brandt's *Ostpolitik* were the Treaty of Warsaw in 1970, which recognised the current European borders including the Oder-Neisse line, and the Basic Treaty of 1972, which established formal relations between the two German states. At the same time, however, Brandt remained careful to balance *Ostpolitik* with a correspondingly proactive *Westpolitik*, believing that a proactive policy towards the East could only be conducted by a FRG firmly anchored in the Western bloc.[78] As such, Brandt also proved a major driving force behind the much-heralded revitalisation of the European integration process at The Hague summit in December 1969, which set in motion an ambitious programme of 'completion, deepening, and widening' of the EC.[79] Crucially, this programme included a commitment to EC enlargement which was at least partially designed to ease Britain's way into the Community. With the newly elected French President Georges Pompidou eventually lifting French opposition, British EC membership suddenly seemed like a more realistic prospect than it had for much of the 1960s.[80]

---

[77] For an excellent recent overview of *Ostpolitik*, see G. Niedhart, 'Ostpolitik: Transformation Through Communication and the Quest for Peaceful Change', *Journal of Cold War Studies* 18/3 (2016), 14–59.

[78] A. Wilkens, 'New Ostpolitik and European Integration: Concepts and Policies in the Brandt Era', in Ludlow, *Ostpolitik-Westpolitik*, 67–80.

[79] C. Hiepel, 'The Hague Summit of the European Community, Britain's Entry, and the New Atlantic Partnership, 1969–1970', in M. Schulz and T. A. Schwartz (eds.), *The Strained Alliance: US-European Relations from Nixon to Carter* (Cambridge: Cambridge University Press, 2010), 105–24.

[80] Britain's EC entry will be discussed more extensively in the next chapter.

42 *The Young Helmut Schmidt, 1945–1974*

These wider changes in international politics boded well for British–German relations for several reasons. First, Brandt's *Ostpolitik* removed a long-standing obstacle that had plagued the bilateral relationship since the late 1950s, namely Germany's previously uncompromising opposition to any British attempts at East–West reconciliation and détente.[81] With both Britain and Germany trying to find a *modus vivendi* with the Eastern bloc, the two countries' foreign policy objectives now seemed rather more congruent than before, even though some latent British suspicions over German interests in the East remained.[82] But even more important for the improvement of British–German relations in the early 1970s was Pompidou's eventual support of British EC membership, reviving both British and German hopes for a united Western Europe embedded firmly within the wider transatlantic alliance. Brandt in particular regarded British membership as a key step in the EC's long-term evolution into a powerful political actor on the global stage, claiming in the British *Guardian* that it was only with Britain as a full EC member that Europe could 'ever learn to speak with one voice'.[83]

Brandt's thoughts mirrored those of his newly appointed Minister of Defence Helmut Schmidt, who similarly claimed at the time that British entry into the EC was a vital prerequisite to transform the EC into a major political actor on the international stage.[84] Schmidt hoped that British EC membership might trigger a lasting rapprochement of British and French visions for post-war European cooperation, eventually leading to a more coherent West European position within the transatlantic alliance as a whole. In a major interview with the German newspaper *Die Welt* in February 1970, for example, he argued that 'stronger cooperation of the Western states in common defence policies can only happen if British entry into the EC succeeds', and that British entry

---

[81] R. G. Hughes, *Britain, Germany and the Cold War: The Search for a European Détente 1949–1967* (London: Routledge, 2007).

[82] G. Niedhart, 'The British Reaction Towards Ostpolitik: Anglo-West German Relations in the Era of Détente 1967–1971', in Haase, *Debating Foreign Policy*, 130–52; R. Morgan, 'Willy Brandt's "Neue Ostpolitik": British Perceptions and Positions, 1969–1975', in A. M. Birke, M. Brechtken and A. Searle (eds.), *An Anglo-German Dialogue: The Munich Lectures on the History of International Relations* (Munich: Saur, 2000), 179–202.

[83] *Guardian*, 6 May 1971.

[84] See his statements to that effect in Bundespresseamt [henceforward: BPA], Das Interview der Woche: DLF, 15 February 1970; BPA, DFS/13.4.1970/20.20h, 13 April 1970; *europäische gemeinschaft* 10 (October 1969); *Die Welt*, 16 February 1970.

British European Community Membership 43

would inevitably 'also have positive effects in the field of defence'.[85] At the annual German *Wehrpolitische Tagung* in November 1970, he even mused off-the-record that British membership might one day create sufficient political pressure to draw France back into the integrated military command of NATO.[86] In light of these hopes, Schmidt decided to intervene personally to shore up British domestic support for EC membership, writing uncharacteristically emotional letters to key members of the Labour Party in which he recalled in a highly personal manner how the SPD had made the grave mistake of missing the train to Europe in the early 1950s and urged his British counterparts not to make the same mistake.[87]

In the late 1960s, then, the climate of the British–German relationship was much more positive and optimistic than it had been for a long time. Schmidt therefore also hoped to use his tenure as Defence Minister to build on British–German cooperation in the pursuit of his long-term objective to strengthen the West European pillar of NATO in light of continuing concerns over the US nuclear guarantee.[88] As early as 1961, Schmidt had become convinced that any credible strategy for the defence of Europe had to be based on a balance of power on all military levels, i.e. conventional, tactical-nuclear, and strategic-nuclear weapons, in order to ensure credible deterrence.[89] Given NATO's comparative weakness in conventional forces, Schmidt therefore aimed to work with Britain to strengthen the alliance's conventional forces, as well as to push more strongly for arms limitation talks.[90] In both quests, he found a congenial British counterpart in Denis Healey, whom he had known and liked since the early 1950s. Like

---

[85] *Die Welt*, 16 February 1970.

[86] PHSA/EA, Band 47, Rede bei Wehrpolitische Tagung bei Ulm [unkorrigierte Bandabschrift], 14 November 1970.

[87] PHSA/Privat-Politisch 1971, A–Z, Band 8, Schmidt to Jenkins, 7 July 1971; Schmidt to Healey, 7 July 1971; Schmidt to Brown, 7 July 1971.
The culmination of Schmidt's charm offensive was his appearance at the 1971 Königswinter conference, where he urged the British participants 'not to run out of breath at the eleventh hour'. See 1/HSAA005538, 21. Deutsch-Englisches Gespräch in Königswinter 1971; Empfang der Bundesregierung durch den Herrn Bundesminister der Verteidigung Helmut Schmidt, Bad Godesberg, 27 March 1971.

[88] Heuser, 'Britain and Germany in NATO', 149.

[89] For the evolution of Schmidt's strategic thinking, see also Spohr, *Global Chancellor*, 34–40.

[90] Ibid., 43–6.

Schmidt, Healey believed in deterrence based on a balance of power on both nuclear and non-nuclear levels, and called repeatedly for both a strengthening of West European conventional forces and greater European influence on the nuclear-strategic planning of NATO.[91] During their brief joint stint in office, Schmidt and Healey thus cooperated extensively in order to align British and German defence doctrines closely with each other, frequently exchanging ideas and manuscripts over nuclear strategy.[92] In 1970, Schmidt even praised Healey's initiative for the creation of NATO's *Eurogroup* as the first step towards 'what may, in time, become the consolidated defense establishment of a politically united Western Europe' in an article for *Foreign Affairs*.[93] Yet, British–German defence cooperation remained equally smooth under Healey's Conservative successor Lord Carrington, showing how the rapprochement of British and German views was largely the result of structural pressures emanating from Britain's eventual acceptance of a more limited European role and Germany's simultaneous gradual opening up to East–West détente.[94] At long last, Britain and Germany seemed ready to embark upon a joint European future together.

Everything Falls Apart? Helmut Schmidt as Minister of Finance During the Multiple Crises of the Early 1970s

Yet, the course of the British–German relationship was again altered by developments largely outside the bilateral realm. The multiple crises of the early 1970s changed not only the context of British–German relations profoundly, but they also affected the wider framework of European and transatlantic cooperation. The collapse of the Bretton

---

[91] See, for example, *Der Spiegel*, 23, 2 June 1965; D. Healey, 'On European Defence', *Survival* 11/4 (1969), 110–15; or D. Healey, 'NATO, Britain and Soviet Military Policy', *Orbis* 13/1 (1969), 48–58. More generally also Macintyre, *Anglo-German Relations*, 122–46.

[92] Healey, *Time of My Life*, 315–6. Unfortunately, few archival materials are available on Schmidt and Healey's cooperation during this period. For some correspondence, see 1/HSAA005482, Healey to Schmidt, 20 April 1970; Schmidt to Healey, 19 June 1970.

[93] H. Schmidt, 'Germany in the Era of Negotiations', *Foreign Affairs* 49 (1970), 42. See also Schmidt's draft foreword to a proposed biography of Healey in 1/HSAA005494, Schmidt to Reed, 30 September 1970.

[94] Morgan, 'Neue Ostpolitik', 200; Hughes, *Britain, Germany, and the Cold War*.

Everything Falls Apart?

1.2 As Minister of Defence, Helmut Schmidt established a close partnership with his British counterpart Denis Healey, pictured here in October 1969. Source: Bundeskanzler-Helmut-Schmidt-Stiftung Archiv.

Woods system in August 1971 and the global economic shock following the Yom-Kippur War of October 1973 suddenly put to a halt two decades of European economic growth and prosperity, triggering sharply rising inflation and unemployment in many European countries.[95]

---

[95] For the wealth of literature on the early 1970s, see as a starting point N. Ferguson et al. (eds.), *The Shock of the Global: The 1970s in Perspective*

46 *The Young Helmut Schmidt, 1945–1974*

The different ways in which the West Europeans dealt with these challenges exposed their sometimes stark differences over fiscal and economic policy, and reopened old rifts between transatlantic and European models of international cooperation.[96] As Finance Minister from July 1972 to May 1974, Schmidt was at the very centre of these wider developments. His thoughts and actions at the time again highlight not only the overriding importance he attached to the FRG's relations with France and the United States, with British–German relations playing a subordinate role at best, but they also reveal the much wider strategic gap in fiscal and economic matters that separated the two countries in the early 1970s.

Schmidt's most immediate task once in office was to tackle the monetary crisis that had triggered the collapse of the Bretton Woods system in August 1971.[97] After the unilateral decision by the United States to float the American dollar, a heated debate had emerged over the appropriate European reaction: whereas France resisted US demands to appreciate European currencies and urged a return to fixed exchange rates with capital controls, the Germans instead lobbied for a limited float against the dollar.[98] Whereas Schmidt's predecessor as Finance Minister, Karl Schiller, had been an outspoken critic of the French position, Schmidt opted for a rather different political strategy by immediately calling for greater international cooperation and a realignment of Franco–German positions.[99] To pursue this quest,

(Cambridge, MA: Belknap of Harvard University Press, 2010); L. Raphael and A. Doering-Manteuffel, *Nach dem Boom: Perspektiven auf die Zeitgeschichte seit 1970* (Göttingen: Vandenhoeck & Ruprecht, 2008); A. Rödder, *Die Bundesrepublik Deutschland 1969–1990* (Munich: Oldenbourg, 2004).

[96] For recent studies of the transatlantic tensions surrounding Kissinger's call, see in particular Möckli, *European Foreign Policy; and Gfeller, Building a European Identity.*

[97] H. James, *International Monetary Cooperation Since Bretton Woods* (New York, NY and Oxford: Oxford University Press, 1996).

[98] For more background, see H. Zimmermann, 'Unravelling the Ties That Really Bind: The Dissolution of the Transatlantic Monetary Order and the European Monetary Cooperation, 1965–1973', in Schulz and Schwartz, *Strained Alliance*, 125–44; W. G. Gray, 'Toward a "Community of Stability"? The Deutsche Mark Between European and Atlantic Priorities, 1968–1973', in ibid., 145–67; W. G. Gray, 'Floating the System: Germany, the United States, and the Breakdown of Bretton Woods, 1969–1973', *Diplomatic History* 31/2 (2007), 295–323.

[99] For the differences between Schiller's and Schmidt's approach, see in particular Gray, 'Community of Stability', 166–7; Gray, 'Floating the System', 317–18.

Everything Falls Apart?   47

he relied closely on cooperation with his French counterpart Valéry Giscard d'Estaing, with whom he quickly established a strong personal rapport as both set out to shape a new Franco–German consensus based largely around stability-orientated and deflationary measures. During the dollar crisis of January 1973, Schmidt and Giscard then translated their words into deeds. Although the technical substance of their eventual solutions was not much different to some of Schiller's earlier suggestions, the political presentation was very different indeed.[100] In marked contrast to earlier episodes under Schiller, both Schmidt and Giscard were keen to stress their close cooperation in public, with Schmidt proclaiming repeatedly that French and German interests in monetary matters were 'almost identical'.[101] The period might thus well be seen to mark the beginning of a joint Franco–German lead in setting the EC's fiscal and economic agenda, something that would become a central feature of Schmidt's chancellorship from 1974 onwards.[102]

As regards the British–German relationship, however, the Franco–German rapprochement rather illustrated the widening gap over fiscal and monetary matters between Britain and its new EC partners. Indeed, the British response to the collapse of Bretton Woods was almost diametrically opposed to the Franco–German emphasis on deflation, as PM Heath decided to embark upon a programme of massive fiscal and monetary expansion.[103] The short-term results were

> For Schmidt's calls for action, PHSA/EA, 21.-30.9.1972, Helmut Schmidt's speech at IMF conference, 26 September 1972; PHSA/EA; 21.-30.9.1972, BPA, Helmut Schmidt: Bericht aus Bonn, DFS 21h, 29 September 1972.

[100] Gray, 'Floating the System', 319–20.

[101] See, for example, PHSA/EA, 4.12.1972–29.1.1973, BPA., Helmut Schmidt zu den deutsch-französischen Konsultationen auf der Ebene von Wirtschaft und Finanzen: Tagesschau 22.30h, 23 January 1973; SPD, Pressemitteilungen und Informationen, 28 January 1973; Pressekonferenz (unkorrigiertes Manuskript), 13 February 1973. For contemporary praise of Schmidt's and Giscard's collaboration, 'Er stand wie ein Fels in der Dollarflut: Helmut Schmidts Hartnäckigkeit ermöglichte eine europäisch-amerikanische Lösung', *Die Zeit*, 16 February 1973; 'Ein Zahlenkünstler mit Charme: Widerpart und Währungspartner des Organisten Schmidt: Ziehharmonikaspieler Giscard', *Die Zeit* 16 February 1973.

[102] Simonian, *Privileged Partnership*, 247–73; Miard-Delacroix, *Partenaires de choix*; Spohr, *Global Chancellor*, 14–32.

[103] J. Tomlinson, 'Economic Policy', in Seldon and Hickson, *New Labour, Old Labour*, 55; R. D. Putnam and N. Bayne, *Hanging Together. Cooperation and Conflict in the Seven-Power Summits* (London: Sage, 1987), 26.

fairly disastrous: by mid-1973, Britain's trade balance had plummeted from +£285 million in 1971 to –£1,184 million.[104] The major short-term international consequence of Britain's comparatively worse performance was that the British government felt unable to return to the so-called European currency 'snake', fearing that it could not risk aligning the weak Pound Stirling permanently to other European currencies against the dollar.[105] As a result, the EC's more ambitious plans for European Economic and Monetary Union (EMU), which would have required participation of all EC member-states, were shelved for the time being, and Germany and France instead opted for a much more limited 'snake' excluding Britain, Ireland, and Italy.[106]

It was an early indicator of the stark discrepancies between the British and most other EC economies, which would continue to trouble the EC for much of the 1970s. To Schmidt, however, these developments merely seemed to confirm his personal long-standing scepticism over the goal of EMU, and he professed to care little about Britain's decision to stay outside the 'snake'.[107] If anything, the episode seems to have reinforced his strong personal conviction that the convergence and harmonisation of fiscal and economic policies by EC member-states always had to precede any more ambitious attempts at further monetary integration. As he put it in an interview with *The Times* in November 1973, it seemed 'quite clear ... that in the present economic situation Britain, Ireland and Italy are not in a position to take such firm action in fighting inflation as Germany and Holland have done'.[108] As far as economic and monetary cooperation was concerned, Britain was

---

[104] Bundesarchiv Koblenz, Bundeskanzleramt [henceforward: B136/], 12550, Wirtschaftspolitische Lage in Großbritannien, 28 September 1973.

[105] For the difference of the British position vis-à-vis the Franco–German ones, see C. Hiepel, 'Willy Brandt, Georges Pompidou und Europa. Das deutsch-franz ösische Tandem in den Jahren 1969–1974', in Knipping and Schönwald, *Europa der zweiten Generation*, 41–3.

[106] C. Hiepel, *Willy Brandt und Georges Pompidou: deutsch-französische Europapolitik zwischen Aufbruch und Krise* (Munich: Oldenbourg, 2012), part. 217–82.

[107] PHSA/EA, 4.3.-12.4.1973, Pressekonferenz 28/73: unkorrigiertes Manuskript, 12 March 1973. In the final months of Brandt's government, Schmidt's stance increasingly came to reflect the more general view of the German government. See Hiepel, *Brandt und Pompidou*, 226–9.

[108] *The Times*, 6 November 1973.

Everything Falls Apart? 49

still toddling far behind the Franco–German tandem during its first year inside the EC.

The political and economic troubles of the early 1970s also raised some more fundamental questions over Western Europe's future relationship with the United States. Whereas previous US governments had by and large been supportive of European integration, the Nixon administrations from 1969 to 1974 harboured open suspicions and public distrust over the EC's growing political ambitions on the international stage, fearing a potential threat to American leadership of the Western alliance.[109] On 23 April 1973, US National Security Adviser Henry Kissinger then famously called for a 'Year of Europe' in a widely-noticed speech, aiming to redefine the transatlantic relationship in light of these changing power dynamics. Yet, the initiative backfired: most European governments interpreted Kissinger's speech as a thinly disguised attempt to call the Europeans back into line, and in response proved rather unusually effective in formulating a joint response. When transatlantic tensions culminated over the Yom Kippur War in October 1973, the EC member-states even formulated a joint European foreign policy position that clearly ran against American objectives for the very first time in their history, declaring their support of the UN Resolution 242 that called for Israeli withdrawal from the occupied territories.[110]

The main reason why such European attempts at coordinating and fostering joint international positions in response to the 'Year of Europe' eventually came to nothing were long-term dependencies in security and economics at the very heart of the transatlantic alliance. From an American perspective, the EC's support for UN Resolution 242 seemed to illustrate a spineless caving in by the Europeans to OPEC economic pressures over energy and oil prices. This was not entirely without foundation. Given the EC member-states' much higher dependencies on Middle East oil, the EC's early attempts at forging

---

[109] There has been an intense historiographical debate on the transatlantic upheavals under Nixon in recent years. Apart from the aforementioned works (Schulz and Schwartz, *Strained Alliance*; Möckli, *European Foreign Policy*; Gfeller, *Building a European Identity*), see in particular L. Nichter, *Richard Nixon and Europe: The Reshaping of the Postwar Atlantic World* (New York, NY and Cambridge: Cambridge University Press, 2015), and – with a tighter focus on European perspectives – S. Kieninger, *Dynamic Détente: The United States and Europe, 1964–1975* (Lanham, MD: Lexington Books, 2016).

[110] D. Möckli, 'Asserting Europe's Distinct Identity: The EC Nine and Kissinger's Year of Europe', in Schulz and Schwartz, *Strained Alliance*, 208–10.

a common policy vis-à-vis the OPEC countries soon faltered, as key member-states increasingly sought refuge in unilateral measures or bilateral deals. By early 1974, it had become painstakingly clear that the quest for a joint EC energy policy had failed, and most member-states had as a result come to favour a new joint transatlantic approach towards the Middle East. The exception was France, which continued to insist on an independent European energy policy without US involvement in order to avoid antagonising OPEC countries and potentially jeopardizing France's traditionally good links with many oil-exporting Arab countries.[111] When the United States decided to invite the major industrial Western powers to a major conference on energy matters in Washington in February 1974 in spite of such French opposition, the scene seemed set for a major confrontation between France and the United States, even though it became quickly evident that all EC member-states except France backed the American proposals. Schmidt, who attended the conference in his capacity as Finance Minister, believed particularly strongly that the West Europeans were ultimately powerless without American support, and that only a concerted approach by all major oil-consuming countries including the United States would stand any chance of success.[112] When the French Foreign Minister Jobert refused to budge on a joint transatlantic strategy, Schmidt thus eventually lost patience and exclaimed that 'if he had to choose between the United States and France, he would choose the former'.[113] Jobert rose to the challenge, afterwards publicly denouncing Schmidt for having betrayed the European cause.[114] This turned out to be the end of the 'Year of Europe'.

While there were few direct British–German dynamics in most of these debates, the episode nonetheless had important indirect consequences for the bilateral relationship, not least because Britain shared the German dilemma of potentially getting caught between France and the United States. The Heath government was also anxious to present itself as a constructive new EC member-state, and Britain had historically quite different interests in the Middle East than the United States.

[111] Hiepel, *Brandt und Pompidou*, 292–3.   [112] Ibid., 294.
[113] The National Archives: Public Record Office (Kew) [henceforward: TNA]/ FCO33/2459, Diplomatic Report: Germany, Europe, and the United States, 27 February 1974; Möckli, 'Asserting Europe's Distinct Identity', 215.
[114] Hiepel, *Brandt und Pompidou*, 298.

Everything Falls Apart? 51

At the same time, however, Britain remained firmly committed to the Anglo–American relationship as the overarching foundation of its foreign policy, a long-term strategic prioritisation that eventually proved decisive in the evolution of the British position between April 1973 and February 1974.[115] By the time of the Washington Energy Conference, Britain was indeed firmly back in the transatlantic camp, and cooperated closely with the American side in the design and run-up to the conference.[116] Given that this evolution of the British position largely mirrored the parallel evolution of the German one, the British even seemed hopeful in early 1974 that they had finally managed to steal France's thunder in the leadership of Europe. A major FCO dispatch following the Washington Energy Conference, for example, claimed that the Germans would 'now be more than ever reluctant to do anything which might alienate the United States for the sake of a French conception of Europe', and that the Germans would 'no longer be such ready material for French blackmail'. Schmidt in particular was portrayed as 'not so much anti-European as agnostic about it', as well as 'certainly not likely to push the Federal Government in the direction of a more forward Western European policy'.[117] This was the British view on the eve of Schmidt's election as German chancellor in May 1974.

As the next chapters show, however, this turned out to be a serious misreading of both Schmidt and the German position more generally. In no way did Schmidt's performance in Washington signify a lasting break from German attachment to the Franco–German relationship, or from the EC more generally. While Schmidt had clearly become disillusioned by Jobert's obstructionism at the conference, he nonetheless remained convinced as ever about the FRG's strategic dependence on the Franco–German relationship and

---

[115] For the evolution of British policy over the Year of Europe, see A. Scott, *Allies Apart: Heath, Nixon and the Anglo–American Relationship* (Basingstoke: Macmillan, 2011); N. H. Rossbach, *Heath, Nixon and the Rebirth of the Special Relationship: Britain, the US and the EC, 1969–74* (Basingstoke: Macmillan, 2009).

[116] T. Robb, 'The Power of Oil: Edward Heath, the "Year of Europe" and the Anglo–American "Special Relationship"', *Contemporary British History* 26/1 (2012), 73–96.

[117] TNA/FCO33/2459, Diplomatic Report: Germany, Europe, and the United States, 27 February 1974. For British scepticism over Schmidt's commitment to European integration, see also Bundesarchiv (Koblenz), Bundesfinanzministerium [henceforward: B102/]264598, London to AA, 30 January 1974.

European integration. Just like during the Gaullist challenge of the mid-1960s, Schmidt therefore again sought to preserve the long-term substance of Franco–German relations against the short-term fallout at Washington, and indeed continued to cooperate closely with Giscard over fiscal policy during his final weeks as Finance Minister in order to repair some of the diplomatic damage. This cautious Franco–German rapprochement following the Washington Energy Conference, which would eventually result in the so-called Gymnich compromise a few weeks later, was the immediate international background against which Willy Brandt resigned as German Chancellor following the Guillaume affair, and Schmidt quickly emerged as his successor.

Conclusions

'The convictions that leaders have formed before reaching high office', Henry Kissinger famously remarked in his memoirs, 'are the intellectual capital they will consume as long as they continue in office'.[118] Indeed, it was during the period from 1945 to 1974 that Helmut Schmidt's main political convictions were formed, not least as regards the British–German relationship. For much of the period, it was, crudely put, a story of German ascent and British decline. The FRG, a divided and semi-sovereign nation at the frontline of the Cold War, managed to reinvent itself as a benevolent Western power through integration in wider multilateral organisations – gaining sovereignty by renouncing sovereignty, as Helga Haftendorn put it.[119] In this strategy, West German foreign policy relied on two main pillars: the EC with the Franco–German relationship at its core, and the transatlantic relationship with the United States. Britain, by contrast, rapidly lost in comparative importance, partly because of its self-exclusion from the European integration process and partly because of the more general decline of British power during that period. The key question remains, of course, whether a different British policy towards Europe in the mid-1950s, particularly as regards the Messina conference and the Treaties of Rome, might

[118] H. A. Kissinger, *White House Years* (Boston, MA: Little, Brown, 1979), 54.
[119] H. Haftendorn, *Deutsche Außenpolitik zwischen Selbstbeschränkung und Selbstbehauptung, 1945–2000* (Stuttgart: DVA, 2001), 436.

Conclusions

perhaps have resulted in a different outcome.[120] By the time Britain changed course and applied for EC membership in the 1960s, however, some powerful path dependencies had emerged, and the importance the FRG placed on British–German relations had already declined markedly in comparison to the Franco–German and US–German relationships.

As a young and ambitious politician rising through the ranks of German politics, Schmidt was a passive observer rather than an active shaper of the British–German relationship for much of the period. As a result, the evolution of his personal views largely reflected the broader currents of post-war British–German relations outlined above. They were shaped by his evolving views on the post-war international system and Germany's role in it, which meant that his early personal attachment to the British–German relationship gradually faded during his political maturation in the 1960s. In light of the FRG's overarching dependence on both transatlantic relations and European integration, Schmidt came to regard British–German relations as largely subordinate to the FRG's relations with France and the United States. From the mid-1960s onwards, he therefore never considered British–German relations as a potential substitute for Franco–German or US–German relations, and correspondingly never thought of breaking ranks with either France or the United States for the sake of the British. Yet, it was a change that was driven primarily by Schmidt's perceptions of and strategic choices about Germany's national interest, rather than by any allegedly flawed or malicious British diplomacy towards Europe that would feature so prominently in Schmidt's later writings. It reflected the long-term decline of British power and influence, rather than any animosity or tensions in the bilateral relationship itself. The evolution of Schmidt's attitudes towards Britain prior to his chancellorship thus shows how and why, by 1974, Britain had already become the sorry third in its triangular relationships with France and Germany.

---

[120] For an excellent summary of the somewhat notorious historiographical debate whether Britain missed a boat and/or bus in 1955, see Ellison, 'Britain and Europe', 525–7.

2 | *Harold Wilson, 1974–1976*

When Helmut Schmidt was elected German Chancellor on 16 May 1974, the scene seemed set for a new phase in the British–German relationship. By the early 1970s, both countries had come to develop largely compatible goals in their security and defence policies, and Britain's belated entry into the EC had removed a further long-standing obstacle against greater bilateral cooperation. The long-envisioned tripartite leadership of Western Europe by Britain, France, and West Germany finally seemed within eyeshot; an impression Schmidt himself was keen to encourage. 'All three countries had an essential voice in Community affairs', he told the British PM Harold Wilson in June 1974, and 'it was the three Governments concerned who really mattered'.[1] Within two years, however, the situation looked very different indeed: Schmidt's FRG was at the heart of a revived EC with a revitalized Franco–German axis at its centre, while Britain was wrestling with severe domestic difficulties on the side-lines. It was a shift in trilateral power dynamics that extended far beyond intra-EC politics: whereas France and Germany increasingly took the lead in shaping a united West European position within the wider transatlantic alliance, Britain seemed marginalised over key issues of macroeconomic policy or energy. The story of British–German relations during Harold Wilson's final term is one of unfulfilled expectations and severe disappointments.

More than anything else, it was the British attempt to renegotiate its terms of EC membership – followed by a nationwide referendum over the question – that caused the deterioration of British–German relations under Wilson. At a time of severe political and economic crises, the Wilson government's preoccupation with the renegotiations raised severe German doubts over Britain's reliability and ultimately its commitment to

---

[1] TNA/PREM16/99, Conversation between PM and Schmidt: Supplementary Record, 19 June 1974.

54

its European partners, which triggered a profound erosion of trust that extended far beyond the concrete issues surrounding Britain's terms of EC membership. At the heart of British–German differences lay deeply conflicting perceptions and irreconcilable concepts of European integration; differences that were exacerbated by Wilson's inadept handling of personal diplomacy on the highest political level.

The Long-Term Origins of Britain's EC Renegotiations

When Britain joined the EC on 1 January 1973, it did so at the worst possible time. The world economic crises triggered by the collapse of the Bretton Woods system and the oil shock drastically ended two decades of almost unprecedented post-war European growth: since 1950, the average growth in the world's Gross National Product (GNP) had been at 4.9 per cent; by 1974 and 1975, it had shrunk to 2.3 per cent and 1.5 per cent, respectively.[2] Whereas the EC's six founding member-states had been able to consolidate the achievements of the early integration process under highly favourable economic circumstances, Britain now had to adjust to the changes brought by membership in a rather less benevolent climate. It did not help that EC membership had been sold to the British public largely on the grounds of potential economic benefits; yet, surging inflation, the miners' strike, and the government-enforced three-day working week painted a rather different picture to domestic observers.[3] Though EC membership had little to do with any of these problems, public support nonetheless plummeted rapidly: whereas only 20 per cent had supported leaving the EC in January 1973, this number had risen to 41 per cent in July.[4] When asked about the main causes of inflation in October 1973, 'Britain joining the EEC' was named by 28 per cent, second only to the 'world situation' with 31 per cent.[5]

---

[2] Sargent, *Superpower Transformed*, 178.
[3] For the domestic context of early 1970s Britain, see J. E. Alt 'The Politics of Economic Decline in the 1970s', in L. Black, H. Pemberton, and P. Thane (eds.), *Reassessing 1970s Britain* (Manchester: Manchester University Press, 2013), 25–40; J. Tomlinson, 'The politics of declinism', in ibid., 41–60.
[4] Politisches Archiv des Auswärtigen Amts, Berlin (henceforward: PAAA/), Zwischenarchiv, Bd. 101400, London to AA, 13 July 1973.
[5] Table printed in J. E. Alt, *The Politics of Economic Decline: Economic Management and Political Behaviour in Britain Since 1964* (Cambridge: Cambridge University Press, 1979), 162.

If wavering public support for EC membership was one problem for the Conservative PM Edward Heath, he was even more troubled by the structural disadvantages of Britain's position inside the EC. During the accession negotiations, he had considered it paramount to demonstrate goodwill and European vocation in the high-level encounters with his European counterparts, paying less attention to the exact terms under which Britain was entering the Community. In particular, Heath accepted that new methods of Community financing, such as the 'own resources' principle, would be negotiated prior to British membership and without British involvement. Once inside the EC, so Heath thought optimistically, such initially disadvantageous policies to Britain could still be adjusted and reworked through regular community mechanisms.[6] He placed high hopes on the proposed European Regional Fund, which was likely to result in substantial payments to Britain.[7] Yet, the worsening financial and economic situation after October 1973 meant that the regional fund did not come into fruition as planned, with the Germans in particular adopting a hardline position.[8] By early 1974, Heath's strategy to improve the terms of entry once inside the EC framework was therefore widely seen to have failed. As the Foreign and Commonwealth Office (FCO) put it in January 1974, Britain's first year inside the EC had made it painfully clear that it was 'not all plain sailing to "join now and negotiate later"'.[9] For a lifelong advocate of British EC membership like Heath, the situation was nothing short of a disaster.

Harold Wilson, leader of the opposition after Labour's electoral defeat in 1970, perceived the membership issue from a very different angle. Contrary to Heath, Wilson had never felt much personal attachment to the European project. Instead, his worldview and outlook had

[6] The most extensive account of British entry under Heath can be found in D. Hannay (ed.), *Britain's Entry into the European Community. Report on the Negotiations of 1970–1972 by Sir Con O'Neill* (London: Cass, 2000), and Wall, *Official History, 332–456*. See also C. Lord, *British Entry to the European Community Under the Heath Government of 1970–4* (Aldershot: Dartmouth, 1993), 147–75. For a recent criticism of Heath's narrative, see D. E. Furby, 'The Revival and Success of Britain's Second Application for Membership of the European Community, 1968–71', unpublished PhD thesis (Queen Mary University of London, 2010), part. 232–88.

[7] PAAA/Zwischenarchiv, Bd. 101398, London to AA, 19 October 1973.

[8] Lord, *British Entry*, 164–5.

[9] TNA/FCO30/2456, 1973: Year I in the European communities, 25 January 1974.

The Long-Term Origins   57

been shaped primarily by the British Commonwealth: as an eleven-year old schoolboy in 1927, he had spent six months visiting his maternal grandfather in Australia, and in later years frequently claimed to have had forty-three relatives there.[10] At the time of Macmillan's first application for EC membership in 1961–3, Wilson came out heavily in opposition, urging the Conservative government to develop alternatives to EC membership based on a revival of the Commonwealth connection.[11] Yet, Wilson was also a shrewd political strategist astutely aware of Britain's decline in post-war influence and power. During his first tenure as PM from 1964 and 1970, he had therefore concluded reluctantly that British EC membership was the only way to secure post-imperial Britain's continuing influence on the global stage. As a result, he launched Britain's second application in 1967, and campaigned energetically and creatively for British membership against at times significant opposition.[12] Yet again, however, the British application was vetoed by the French President Charles de Gaulle in November that year.

Harold Wilson may have been personally disappointed by the application's failure, but he was even more worried about its effects on the Labour Party. Ever since the late 1940s, the European question had aroused passionate debates and emotions, feeding into wider internal debates over the party's economic doctrine and internationalist outlook. Whereas supporters of British membership saw the EC as an opportunity to retain international influence and to pursue economic reforms along the lines of Continental-style European social democracy, its opponents

---

[10] B. Pimlott, *Harold Wilson* (London: HarperCollins, 1993), 18–20; R. Jenkins, 'Wilson, (James) Harold, Baron Wilson of Rievaulx (1916–1995)', in *Oxford Dictionary of National Biography* (Oxford: Oxford University Press, 2004).

[11] The headlines of some of Wilson's articles against EC membership in the *Daily Express* are telling about the interconnections between Europe and Empire in his thought at the time. See, for example, 'A New Deal Now for the Commonwealth', *Daily Express*, 26 February 1962; 'I Say There Is Still Time to Save the Empire', *Sunday Express*, 10 June 1962.

[12] H. Parr, *Britain's Policy Towards the European Community: Harold Wilson and Britain's World Role, 1964–1967* (London: Routledge, 2006); M. Pine, *Harold Wilson and Europe: Pursuing Britain's Membership of the European Community* (London: Tauris Academic Studies, 2007). See also the essays in Daddow, *Harold Wilson and European Integration*. For a more positive reading of Wilson's move towards Europe, K. Steinnes, *The British Labour Party: Transnational Influences and European Community Membership, 1960–1973* (Stuttgart: Steiner, 2014).

tended to regard the EC as a US-inspired capitalist club preventing the march of British democratic socialism. Though most party members had occupied a more pragmatic middle ground during the 1950s and 1960s, Labour's increased factionalism following its electoral defeat in 1970 now put the European question at the very centre of its internal divisions.[13] The upsurge in post-1970 anti-EC sentiment was further strengthened by a degree of electoral opportunism, since the close identification of PM Heath with Britain's eventual EC membership offered Labour a major opportunity to attack one of the Conservative government's key policies. To Wilson, who later described holding his party together over Europe as the most difficult task of his premiership, Labour's increasingly hostile attitude towards British EC membership also posed a challenge to his own authority.[14] A motion calling for unconditional opposition to British EC entry was only narrowly defeated at the Labour party conference in October 1970, and things looked even worse once James Callaghan, regarded at the time as Wilson's strongest rival for party leadership, declared his own opposition to EC membership in a well-publicised and highly populist speech in May 1971. 'If we have to prove our Europeanism by accepting that French is the dominant language in the Community', he exclaimed in reference to a recent claim made by the French President Pompidou, 'then my answer is quite clear, and I will say it in French in order to prevent any misunderstanding: *Non, merci beaucoup*'.[15]

Wilson's lack of personal attachment to the European question, combined with his sensitivity towards Labour's internal divisions, determined his position on the European question during the early 1970s. Convinced that EC membership remained in Britain's national interest but also

---

[13] C. Cotton, 'The Labour Party and European Integration, 1961–1983', unpublished PhD dissertation (Cambridge: University of Cambridge, 2010). Other studies are R. Broad, *Labour's European Dilemmas Since 1945: From Bevin to Blair* (Basingstoke: Macmillan, 2001), and the more explicitly political A. Mullen, *The British Left's Great Debate on Europe* (London: Continuum, 2007). For the evolution of British Euroscepticism more generally, A. Forster, *Euroscepticism in Contemporary British Politics: Opposition to Europe in the British Conservative and Labour Parties Since 1945* (London: Routledge, 2002).

[14] H. Wilson, *Final Term: The Labour Government, 1974–76* (London: Weidenfeld and Nicolson, 1979), 51.

[15] *Guardian*, 26 May 1971. For an in-depth analysis of Callaghan's turn against EC-membership in opposition, see P. J. Deveney, *Callaghan's Journey to Downing Street* (Basingstoke: Macmillan, 2010), 156–90.

Initial German Reactions 59

adamant to prevent an intra-party split at almost all cost, he eventually came up with a shrewd ploy to divert the issue away from the Labour party into the realm of national politics. In October 1971, he publicly spoke out against Heath's *terms* of entry, proposing to 'renegotiate' them and then putting the membership question to the British people in a nationwide referendum or an election. In so doing, Wilson hoped to appease the party's anti-Europeans by speaking out against the current terms of EC membership while, crucially, also avoiding committing himself personally to withdrawal – it would all depend on the terms achieved in the renegotiations. Labour's election manifesto in March 1974 correspondingly called for a 'fundamental renegotiation of the terms of entry', spelling out seven objectives: major changes in the Common Agricultural Policy (CAP), fairer methods of financing the Community budget, the withdrawal from proposals for Economic and Monetary Union (EMU), retention of national powers for regional, industrial and fiscal policies, no harmonisation of Valued-Added Tax (VAT), and safeguards for the economic interests of the Commonwealth and developing countries.[16] When the March 1974 election surprisingly returned Wilson to Downing Street, however, he suddenly had to deliver on these far-reaching pledges made in opposition. This dilemma more than anything else determined his policy towards Europe during his final term as PM, as well as the course of the British–German relationship during that period.[17]

Initial German Reactions: Conflicting Priorities and Mutual Misunderstandings

In Bonn, the dominant reaction to Labour's European policy was one of scepticism and disbelief. Having experienced the perceived benefits of European integration at first hand for almost two decades, most

[16] Labour Party, 'Let Us Work Together – Labour's Way out of the Crisis', February 1974.

[17] For general studies of the renegotiations, see Wall, *From Rejection to Referendum*, 511–90; B. Donoughue, 'Harold Wilson and the Renegotiation of the EEC Terms of Membership, 1974–75: a Witness Account', in B. Brivati and H. Jones (eds.), *From Reconstruction to Integration: Britain and Europe Since 1945* (Leicester: Leicester University Press, 1993), 191–206; Pimlott, *Wilson*, 648–68. Also, my own M. Haeussler, 'A Pyrrhic Victory: Harold Wilson, Helmut Schmidt, and the British Renegotiation of EC Membership, 1974–5', *The International History Review* 37/4 (2015), 768–89, on which parts of this chapter are based.

German policy-makers simply did not believe that the new British government would sacrifice its EC membership simply for the sake of an internal party-political feud, particularly after Britain had unsuccessfully tried to get into the EC for over a decade. Instead, the Germans predicted that the alleged advantages of membership would become clearer to the new British government once it was in power: after all, the assumption of governmental responsibilities usually tended to strengthen more moderate voices within political parties, and, in any case, the British had much more to lose than the Germans did.[18] As the British Ambassador to Bonn Nicholas Henderson, himself an ardent advocate of British EC membership, put it in a dispatch from Bonn, the Germans were 'convinced that the British interest lies in remaining within the Community, and that, unless irrationality prevails, we are bound to stay in, if not out of any belief in the idea of Europe, at any rate from the hard calculation of where our own national interest lies'.[19] This was also the initial position of Schmidt, who coolly told the French newspaper *Le Monde* in June 1974 that Labour had 'set about re-examining a number of problems which take on quite a different aspect depending on whether you try to analyse them from the opposition benches or from those of the government'.[20] In the end, Schmidt believed, the powerful strategic reasons for British EC membership would inevitably trump narrow-minded party-political calculations.

The Labour government's initial diplomacy, however, gave little credibility to such hopes. Having fallen just short of an overall majority in the House of Commons, Wilson thought it pivotal to avoid an open intra-party rift in order to consolidate his own position, whatever the side-effects on Britain's relations with its European partners. It mirrored the attitude of his new Foreign Secretary Callaghan, who similarly believed that it was 'necessary, if the Government was to survive intact, to test all we did against the manifesto on which we had fought the election'.[21] As a result, Wilson's and Callaghan's key aim was to convince both Britain's partners and the wider British public that they meant business with the renegotiations. Heading the

---

[18] B136/17103, Kurz- und mittelfristige Aussichten der Entwicklung der Europäischen Gemeinschaften, 19 March 1974.

[19] TNA/PREM16/73, Bonn to FCO, 27 May 1974.

[20] *Le Monde*, 11 June 1974.

[21] J. Callaghan, *Time and Chance* (London: Collins, 1987), 305.

Initial German Reactions 61

traditionally pro-EC Foreign Office, Callaghan even found himself in direct confrontation with many officials who worried about the effects of the new government's policies on Britain's standing inside the Community.[22] Having just received the draft speech for his first appearance at the EC Council of Foreign Ministers, for example, he complained that it was 'too warm' and did not take into account the 'substantial concessions from the Community' the new government wanted. He also professed to be particularly 'worried about personalities in the FCO: were the FCO zealots for integration? . . . [T]he Labour Party, and he himself, were much less European than the FCO'.[23] A few days later, Callaghan assembled a group of British Ambassadors to EC countries to impress on them the seriousness of Labour's demands, exclaiming that 'if the French wanted a showdown they would have one', and that 'de Gaulle had been right in thinking that it was against French interests to let us into the Community'.[24] At the subsequent Council of Ministers meeting, Callaghan read out Labour's election manifesto almost word by word; a few weeks later, he again alienated most of his European counterparts by professing to seek 'enlightenment' about what exactly they meant by their language of European unity.[25] 'Is it not enough that we are all sitting here?', he exclaimed according to the German record, 'does one have to have a European Union?'[26]

Callaghan's strategy worked insofar as the Germans now began to seriously worry about the effects of the renegotiations on their own European policies. After Callaghan's first visit to Bonn in mid-March, for example, senior officials told the British Embassy how they had 'sat up to 2 o'clock in the morning discussing the situation in the gravest way'.[27] Yet, the German reaction to Callaghan's hard-line stance was

[22] TNA/FCO33/2459, Killick to Wright and Wiggin, 13 March 1974.
[23] TNA/FCO33/2456, Record of Telephone Conversation between PUS and Mr J. O. Wright, 5 March 1974.
[24] TNA/PREM16/72, Meeting of Ambassadors to EEC Countries, 20 March 1974.
[25] TNA/CAB129/175, Renegotiation of the terms of entry into the European Economic Community: Text of Statement delivered by the Secretary of State for Foreign and Commonwealth Affairs in the Council of Ministers of the European Communities in Luxembourg, 1 April 1974; TNA/PREM16/73, Meeting of Foreign Ministers of EC at Schloss Gymnich, 20/21 April 1974, 24 April 1974.
[26] *AAPD 1974*, Doc. Nr. 128, Aufzeichnung des Ministerialdirektors van Well, 22 April 1974.
[27] TNA/PREM16/92, Bonn to FCO, 22 March 1974.

quite different to British expectations: rather than trying to accommodate the new British government's far-reaching demands, they were instead driven by a political instinct to preserve the substance of the current state of the EC against what they perceived as an opportunistic British onslaught. As an internal German assessment put it, any change of the EC's institutional shape and basic political character would simply be 'too high a price' for continuing British membership.[28] Thus, Bonn stuck to a 'wait-and-see' policy, appearing sympathetic towards some limited British demands while strictly rejecting anything that would go against the established principles of the Community or involve treaty changes.[29] Faced with such a restrictive German position, it was hoped, the British might well swing towards a more pragmatic and limited negotiating position in due course.

These German predictions were not entirely unfounded. For while Wilson and Callaghan continued to put on the faces of uncompromising doughty fighters for British interests in public, they had in fact already begun to work towards an eventual deal behind the scenes. One of Wilson's first moves as PM, for example, was to move responsibility for the renegotiations to two Cabinet committees chaired by him and Callaghan, allowing the two Labour heavyweights to side-line sceptics like Tony Benn whilst presiding seemingly dispassionately over the outcome. They also dealt a major blow to the more hard-line opponents of British EC membership by quickly ruling out changes to the Treaties of Rome or the Treaty of Accession as part of the renegotiations, thereby making any substantial changes in the EC's basic rules and methods highly unlikely.[30] Even the publicly ebullient Callaghan seems to have contemplated the framework of a potential deal already during his first weeks as Foreign Secretary. It was important to know 'whether the Community was serious about EMU and European Union', he confided in a quiet moment during his March 1974 meeting with Britain's EC Ambassadors, 'if these items could be left out of the account, it might be possible to do a deal on such matters as the CAP

[28] B136/17103, Kurz- und mittelfristige Aussichten der Entwicklung der Europäischen Gemeinschaften, 19 March 1974.
[29] *AAPD 1974 I*, Doc. Nr. 133, Betr.: Britische Mitgliedschaft in der EG, 25 April 1974.
[30] For Wilson's and Callaghan's early domestic manoeuvring, see also A. Collins, 'The Cabinet Office, Tony Benn and the Renegotiation of Britain's Terms of Entry into the European Community, 1974–1975', *Contemporary British History* 24/4 (2010), 471–91.

and the budget'.[31] The trouble for the British–German relationship, however, was that such deliberations could only take place behind closed doors, rather than in public.

Franco–German Rapprochement and British Self-Exclusion

The renegotiations might have been the key issue in European politics from a British perspective, but for the Germans, another development seemed much more important: the election of Valéry Giscard d'Estaing as French President on 27 May 1974. Giscard, an essentially techno-cratic centrist from aristocratic background, was a rather different character to his predecessors de Gaulle and Pompidou, and pursued markedly different European policies as well. Whereas de Gaulle had been an ardent advocate of an intergovernmental Europe of sovereign nation-states led by an independent France, and his erstwhile protégé Pompidou had remained severely constrained by this Gaullist legacy throughout his time in office, Giscard came to office holding undogmatic but rather more positive views towards European integration.[32] As former finance minister and graduate of the Ecole Polytechnique, he firmly believed in the need for greater European macroeconomic coordination, hoping to reform and revitalize the EC in order for it to meet the political and economic challenges. It was an agenda supported strongly by his – highly Germanophile – Foreign Minister Sauvagnargues, who was close to Jean Monnet and had already played a key part in France's 1950s European policy as one of the fathers of the ill-fated EDC treaty and adviser of Antoine Pinay.[33] Importantly, the new Giscard administration defined its strong commitment to the EC not against partnership with the United States, but instead connected it to a renewed emphasis on transatlantic cooperation.[34] This closely mirrored the convictions of the German government, as well as Schmidt's own long-standing personal beliefs. Having already cooperated closely with Giscard during their joint stint as finance ministers in the early 1970s, the two leaders

[31] TNA/PREM16/72, Meeting of Ambassadors to EEC Countries, 20 March 1974.
[32] S. Berstein and J. P. Rioux, *The Pompidou Years, 1969–1974* (Cambridge: Cambridge University Press, 2000), 22–7; Soutou, 'The Linkage Between European Integration and Détente', 11–35.
[33] Gfeller, *Building a European Identity*, 180.
[34] The 'Giscard effect' in transatlantic relations will be discussed in later parts of the chapter.

therefore quickly struck up a remarkably close personal relationship, regularly meeting up and exchanging messages and telephone calls to coordinate their responses to the key political issues.[35] Immediately after his first meeting with Giscard as President, for example, Schmidt told the German Ambassador in Paris that the meeting had contrasted with earlier Franco–German encounters 'like day and night',[36] and wrote an even more euphoric letter to US President Nixon professing 'how pleased' he was 'with the looming possibilities of closer Franco–German cooperation in European and Atlantic matters'.[37]

Over the following months, Schmidt and Giscard sought to translate their theoretical commitment to a revival of the European Community into more concrete initiatives for institutional reform and greater intra-European fiscal and economic cooperation. At the heart of their agenda was an attempt for greater macroeconomic coordination of European economies, which were suffering from quite different fates. Whereas German inflation was comparatively modest with 7.2 per cent, the situation was significantly worse in France (12.0 per cent), Britain (13.2 per cent), and Italy (14.2 per cent). Even more divergent were the fluctuations of European currencies, with the Deutschmark revalued by 25.7 per cent between 1969 and March 1974 whereas the British Pound dropped by 12.7 per cent and the French Franc by 2.2 per cent during the same period. Schmidt, like Giscard, attributed these divergent national trends to the largely uncoordinated and sometimes outright contradictory economic and fiscal policies by key EC member-states, often pursued with little regard for their wider international ramifications. In response, the two leaders thus sought to revitalize the EC in order to shape a West European consensus based largely on fiscal restraint and budgetary consolidation.[38] They also pushed for more concrete institutional reforms, proposals that included direct elections to the EP, more frequent use of majority

---

[35] On the Schmidt–Giscard relationship, see Waechter, *Helmut Schmidt und Valéry Giscard d'Estaing*; Miard-Delacroix, *Partenaires de choix*; Simonian, *Privileged Partnership*.

[36] *AAPD 1974 I*, Doc. Nr. 157, von Braun an Genscher, 4 June 1974.

[37] 1/HSAA006579, Schmidt to Nixon, 4 June 1974. See also ibid., Schmidt to Kissinger, June 1974.

[38] See in particular Schmidt's now famous memorandum on economic policy, from which the above numbers are also taken. 1/HSAA010072, Memorandum, 7 May 1974.

decisions within the Council of Ministers, a passport union, as well as the institutionalization of EC heads of government summitry.[39]

For Britain, the main consequence of such renewed Franco–German cooperation was that it suddenly found itself on the margins of EC politics, less than two years after its belated entry into the Community. In the realm of economic policy, Wilson proved particularly hesitant to follow the new Franco–German consensus. Not only was Britain suffering from a profits and inflation crisis that was significantly worse than that of most other EC member-states, but the Labour government was also reluctant to upset the powerful trade unions, given the party's previous experiences in the 1960s as well as Heath's more recent political difficulties over industrial relations.[40] In German eyes, however, such British hesitancy over macroeconomic policy contrasted unfavourably with the new French dynamism under Giscard, who had embarked upon substantial economic reforms against similar domestic opposition.[41] This, at least, was the personal impression of Schmidt, who asserted in conversation with EC Commission President Ortoli in June 1974 that, while France and Germany shared 'the same will and the same goals' in their economic policies, he was 'not sure whether that applied to England as well', doubting whether Wilson was 'ready to take really tough measures'.[42] To Schmidt, the EC renegotiations even seemed like a smokescreen to distract the British public from the very real economic problems the country faced. There was a 'fatal tendency of the English to regard their EEC-membership as cause of all their economic ills', he mused in an internal German memorandum in May 1974, which had not only 'negative effects inside the EEC' but also engaged 'the strength of purpose in economic policies in the wrong directions'.[43]

Britain was even more isolated on the issue of institutional reform, since the British government felt unable to agree to any proposals until the question of its membership was settled. This, of course, ran directly against Franco–German attempts to make quick progress in order to translate their newly found political agreement into lasting changes.

---

[39] Gfeller, *European Identity*, 171–94; Waechter, *Schmidt und Giscard*, 78–97.
[40] Tomlinson, 'Economic Policy', 57–8.
[41] Waechter, *Schmidt und Giscard*, 61–3.
[42] *AAPD 1974*, Doc. Nr. 16M2, Gespräch BK Schmidt mit EG-Kommissionspräsident Ortoli, 11 June 1974.
[43] 1/HSAA10072, Memorandum, 7 May 1974.

The extent of British self-marginalization became evident when Schmidt and Giscard unveiled their reform ideas at an informal dinner of EC heads of government and state in September 1974.[44] Afterwards, Schmidt noted internally how 'Giscard's strong engagement for further European progress, which had been completely evident to me for quite some time, has certainly impressed the other participants', whereas the British position had been 'explicitly criticized from all sides. . . . Wilson has undoubtedly left the impression of a still uncertain English position'.[45] Such discord did not go unnoticed by Wilson himself, who afterwards recorded his impressions 'that some of our partners thought that renegotiation was a "bore"', as well as 'the slight feeling that some of them were assuming that Britain would leave the Community' in any case.[46] These impressions mirrored FCO Minister of State Roy Hattersley's experiences at the EC Council of Foreign Ministers the week before; he had similarly detected a 'feeling on the part of the others that Britain was not really part of the process under discussion. This was never stated but there was an implicit, if disguised, assumption that Britain would not be there when these developments were realized'.[47] By the autumn of 1974, the renegotiations were thus not only seen to hold up the process of the EC's institutional reform, but they were also increasingly regarded as a symptom of a more general British ambivalence about the EC – precisely at a point when France and Germany were anxious to revitalize the European integration process.

Shaping the Domestic Debate: Helmut Schmidt's Labour Party Conference Speech

If things looked bad for Wilson in Europe, they were beginning to look even worse at home. Though the October 1974 elections returned his government with a small majority of three, they also saw the left gaining further ground: nearly half of the fifty-four newly elected

[44] For Schmidt and Giscard's coordination in preparation of the informal summit, see *AAPD 1974 II*, Doc. Nr. 249, Aufzeichnung des Bundeskanzlers Schmidt, 3 September 1974.

[45] *AAPD 1974 II*, Doc. Nr. 268, Aufzeichnung des BK Schmidt, 16 September 1974.

[46] TNA/PREM16/78, Record: Heads of Government Dinner, 16 September 1974.

[47] TNA/PREM16/75, Hattersley to FCO 17 September 1974. Hattersley had stepped in for Callaghan at this particular meeting.

Shaping the Domestic Debate 67

MPs joined the Tribune Group, and the leading anti-EC Tony Benn got voted top of the Labour Party's National Executive Council [NEC] elections in November 1974.[48] For Wilson and Callaghan, this meant that the delicate intra-party balance over the European question now seemed even more fragile than before. As a result, they stuck rigidly to the line that their own position would be determined solely by the results of the renegotiations. This enabled them to project themselves as neutral arbiters for British national interests, seemingly detached from the virulent party-political and public debates at the time. Any departure from this strategy, they thought, would make them susceptible to domestic charges of not taking the renegotiations seriously enough, or of having somehow wanted to trick the British people into continuing membership from the very beginning.[49]

In Germany, however, Wilson's and Callaghan's sitting on the fence only served to increase doubts over their ultimate intentions further. Schmidt in particular appeared puzzled over the British government's public apathy. Convinced as ever that Britain's national interests demanded its continuing EC membership, Schmidt increasingly came to regard Wilson's public indifference as a cynical prioritisation of narrow party-political interests. In October 1974, Schmidt put his doubts to his old friend Alastair Buchan in a conversation that was subsequently leaked to the British FCO. 'What was wrong with Britain?', he asked, appearing particularly worried about Wilson: 'From discussions with him, he no longer knew whether the PM still wanted Britain in the Community or not. ... He [Schmidt] was an Anglophile and would see Britain leave the Community with real regret, but the French would be happy to see her go; they were convinced that the British were not yet really committed to Europe and should not be allowed to hold up European business until they had properly made up their minds'.[50] More precisely, Schmidt criticised Wilson's refusal to take a stronger pro-EC position in public, dismissing the British argument that the issues at stake in the renegotiations were so important as to make the country's continued membership dependent on them. Whatever the results of the renegotiations, Schmidt believed, a stronger public pro-EC stance by the government

---

[48] Pimlott, *Wilson*, 636; Donoughue, 'Renegotiation', 195.   [49] Ibid.

[50] TNA/FCO33/2460, Professor Buchan's Conversation with Helmut Schmidt, 30 October 1974.

would eventually be decisive during the referendum campaign.[51] As he put it to German journalists in November 1974, the referendum outcome would depend 'very much ... on the recommendation made by the British government', and the 'actual decision' therefore had to 'be made in the bosom of the government and one hopes that the British nation will follow the government and their recommendation'.[52]

From today's perspective, it seems clear that Wilson's public ambiguity were part of his strategy to ultimately keep Britain inside the EC from the very beginning. At the time, however, Schmidt's doubts also mirrored internal British concerns about the lack of governmental steering of public opinion by some ministers and officials. Callaghan, who as Foreign Secretary was more exposed to the views of Britain's EC partners than most of his colleagues, had by the autumn of 1974 already come to display a much more positive attitude towards the British membership question, and indeed now seemed anxious to influence public opinion even though his exposed role in the renegotiations meant that he felt unable to do so himself. A particular problem concerned Labour's upcoming special conference on Europe, which ran the risk of turning into yet another public demonstration of Labour grassroots opposition to EC membership. To prevent this, Callaghan came up with the highly unusual idea of inviting Schmidt as a guest speaker, hoping that the rhetorically gifted German Chancellor might be able to somehow influence the debate in positive ways.[53] Schmidt accepted, not least because of the extensive lobbying of long-standing friends and colleagues in Britain. Indeed, even the drafting of Schmidt's speech was very much a transnational collaborative effort: Callaghan in particular supplied Schmidt with several long drafts, many parts of which found their way into the final script,[54] his old friend Denis Healey advised him to pitch the European issue by dwelling on the Labour Party's internationalist tradition,[55] and the German Ambassador to London was behind an eloquent Shakespeare quotation that Schmidt eventually used to round off his speech.[56] Even the Germanophile – though

---

[51] See Schmidt's remarks quoted in 1/HSAA006642, BPA an Ref IV, 21 November 1974.

[52] Records of the meeting were – perhaps deliberately – leaked to the British. TNA/PREM16/76, Bonn to FCO, 16 November 1974.

[53] TNA/PREM16/100, Callaghan to FCO and No.10, 16 October 1974.

[54] See various correspondence in 1/HSAA006642 and B136/16866.

[55] B136/16866, London to AA, 20 November 1974.

[56] 1/HSAA006642, London to AA, 24 November 1974.

Shaping the Domestic Debate 69

virulent anti-EC – Barbara Castle offered some valuable advice: 'The only way to keep Britain inside the Community was to not remind her that she was already in it'.[57] Schmidt may have addressed the conference in his capacity as German Chancellor; but he was also articulating the voices of many in Britain who felt too constrained to take a similarly strong stand themselves.

Schmidt's speech, broadcasted live on nationwide TV and discussed prominently in all major newspapers, was a major success.[58] Though Schmidt had been greeted by a largely hostile and angry crowd outside the conference venue and some prominent Labour figures had even threatened to walk out during his speech,[59] the German Chancellor managed to transform the mood of the conference with a witty masterpiece delivered in fluent English, embedding the European topic in a lengthy plea for international cooperation in light of the dangers of a worldwide recession. He did not even shy away from using some socialist rhetoric with which he was usually uncomfortable, stating unequivocally 'the desire of your German comrades to have you British comrades on our side within the Community'.[60] Though claiming to put himself 'in the position of a man who, in front of ladies and gentlemen from the Salvation Army, tries to convince them of the advantages of drinking' (also a line borrowed from Callaghan),[61] he nonetheless stated his case bluntly: 'All I really want to say – even at the risk of a walk-out – is that your comrades on the Continent want you to stay, and you will please have to weigh it. If you talk of solidarity, you have to weigh it. *(Applause)* Your comrades on the Continent believe that it is in their interest as well as in yours, too'.[62] Afterwards, Schmidt received several rounds of applause, with the *Guardian* commenting that the German Chancellor had talked 'more sense' than Britain's 'impassioned

---

[57] 1/HSAA006642, Focke zu BK, 18 November 1974.
[58] For an in-depth historical reconstruction of Schmidt's speech and its perception, as well as a full transcript, see Birkner, *Comrades for Europe*, 88–123. For examples of positive recollections by key participants, Wilson, *Final Term*, 88; Callaghan, *Time and Chance*, 311–12; Healey, *Time of My Life*, 454.
[59] TNA/PREM16/101, Henderson to Wright, 4 December 1974.
[60] Labour Party, *Report of the Seventy-third Annual Conference* (London, 1974), 315–18.
[61] Ibid.; B136/16866, London to AA, 27 November 1974.
[62] Labour Party, *Report of the Seventy-third Annual Conference*, 318.

European advocates – both pro and anti – have contrived in a year'.[63] Such praise was mirrored in the German press, which according to the British Embassy in Bonn indulged in a 'minor orgy of self-congratulation'.[64] The summary by the British Ambassador Henderson almost reads like a heroic tale, concluding 'that if any single speech could have made a difference to opinion and events Herr Schmidt's should have done so'.[65] Indeed, Schmidt's unequivocal and positive pro-EC argument contrasted starkly with Wilson's and Callaghan's steadfast refusal at the time to take up a clear public position themselves. As Schmidt himself would recall in his memoirs, the episode had illustrated to him that 'a good speech' could 'influence the political mood in England' – a thinly disguised criticism of the British government's public ambiguity at the time.[66]

The Wilson Factor: The Failure of Personal Diplomacy at Chequers

German concerns over Wilson's apparent lack of personal involvement had by now come to be shared by most British ministers and officials keen to keep Britain inside the EC. In advance of Schmidt's visit, for example, the PM's Office urged Wilson to 'reassure Schmidt, to the extent he [Wilson] considers possible, about the Government's intention to secure a positive decision on continued membership of the Community if renegotiation is successful'. This, it claimed, would be 'crucial in determining the extent to which Schmidt is prepared to be helpful to us'.[67] Callaghan too pleaded with Wilson to become personally involved. 'You said you would prefer to keep these matters within

[63] *Guardian*, 2 December 1974.
[64] TNA/PREM16/101, Bonn to FCO, 4 December 1974.
[65] TNA/PREM16/101, Henderson to Wright, 4 December 1974. For ample evidence of Henderson's own pro-EC commitment, as well as his retrospective views on the renegotiation episode, see in particular Churchill College Cambridge, British Diplomatic Oral History Project [BDOHP], Sir Nicholas Henderson, 24 September 1998, 12–13; as well as his books N. Henderson, *The Private Office: A Personal View of Five Foreign Secretaries and of Government from the Inside* (London: Weidenfeld and Nicolson, 1984); N. Henderson, *Mandarin: The Diaries of an Ambassador, 1969–1982* (London: Weidenfeld and Nicolson, 1994).
[66] Schmidt, *Die Deutschen und ihre Nachbarn*, 96.
[67] TNA/PREM16/100, UK Objectives, 28 November 1974.

2.1 Helmut Schmidt speaking to the Labour Party Conference on Europe, 30 November 1974. Source: Photo by Roger Jackson & Peter Cade/Central Press/Hulton Archive/Getty Images.

the negotiating channels where they have been so far', he wrote to him in October 1974, 'but I hold the view that Schmidt and Giscard will wish to play a large personal part and that at a later stage you will have to come in on things'.[68] Indeed, Wilson's continuing dithering in high-level encounters with European counterparts had by that stage come to contrast starkly with Callaghan's personal diplomacy, whose more frequent European contacts had impressed on him the need for plain-spokenness and confidential bargaining behind the scenes. In November 1974, for example, Callaghan told the French President Giscard bluntly that he was 'negotiating for success', and that the question of Britain's budget contributions in particular was 'not of very great importance measured in terms of money' but 'of the greatest importance' in terms of the British domestic debate.[69]

Yet, the decisive shots would still have to be called by the PM, and Wilson continued to show preciously little personal interest in the EC

---

[68] TNA/PREM16/85, Callaghan to Wilson, 14 October 1974.
[69] TNA/PREM16/76, Secretary of State's visit to Paris: meeting with the French President, 19 November 1974.

question: party-political perspectives still dominated his views on the renegotiations almost completely. As his personal adviser Bernard Donoughue recalls, it seemed like Wilson 'did not seem to care too much about the policies as policies, and might happily have argued a different position had the manifesto required it'.[70] It matched what Peter Hennessy has described as the general air of 'lassitude verging on melancholy' surrounding Wilson's final years in office.[71] With secret plans for retirement well under way, Wilson consciously adopted a 'hands-off' approach for his last term in office, with ministers being largely free to run their own departments.[72] It became increasingly evident to insiders that Wilson, as his biographer put it, 'had been slowing up, psychologically and perhaps also physically ... the demonic energy of the 1960s was gone, and he no longer had the desire, or the conceit, to take everything upon himself'.[73] It is likely that such detachment from the renegotiations was further intensified by the state of Wilson's health, as well as perhaps by the first signs of Alzheimer disease that he suffered from in his final years.[74]

Whatever the deeper reasons behind Wilson's aloofness, it was a striking contrast to the energy and restlessness with which he had pursued the membership question during the 1960s. If any subject arose his interest during the renegotiations at all, it was usually the role of Commonwealth, the one issue about which he cared deeply. Although both Callaghan and Whitehall officials concluded repeatedly to focus the renegotiations primarily on Britain's EC budget contributions,[75] Wilson frequently interfered to push the question of Commonwealth food imports back on the agenda. During one internal meeting prior to Schmidt's visit, for example, Wilson exclaimed that a 'mistake' had been made attaching 'so much importance' to the budget problem. Instead, as the present British Ambassador to Bonn

---

[70] Donoughue, 'Renegotiation', 194.

[71] P. Hennessy, *The Prime Minister: The Office and Its Holders Since 1945* (London: Allen Lane, 2000), 370.

[72] B. Donoughue, *Prime Minister: The Conduct of Policy Under Harold Wilson and James Callaghan* (London: Jonathan Cape, 1987), 48.

[73] Pimlott, *Wilson*, 617.

[74] Donoughue, 'Renegotiation', 196. It has been suggested that Wilson may also have suffered from first signs of Alzheimer disease during his final term in office. See P. Garrard, 'Cognitive Archaeology: Uses, Methods and Results', *Journal of Neurolinguistics* 20 (2008), 9–13.

[75] Wall, *Official History*, 563, 569–70.

The Wilson Factor   73

Henderson recalled in his diary, Wilson suddenly professed that 'New Zealand and Australia were important. The British people minded a lot about them'.[76] Again, it was a striking reversal to his position in 1967, where he had worried deeply about the long-term implications of the EC's agricultural payment structures but appeared relatively optimistic about the Commonwealth trade issue.[77]

Wilson's ambiguity may well have been the only way to remain on top of the domestic debate, but his secrecy and aloofness in his dealings with his European counterparts had nonetheless come to constrain Britain's negotiating position in the renegotiations. The British–German meeting at Chequers which immediately followed Schmidt's conference speech is a case in point. The Germans, having come to Britain with the firm aim to finally receive an unequivocal personal commitment from Wilson 'that he would personally support Britain remaining in the EC', were deeply disappointed by Wilson's evasive and ambiguous answers.[78] Though Wilson claimed, according to the British record, to be 'absolutely prepared to give ... the assurance that the Federal Chancellor had sought on his position in relation to continuing British membership: if the outcome of the renegotiation produced terms of membership which were satisfactory, continuing British membership would be good for Britain and good for Europe, and he would be prepared to put his weight behind acceptance of continuing British membership',[79] it was a highly conditional and vague statement that clearly stepped short of German hopes for a more unequivocal assurance. Indeed, the German record noted afterwards how Wilson had appeared 'interested in Britain remaining member of the EC, but <u>without</u> strong involvement; <u>uniformed</u> about details', complaining that Wilson had shown '<u>no</u> readiness to publicly declare the wish to remain inside the EC before final renegotiation results were known'.[80] Callaghan, by contrast, was perceived by the Germans as both 'interested <u>and</u> engaged; starting to identify himself with the success of the renegotiations'.[81] It was a perception that was shared by the French side. When US Secretary of State Henry Kissinger

---

[76] Henderson, *Diaries*, 78.

[77] Parr, *Britain's Policy Towards the European Community*, 134–62.

[78] 1/HSAA006642, Britische Wünsche zur Verminderung der Haushaltsbelastung, 27 November 1974.

[79] TNA/PREM16/77, Record of conversations at Chequers, 30 November 1974.

[80] 1/HSAA006642, Vermerk über das Gespräch des Bundeskanzlers mit PM Wilson, 2 December 1974. Emphases in original.

[81] Ibid.

74   *Harold Wilson, 1974–1976*

told Giscard that his impression was that the Labour government wanted to keep Britain in the EC, Giscard replied that this clearly applied only to Callaghan: 'Wilson wants a satisfaction he can't get'.[82] By December 1974, the British PM was thus seen as an obstacle rather than an asset in the German quest to keep Britain in the EC.

Perhaps even more worryingly from a German perspective, the British–German talks at Chequers also revealed to them the highly confused policy-making process in Britain, with different voices telling the Germans different things at different times. Particularly striking were Wilson's repeated attempts to discuss the issue of Commonwealth food imports, even though the British had briefed the Germans beforehand that they wanted to focus the talks primarily on the budget question. But Wilson's performance at Chequers left them with very different impressions. 'It had been wrong to focus so much attention on the budget', Wilson declared, expanding that he 'did not think that any general budgetary formula that could be obtained would be of any use in winning votes amongst the British people ... New Zealand had supplied butter and cheese for over one hundred years to the UK. .... He was appalled by the "weevils or rather moles" working away in Brussels trying to undermine this'.[83] Taken aback by Wilson's outburst and sudden prioritisation of the Commonwealth issue, Schmidt responded that he was still 'willing to help [Britain] to stay in', but that he 'really did not quite know what it is that Britain wanted out of the renegotiation'. At that stage, Callaghan stepped in as mediator, promising to provide Schmidt with a concrete point-by-point list of British demands that still had to be achieved in the renegotiations.[84]

Wilson's personal campaign over Commonwealth food imports might have confused the Germans, but it is clear from today's perspective that the haphazard and somewhat erratic nature of British policy-making stemmed primarily from the fact that the renegotiations actually did not matter in terms of the policy issues at stake: at least to Wilson and Callaghan, they had always been a tool to appease and divert the more

---

[82] Gerald Ford Presidential Library, Ann Arbor, MI, National Security Advisor (henceforward: GRFL/NSA), Memoranda of Conversations, 1973–7, Box 8, Memorandum of conversation Ford-Giscard-Kissinger, 16 December 1974.

[83] TNA/PREM16/101, Henderson to FCO, 4 December 1974. This was a supplementary record provided to the FCO by Henderson, who was present at the talks.

[84] Ibid.

British Isolation in Europe 75

fundamental issues that underlay both the Labour Party's internal divisions and the wider public debate over Britain's EC membership. One revealing moment of the Chequers talks reveals this basic contradiction at the very core of the whole renegotiation exercise. In an unguarded moment, Callaghan asserted that 'what happened in the referendum' would 'depend not so much on the results of the renegotiation as on the atmosphere and situation at the time'.[85] Schmidt was quick to jump on these off-the-cuff remarks. He 'had understood the Foreign and Commonwealth Secretary to imply that in many respects psychology mattered more than the detailed "fine print" of negotiation', he replied. 'If the psychological needs were of that weight', however, then 'the British Government might want to ask themselves whether they were proceeding psychologically prudently in filling in their needs only step by step'.[86] In effect, this meant that Schmidt had called the British bluff: the renegotiations were a party-political tool to appease the domestic debate, rather than a genuine attempt to remedy British grievances with its EC membership. It was a realisation that did little to counter German suspicions over the Wilson government's basic reliability and trustworthiness. The Chequers meeting may have been successful from a British point of view, but the German delegation came away disillusioned and annoyed.

British Isolation in Europe: The Paris Summit

To Schmidt, the first-hand experience of Wilson's ambiguity at Chequers had reinforced his conviction that Britain could not be relied upon in European politics for the time being, whatever the eventual outcome of the renegotiations. As a result, he decided to lean even more strongly on the Franco–German relationship. Already at Chequers, Schmidt had made it clear that he was not willing to act as broker between London and Paris, stressing the formidable obstacles in France to any potential renegotiation deal.[87] After his return to Bonn, Schmidt then immediately phoned up President Giscard to convey his impression that Wilson seemed to 'realize, but doesn't admit, that he had made a bad mistake by calling for "renegotiation" in opposition. At the moment, he prioritizes the manifesto and party unity; Callaghan is, in

---

[85] TNA/PREM16/77, Record of conversations at Chequers, 30 November 1974.
[86] Ibid.   [87] TNA/PREM16/101, Henderson to FCO, 4 December 1974.

comparison, markedly pro-European'.[88] The two leaders also joked about Wilson's preoccupation with Commonwealth food imports, musing whether the British PM actually realized 'that the period of cheap food prices on the world market is over for the time being'.[89] By that stage, an evident confidence gap had emerged between Schmidt and Giscard on the one hand and Wilson on the other, with the two leaders having established a personal relationship of mutual trust and confidence that was clearly lacking in their dealings with Wilson.[90] For the British renegotiation prospects this was an unfortunate development, since the final outcome would inevitably depend on a high-level multilateral deal.

Wilson's bilateral meeting with Schmidt, as well as a subsequent meeting with Giscard, had deliberately been scheduled just prior to the summit of EC heads of government and state in Paris from 9–10 December 1974, a meeting originally proposed by Giscard to make headway on the reform ideas he had developed with Schmidt over the summer. In particular, Giscard was looking to institutionalise regular meetings of heads of government, to reintroduce Qualified Majority Voting (QMV) in non-essential matters, and to establish direct elections to the European Parliament.[91] Since most of these proposals ran against the grain of traditional Gaullist French positions, the Germans were keen to make early progress, hoping to 'irrevocably codify' what they regarded as a 'significant change' in French European policies.[92] The problem, of course, was Britain's still uncertain future inside the EC. Completely preoccupied with the renegotiations, the British argued that they could not even contemplate any decisions in the institutional field until the membership question had been settled. They were also highly apprehensive about any potentially 'over-ambitious commitments to an undefined European Union', fearing that such grandiose rhetoric coming out of Paris might antagonise domestic opinion over EC

---

[88] 1/HSAA006586, Telefongespräch Bundeskanzler / Giscard d'Estaing, 3 December 1974.

[89] Ibid.

[90] For the way in which Schmidt and Giscard set in store close, personal cooperation through informal telephone conversations and confidential tête-a-têtes right from the beginning of their time in office, see Waechter, *Helmut Schmidt and Valéry Giscard d'Estaing*, 66–9.

[91] Gfeller, *Building a European Identity*, 199.

[92] PAAA, Zwischenarchiv, 108867, Vorbereitung einer Präsidentschaftskonferenz in Paris, hier: Institutionelle Fragen, 22 November 1974.

British Isolation in Europe 77

membership even further.[93] The conceptual gulf separating Britain from most other member-states was now evident to everybody. As Callaghan revealingly told Genscher a few weeks prior to the summit, the larger issues behind the European integration process were in fact 'much more difficult than practical ones. The deeper we got into institutional questions the further apart we got with our colleagues in the Community'.[94]

Rather than contemplating far-reaching institutional reforms, the British delegation instead hoped to use the summit in order to make progress on the renegotiations, particularly as regards the budget question.[95] The underlying problem was a structural one: as a result of the EC's financing methods, Britain was likely to shoulder a disproportionate financial burden in its contributions to the EC budget after the end of its transitionary membership period in 1978. This was due to the fact that, under the EC's 'own resources' system, Britain's traditionally high external tariff revenues went directly into the EC budget, whereas its returns from the budget amounted to a significantly lesser sum because of the EC's heavy spending on the agricultural sector which was comparatively small and efficient in Britain.[96] Simply put, Britain would soon pay significantly more into the EC budget than it was likely to get out: the Treasury had calculated that Britain's proportion of the budget would rise to 24 per cent by 1980, but that its eventual share of the EC's GNP would be only 14 per cent.[97] Though the political problem was plain to see for everybody, formidable structural obstacles stood in the way of any potential solution: any sort of refund would have to be paid for by the other member-states, and more general changes to the EC's financing system would require a far-reaching and potentially highly divisive reforms that would preoccupy the EC for a long period of time.[98] Thus, there was little incentive for the other

[93] TNA/PREM16/100, Schmidt Visit to Chequers: UK Objectives, 28 November 1974.
[94] TNA/PREM16/76, Record of private conversation between Callaghan and Genscher, 10 November 1974.
[95] For the most extensive account, see again Wall, *Official History*, in particular 561–3, 571–7.
[96] B136/7913, Britischer Wunsch nach Verringerung der finanziellen Belastung des VK durch die Finanzverfassung der EG, 22 November 1974.
[97] PAAA, Zwischenarchiv, 108867, Vorbereitung einer Präsidentschaftskonferenz in Paris, 31 October 1974.
[98] See Giscard's non-compromising remarks to Wilson in early December 1974, TNA/PREM16/84, Record of Conversation at Dinner, 3 December 1974. Giscard had in fact been one of the main architects of the 'own resources' system during his time as Finance Minister.

EC member-states to meet British demands, not least given the British government's continuing dithering and complacency over the principle of EC membership in public. As Schmidt bluntly told journalists in an off-the-record discussion at the time, he considered it politically extremely risky to burden the German taxpayer with additional financial commitments without having anything to show for in return.[99]

Thus, it is somewhat surprising that the Paris Summit in fact managed to make some progress on both institutional reform and the budget question. Publicly, the summit projected the desired image of a relaunch of the European project, illustrated by agreements to re-introduce QMV and to have direct elections to the EP by 1978. Of even more lasting significance was the decision to institutionalise meetings of the EC's heads of state and government in the form of the newly created European Council, perhaps the most significant reform of the EC's structures since its creation in the 1950s.[100] But there was also some simultaneous movement on the question of Britain's budget contributions: for the first time, the EC member-states put on paper their acceptance that the budget question constituted a serious problem, and instructed Council and Commission to set up 'as soon as possible a correcting mechanism of a general application' that could prevent 'the possible development of situations unacceptable for a member-state and incompatible with the smooth working of the Community'.[101] In turn, Britain supported all institutional reforms, even though it reserved its position on direct elections until after the referendum. For once, Britain seems to have played the EC game of compromise and consensus well; and it resulted in significant advances for all participants.

Perhaps even more important than the actual result of the summit, however, was that the first-hand experience of high-level EC politics seems to have changed Wilson's personal perceptions of the European integration process significantly. Contrary to cliché-laden perceptions of empty phrase-mongering and lofty rhetoric, the dealings between the

---

[99] PHSA/EA, 4.10.-7.11.1974, BPA, Hintergrundgespräch (off the record), 9 October 1974.

[100] Mourlon-Druol, 'Filling the EEC Leadership Vacuum', 315–39.

[101] L. Radoux, 'Report drawn up on behalf of the Political Affairs Committee on the results of the Conference of Heads of Government held in Paris on 9 and 10 December 1974', Working Documents 1974–1975, Document 436/74, 13 January 1975. [EU EP Document]. Accessed through University of Pittsburgh, Archive of European Integration (AEI): http://aei.pitt.edu/1740/ [accessed on 13 June 2018].

British Isolation in Europe 79

European leaders had in fact been highly pragmatic, solution-oriented, and addressed real issues of concern. This was the sort of EC Britain could work with. The creation of the European Council was particularly welcomed, seen by the British as part of a 'concept of progress towards a European power of decision that was positive, pragmatic, and, moreover, acceptable to ourselves' by shifting the power balance between member-states and the supranational institutions towards the former.[102] And though the heads of state and government reaffirmed their theoretical long-term commitment towards EMU in their final declaration, it was a vision that appeared to be far removed from the day-to-day realities of EC politics. 'He and M. Giscard D'Estaing had known in 1972 that EMU was an illusion fostered by idealists who did not understand the problem', Schmidt bluntly told his colleagues at the summit, and while it 'was not possible to withdraw from their predecessors' statement ... he would feel intellectually dishonest if Heads of Government pretended that EMU was likely to happen'.[103] This mirrored Schmidt's statements at the Chequers meeting a few days earlier, where he had already dismissed the subject as mere 'theology'.[104] Wilson, of course, was only too happy to believe in such assertions. In the House of Commons, he claimed afterwards that there was 'not a hope in hell ... of EMU taking place in the near future';[105] in Cabinet, he similarly suggested that the issue 'should be seen in the same light as the commitment to "general and complete disarmament" to which Governments were always ready to subscribe'.[106] But his judgement may well have been affected by more than one degree of wishful thinking. Already at Chequers, it was evident that Schmidt's views did not fully reflect German opinion, with Schmidt's confidant Per Fischer warning the British Cabinet Secretary Robert Armstrong afterwards that Schmidt's outburst on EMU should not be taken at face value. 'Herr Fischer seemed rather to regret what the Federal Chancellor had said', Armstrong noted, 'and remarked that the trouble was that there was a Government

---

[102] TNA/PREM16/382, Summary: The Conference of the Heads of Government of the Nine, 23 December 1974.
[103] TNA/PREM16/382, Record of a meeting of Heads of Government/State and Foreign Ministers at 9.00 on Tuesday 10 December, 16 December 1974.
[104] TNA/PREM16/101, Henderson to FCO, 4 December 1974.
[105] Hansard, *House of Commons Debate* 16 December 1974, vol. 883 cc. 1139.
[106] TNA/CAB128/55/26, CC (74) 51st Conclusions, 12 December 1974.

80   *Harold Wilson, 1974–1976*

commitment, and the Free Democratic Party (FDP) partners in the German Government'.[107] The Paris summit may have been a short-term success, but there remained many bigger British–German differences looming behind the façade of the renegotiations.

Harold Wilson Against the Franco–German Axis: The European Council at Dublin

With the Paris summit acknowledging the British budget problem in principle, it was clear that the renegotiations would be finalised at the inaugural session of the European Council on 10–11 March 1975 in Dublin. In Britain, it became evident to attentive observers that Wilson was now clearly working towards a successful renegotiation deal, performing, in the words of his biographer Ben Pimlott, 'the subtle art of making it gradually clear to the world, with a series of hints, nudges and nuances, that he had changed his mind about the Common Market'.[108] Again, however, Wilson stance constituted anything but a clear and coherent position, as EC membership remained a tough sell to both party and the wider public. Wilson therefore continued to play the role of a doughty fighter for British interests in public as well as internally. When he was challenged in Cabinet by the anti-EC Peter Shore about Britain's institutional commitments at the Paris summit, for example, he sharply brushed him off. As Tony Benn recalled in his diary, Wilson exclaimed that he 'strongly resent[ed] the idea that I was an innocent abroad, that I went there and was just swept along. I've been negotiating since some members of this Cabinet have been at school. ... I've been standing absolutely firm on the Manifesto, more than other people'.[109] The British Cabinet indeed remained as deeply divided as ever over the question. On 21 January 1975, Wilson therefore brokered what became known as the 'agreement to differ', allowing Cabinet members to articulate their personal views on membership without reference to the Government's eventual official recommendation during the period between the end of the renegotiations and the referendum.[110] Wilson's ultimate pro-EC intentions may have become

---

[107] TNA/PREM16/77, Note for the Record, 1 December 1974.
[108] Pimlott, *Wilson*, 655.
[109] T. Benn, *Against the Tide: Diaries 1973–6* (London: Hutchinson, 1989), 283.
[110] TNA/CAB128/56, Conclusions CC (75), 21 January 1975.

Harold Wilson Against the Franco–German Axis

evident to some Whitehall insiders by that stage,[111] but his public stance remained as ever determined by domestic pressures.

On the other side of the Channel, the conflicting signals coming out of Britain made a potential renegotiation deal a highly divisive issue in Germany as well. By early 1975, a serious split had emerged between those supporting a substantive offer to Britain on the budget for political reasons, and those fearing the likely economic costs of any deal to Germany. Finance Minister Hans Apel predictably belonged to the latter camp, being anxious to reduce German spending in light of the global economic downturn. In this quest, Wilson's public dithering allowed him to cleverly play into widespread German perceptions of British indecisiveness and opportunism. Already at a dinner party in July 1974, for example, Apel had exclaimed that 'the British no longer counted; it was worth little or nothing to the Federal Republic to keep the British in the Community and if they made what he considered to be the cardinal error of deciding that they were better off outside the Community then he, Apel, for one was not going to stop them. They could return to their historical position as a small island off the shore of North Eastern [sic!] Europe'.[112] Other German voices, however, were more moderate. The *Auswärtiges Amt*, for example, strongly stressed Wilson's domestic constraints in various internal assessments, urging the government to accommodate British demands as fully as possible in order to secure the FRG's long-standing strategic objective to keep Britain inside a united and outward-looking European Community.[113] Indeed, the different positions of the foreign and finance ministries could not be reconciled throughout the renegotiation period. Prior to the Dublin European Council, the two ministries were even unable to agree on a joint brief for Chancellor Schmidt, instead submitting two separate and contradictory briefs to the *Bundeskanzleramt*.[114]

It was therefore up to Schmidt to determine the final German position, and he seemed to place more importance on the political imperative of holding the EC together than on the potential financial costs of a deal. In various speeches during the early months of 1975, for

[111] Donoughue, 'Renegotiation', 197–8.
[112] TNA/FCO33/2469, Brussels to FCO, 24 July 1974.
[113] B136/7917, AA, Tagung der Regierungschefs und Außenminister in Dublin; hier: Unannehmbare Situation und Korrekturmechanismus, 7 March 1975.
[114] Ibid.

example, he emphasized that it was Germany's political responsibility to make financial sacrifices in order to preserve European integration, even if this meant curbing social spending or stalling reforms in education, youth, health, or social policies.[115] In order to do so, however, Schmidt needed to be sure that Wilson too would ultimately work towards continuing British membership. In February 1975, Schmidt's close adviser Hans-Jürgen Wischnewski therefore told Henderson that Schmidt 'would want to show great readiness to help the UK over the renegotiation terms', but that he also needed 'some further assurance from the Prime Minister, perhaps in restricted session, that he was prepared to throw himself wholeheartedly behind the new terms in submitting the issue to the people in the referendum'.[116] But the British government had little intention to reveal its cards prior to the decisive negotiations. Immediately prior to Dublin, Callaghan declared that Wilson would 'not even give his "private assurance" that he would push through a successful negotiating outcome, as such an assurance would eventually become public and negatively prejudice all hopes for a positive decision in Cabinet, majority of the party, and Parliament'.[117] It was a message to which Manfred Schüler, another member of Schmidt's inner circle, reacted 'immediately and strongly'. He wondered 'what sense summit meetings had if Heads of Government did not have authority to make decisions on behalf of their countries', Schüler told Callaghan in response, 'this struck him and he had no doubt it would strike the Federal Chancellor as an absurdity'.[118] Wilson may well have worked to assure Britain's continuing EC membership behind the scenes, but his continuing public complacency and secrecy only served to erode German trust in the British government further.

Partly as a result of such uncertainty over Wilson, Schmidt now started to cooperate even more closely with Giscard in order to transform the renegotiations into a presentable outcome for themselves.

---

[115] PHSA/EA, 1.1.-7.2.75, Rede Helmut Schmidt, auf außenpolitischer Konferenz der SPD in Bonn, 17 January 1975; Rede auf SPD Parteitag der SPD des Landes Rheinland-Pfalz in Kaiserslautern, 25 January 1975. See also PHSA/EA, Band 81, Bericht von Bundeskanzler Schmidt in der gemeinsamen Sitzung von Parteivorstand, Parteirat und Kontrollkommission [unkorrigierte Bandabschrift], 16 February 1975.

[116] TNA/PREM16/397, Bonn to FCO, 20 February 1975.

[117] B136/7916, London to AA, 7 March 1975.

[118] TNA/PREM16/409, Bonn to FCO, 6 March 1975.

Harold Wilson Against the Franco–German Axis

Their now firmly established pattern of private phone calls as well as the more formalised bilateral consultations at regular intervals clearly helped foster the emerging consensus. At a Franco–German plenary session in February 1975, for example, Giscard and Schmidt agreed with the assembled ministers to set up a secret Franco–German expert group, comprising one official each from the respective foreign and finance ministries, in order to work out a joint position for Dublin that would minimize financial contributions of both countries. If anything leaked, the group's objective should be described as merely a 'comparison of financial tables'.[119] For Schmidt, the prime objective had by now become to ensure that the revigorated Franco–German axis under Giscard would not be compromised by the renegotiations. At a final internal meeting with foreign minister Hans-Dietrich Genscher and finance minister Apel, Schmidt even stated bluntly that it was 'not sure whether one could bring Great Britain to positive behaviour. This makes it all the more important that there would be no rift in our relationship with France too, which is why we have to clear our behaviour with France at every stage'.[120] Schmidt then ruled that the total financial impact of German contributions should be held at 250 million European Units of Account (EUA) first; if necessary, it could be upgraded to 275 million EUAs. The final German fall-back position would be 300 million EUAs, significantly less than the compromise formula suggested by the EC Commission which the Germans had estimated to cost them at least 420 million EUAs.[121] Immediately prior to the summit, Schmidt cleared these numbers with Giscard,[122] and phoned Wilson to warn him that 'the size of the refund is the thing which matters more than other things. And we are figuring a size of not more than one quarter billion units of account which means 250 million units of account … I am pretty sure that Valery Giscard will buy that order of magnitude'.[123]

The eventual negotiations at the European Council at Dublin thus quickly became dead-locked, with Wilson facing yet again a united

[119] PAAA, Zwischenarchiv, 111198, Deutsch-Französische Außenministerkonsultationen in Paris, 4 February 1975.
[120] 1/HSAA006648, Vermerk: Ministergespräch vom 3.3.1975, 5 March 1975.
[121] Ibid.
[122] B136/7917, Betr.: Tagung der Regierungschefs und Außenminister in Dublin, 8 March 1975.
[123] TNA/PREM16/397, Record of a telephone Conversation between PM and FRG Chancellor, 9 March 1975.

84 *Harold Wilson, 1974–1976*

front by Schmidt and Giscard. According to the British record, Schmidt started off by brusquely asserting that 'the order of magnitude of the refund was too big for him', and that Germany 'could not finance all the costly inventions of the Commission at a time when their GNP was stagnating'. 'He was facing elections in Germany also', he then exclaimed, and in any case had 'no intention of losing his Minister of Finance'.[124] Throughout the discussions, Schmidt would not budge from this hard-line position; even in his handwritten notes, he scribbled down and underlined repeatedly that this was not a question for Brussels technocrats but about German taxpayers' money.[125] Paradoxically, however, Wilson seems to have lost all interest in the budget question at that stage. When Michael Butler, the FCO's senior official present at Dublin, warned the PM that the restrictive conditions attached to the proposed corrective mechanism by the Germans meant that it could probably never be triggered, Wilson appeared indifferent. As Butler recalls, Wilson simply accepted the final draft, before once again trying to shift focus on the question of Commonwealth trade.[126]

It was therefore not least due to Wilson's personal performance that the actual results of the renegotiations were rather minimal. On the Commonwealth issue, Britain gained continued preferential access to New Zealand butter until 1980, but the question of other dairy and food imports including cheese was left open.[127] Even more disappointing, however, was the deal on the budget: the final corrective formula was capped at a ceiling of 250 million EUAs, the Franco–German starting position, and attached with so many conditions that it never produced any benefit to the United Kingdom in practice.[128] A few years later, the issue would thus resurface rather more violently under Margaret Thatcher.

Not that any of this mattered in the short-term. The renegotiations had always been first and foremost a tool to hold party and public together over the European question, and that strategy worked out very well indeed. On 18 March 1975, the Cabinet decided with a majority of

---

[124] TNA/PREM16/397, Record of EEC Heads of Government meeting, 10 March 1975.
[125] PHSA, EA, Band 81, Dublin – handwritten notes, undated.
[126] Wall, *Official History*, 576–7.
[127] Hansard, *House of Commons Debate* 18 March 1975, vol. 88 cc. 1456–60.
[128] For the conclusions, see European Council, 'The European Council [Dublin Summit 1975]', 10–11 March 1975, *AEI*, http://aei.pitt.edu/1921/ [accessed on 8 November 2017].

sixteen to seven to recommend continuing EC membership on the basis of the renegotiated terms to the British public.[129] The public heeded their government's advice. On 5 June 1975, a total of 17.4 million Britons voted that Britain should remain an EC member, against a 'no' vote of only 8.5 million. This huge majority of 67.2 per cent, as Wilson was keen to point out in his memoirs, was bigger 'than has been received by any Government in any general election', even though the commitment of the British electorate to the EC soon proved to be wide rather than deep.[130] After almost two decades of virulent debate, the question of Britain's EC membership finally seemed settled, at least for the time being. In conversation with US President Ford shortly after-wards, Wilson even claimed that this had been his deliberate strategy all along. 'We couldn't have gotten that vote earlier', he boasted, 'We played it cool, acted as though we had to be convinced and only pulled out the stops at the end'.[131] Yet, while the episode undoubtedly marked an important domestic success, at least in the short-term, it also came at a heavy price internationally – the marginalization of Britain in its triangular relationship with France and Germany, a dynamic that eventually extended far beyond purely intra-EC matters.

Britain Remains in the Doghouse: The Legacy of the Renegotiations in Intra-EC Politics

In Britain, it was painfully clear to many Whitehall observers that the lengthy renegotiations had inflicted lasting damage on Britain's rela-tions with its EC partners. The weeks following the referendum there-fore saw hectic attempts by the British government to display its now allegedly full-hearted commitment to EC membership. Apart from finally sending off Labour MPs to the EP,[132] Wilson also initiated a series of bilateral visits to Germany and France in order to improve his personal relationships with his respective counterparts, with the

[129] TNA/CAB128/56, CC (75) 14th Conclusions, 17 and 18 March 1975.
[130] Wilson, *Final Term*, 108; D. Butler and U. Kitzinger, *The 1975 Referendum* (Basingstoke: Macmillan, 1976). For an excellent new study of the referendum, see R. Saunders, *Yes to Europe! The 1975 Referendum and Seventies Britain* (Cambridge: Cambridge University Press, 2018).
[131] GRFL/NSA, Memoranda of Conversations, 1973–1977, Box 14, Memorandum of conversation Wilson-Ford, 30 July 1975.
[132] The Labour Party had refused to fill its seats at the European Parliament while the renegotiations and referendum were taking place.

FCO still hoping that these meetings would somehow contribute towards the development of 'the triangular relationship which remains in our interest to establish'.[133] Yet, it soon became evident that the erosion of trust triggered by the renegotiations could not simply be glossed over by Wilson's sweet talk. It did not help that the deeper underlying visions of European integration in Britain and Germany remained as far apart as ever: the two countries continued to be at loggerheads over almost all aspects of Community policy, tensions fuelled as much by the two governments' conflicting domestic needs as by the erosion of bilateral trust over the past twelve months.

In spite of the advances at the Paris summit, for example, the Germans remained concerned about the more general lack of European dynamism and revitalization at a time of global economic crises. By June 1975, the alleged lack of progress inside the EC had started to feature in the German domestic debate as well. To many, Schmidt's support of a largely pragmatic and intergovernmental concept of European integration – as institutionalised in the European Council – seemed a far cry from the lofty integrationist rhetoric his predecessors Adenauer and Brandt had drawn upon so frequently.[134] During a high-profile *Bundestag* debate in early 1976, for example, Christian Social Union in Bavaria (CSU) party leader Franz-Josef Strauss went at great lengths to criticise the 'grave setback' European unification had allegedly suffered under Schmidt, proclaiming that the CDU/CSU opposition was the only German party still committed to the 'United States of Europe'.[135] Even the SPD's coalition partner FDP now tried to portray itself as the more pro-European party in government, publishing much-noticed 'guidelines' for a federal Europe at its party conference in October 1975.[136] As the trusted trouble-shooter Wischnewski warned Schmidt in a handwritten letter afterwards, the FDP was keenly aware that the European question remained 'highly important in public opinion', and therefore consciously sought to cultivate a pro-EC image in time for the upcoming national elections of

[133] TNA/PREM16/427, Meetings between the PM and President Giscard and Chancellor Schmidt, 30 June 1975; TNA/PREM16/427, FCO to PREM, 30 June 1975.
[134] Haeussler, 'The Convictions of a Realist', 955–72.
[135] *Protokolle des Deutschen Bundestages*, 7. Wahlperiode, 235. Sitzung, 8 April 1976, 16369, 16371.
[136] For more detail, see H. D. Lucas, 'Politik der kleinen Schritte – Genscher und die deutsche Europapolitik 1974–1983', in H. D. Lucas (ed.), *Genscher, Deutschland und Europa* (Baden-Baden: Nomos, 2002), 90, 102–3.

1976.[137] Schmidt, by contrast, still believed that the continuing discrepancies between member-states' domestic policies made any effort at greater integration in the economic and fiscal realm doomed to fail. Partly to make up for such standstill, he thus sought to utilise the issue of direct elections to the European Parliament, a long-standing demand of German European policy, in order to bolster his European credentials at home.[138] As one of Schmidt's advisers put it in preparation of a Cabinet meeting, Schmidt's strong support of direct elections might well function as a 'sort of compensation' for the 'standstill' over economic integration in the eyes of public opinion.[139]

Yet again, the British domestic debate over the issue was almost diametrically opposed to the German one. Ever since the 1950s, British discourses over European integration had frequently been dominated by the theme of national sovereignty. In the virulent parliamentary debate over EC membership in 1971, for example, Britain's past and future ability to govern itself had featured prominently; during the 1975 referendum campaign, opponents of EC membership like Enoch Powell and Tony Benn had again tried to portray the EC as a threat to Britain's centuries-long constitutional and parliamentary history.[140] In this context, a directly elected EP was commonly seen not as an opportunity to democratise the EC, but rather as a threat to Westminster and other national parliaments. The contrast between British opinion and that of many other member-states was stark indeed: a *Eurobarometer* poll in May 1975 showed that only 41 per cent of Britons favoured direct elections to the EP, against an average of 71 per cent in the founding member-states.[141] This mirrored

[137] 1/HSAA009003, Wischnewski to Schmidt, 30 October 1975.

[138] For German attitudes towards direct elections in the 1970s, see Q. Jouan, 'Narratives of European Integration in Times of Crisis: Images of Europe in the 1970s', *Journal of European Integration History*, 22/1 (2016), 24–5. For more general background, see the respective chapters in D. M. Viola (ed.), *Routledge Handbook of European Elections* (Abingdon: Routledge, 2016).

[139] 1/HSAA007114, Vermerk für Sondersitzung des Bundeskabinetts, 25 September 1975.

[140] N. P. Ludlow, 'Safeguarding British Identity or Betraying It? The Role of British "Tradition" in the Parliamentary Great Debate on EC Membership, October 1971', *Journal of Common Market Studies* 53/1 (2015), 18–34; R. Saunders, 'A Tale of Two Referendums: 1975 and 2016', *The Political Quarterly* 87/3 (2016), 318–22.

[141] Commission of the European Communities, *Euro-Barometre: Public Opinion in the European Community* 3 (June–July 1975), 23, http://ec.europa.eu/com mfrontoffice/publicopinion/archives/eb/eb3/eb3_en.pdf [accessed on 13 June 2018].

some of the more general British unease over European integration that had at times surfaced during the renegotiation and referendum period. In April 1975, for example, Callaghan professed at a meeting of foreign ministers to be 'more aghast than ever before' by the ideas of some of his colleagues over economic and monetary union, wondering whether he actually had to 'deceive the British people about the ultimate goals of the Community' during the referendum campaign. Britain, he asserted, 'had signed the Treaty of Rome and nothing more'.[142]

These very different domestic contexts now put the British and the Germans again at odds with each other, particularly once Wilson seemed to backtrack from his earlier promise at the Paris summit to lift his reservations on direct elections after the referendum. Schmidt in particular was furious. When Wilson told him confidentially in July 1975 that he 'still needed time' on the issue 'in consideration of British public opinion', Schmidt responded fumingly. 'I have expressed my regret about this and said that I think it would be best if he could get that problem off the table with one big push', he noted afterwards, adding that Giscard had subsequently 'expressed himself in even more indignant terms than I have done'.[143] Indeed, Wilson's stake amongst his European counterparts continued to run dangerously low. The following month, Schmidt and Giscard again cross-examined Wilson's newly found commitment to European integration at the European Council in Brussels. Referring to Wilson's opening statement that Britain's role in Europe was now 'committed and total', Giscard asked Wilson specifically whether this also meant that he was now 'prepared to withdraw' the British reservation over direct elections. Yet again, however, Giscard only received an evasive answer from Wilson, and the British PM only lifted his reservation after repeated urgings by his European counterparts.[144] Not only did such dithering reinforce German perceptions of British aloofness and reluctance to identify with the European cause, but it also offered Schmidt a welcome opportunity to talk up his own commitment to European integration at the expense

[142] *AAPD 1975* Doc Nr. 76, Konferenz der Außenminister der EG-Mitgliedstaaten in Dublin, 12–13 April 1975.

[143] 1/HSAA007095, EG-Institutionelle Ergebnisse meiner Vier-Augen-Gespräche mit Premierminister Wilson und Staatspräsident Giscard d'Estaing, 27 July 1975.

[144] TNA/PREM16/393, Record of Discussion at European Council held in Brussels, 16 and 17 July 1975.

of the British. In an interview with a German radio station after the Brussels Council, Schmidt dwelt at length on his personal performance. He had made 'many interventions in favour of ... taking a step forward by the end of this year with direct elections to the European Parliament', he claimed, whereas the British had lifted their reservations only reluctantly 'after direct approaches by us and the French'. '[E]qually, on my lead', Schmidt continued boastfully, 'the earlier British reserve on passport union was lifted'.[145] The picture presented to the German audience was clear: Schmidt and Giscard were at the very heart of the EC, whereas Wilson drifted on its margins. It was a most worrying picture for Britain, not least because such notions of a Franco–German lead now increasingly extended beyond the realm of purely intra-EC politics.

The Changing Transatlantic Environment: US–European Rapprochement and British Aloofness

After the transatlantic disarray following Kissinger's ill-fated 'Year of Europe' in 1973, the almost simultaneous elections of Schmidt, Giscard, and Wilson had managed to calm the storm almost overnight.[146] In Britain, Wilson and Callaghan were self-proclaimed transatlanticists who professed themselves eager to repair the alleged damage done by Heath's Europeanism; Schmidt too had just demonstrated his personal attachment to the transatlantic alliance at the Washington Energy Conference. Most significant, however, was the election of Giscard d'Estaing in France. In sharp contrast to his predecessors, Giscard was not interested in constructing a European polity independent of the United States, but instead sought to advance the process of European integration in close harmony with the Americans. Speaking fluent English and having travelled the United States extensively in his twenties, Giscard was not only personally predisposed towards the transatlantic alliance, but his professional education also meant that he was acutely aware of France's ultimate military and economic dependence on it.[147] In August 1974, the circle of transatlantic renewal was completed by

[145] As quoted in TNA/PREM16/393, Bonn to FCO, 19 July 1975.
[146] N. P. Ludlow, 'The Real Years of Europe? U.S.-West European Relations During the Ford Administration', *Journal of Cold War Studies* 15/3 (2013), 142–3.
[147] Gfeller, *Building a European Identity*, 143–63.

US President Nixon's resignation following the Watergate affair, and his replacement by Gerald Ford. It triggered a surprisingly drastic change in the transatlantic climate: whereas the Nixon administration had been frequently sceptical and at times openly hostile towards its West European allies, Ford and his Secretary of State Henry Kissinger now seemed eager to bolster US–European unity and 'hold the West together' in light of the severe military, political, and economic challenges the alliance faced.[148]

The years 1974 to 1976 indeed saw some remarkable examples of successful transatlantic cooperation that stand in stark contrast to the more troubled period under his predecessor Nixon.[149] Apart from the successful conclusion of the Conference on Security and Cooperation in Europe (CSCE) with the signing of the Helsinki Final Act in August 1975,[150] the establishment of the G7 world economic summits stands as the period's most lasting achievement. It was a development yet again driven primarily by Schmidt and Giscard, who both sought to overcome the disarray in global politics brought by the end of the Bretton Woods system through informal cooperation and governance on the highest political level.[151] The Franco–German tandem was also at the core of what eventually became the inaugural summit at Rambouillet, with the discussions dominated by Schmidt's and Giscard's pronounced agreement over most fiscal and economic matters.[152] Britain, by contrast, played a benevolent but subordinate

---

[148] See in particular Sargent, *Superpower Transformed*, 165–97.

[149] Ludlow, 'The Real Years of Europe?', 136–61.

[150] Most details of the CSCE had already been settled prior to Schmidt's and Wilson's assumption of office, which is why it is not discussed in great detail here. Schmidt's most important input was his promise to the Soviets to keep a low profile on Basket III in a quid pro quo over the 'peaceful change of frontiers' in Basket I. See G. Niedhart, 'Peaceful Change of Frontiers as a Crucial Element in the West German Strategy of Transformation', in O. Bange and G. Niedhart (eds.), *Helsinki 1975 and the Transformation of Europe* (New York, NY and Oxford: Berghahn, 2008), 23–38; and L. Ratti, 'Britain, the German Question and the Transformation of Europe: From Ostpolitik to the Helsinki Conference, 1963–1975', in ibid., 83–97. More generally, Romano, *From Détente in Europe to European Détente.*

[151] There has been an explosion of recent literature on 1970s summitry. As a starting point, see Mourlon-Druol and Romero, *International Summitry and Global Governance.*

[152] For Schmidt and Giscard's joint initiative for the Versailles summit, see Waechter, *Schmidt Giscard,* 98–103; Spohr, *Global Chancellor* 18–23. More generally, von Karczewski, *Weltwirtschaft ist unser Schicksal,* 111–210.

2.2 French President Giscard D' Estaing invites Prime Minister Harold Wilson to move in closer for 'La Photo de Famille' at the first world economic summit at Rambouillet, 17 November 1975. Source: Bettmann/Getty Images.

role, still preoccupied with the renegotiations and suffering from much more severe economic problems than its partners. In January 1975, Kissinger even told President Ford that Britain no longer mattered in his eyes. 'Britain is a tragedy', he exclaimed, 'it has sunk to begging, borrowing, stealing until North Sea oil comes in ... That Britain has become such a scrounger is a disgrace'.[153] At Rambouillet, Wilson indeed seemed largely detached from the other participants, with Giscard at one point slipping a note to Schmidt wondering how Wilson could still profess to be satisfied with Britain's disastrous economic situation.[154]

Newly found Franco–American unity coupled with severe economic difficulties therefore threatened to isolate Britain not only inside the EC, but also within the wider transatlantic framework. Whereas Britain traditionally saw itself as a transatlantic bridge between American and European positions,[155] the French and German governments' close links

---

[153] GRFL/NSA, Memoranda of Conversations, 1973–1977, Box 8, Conversation Ford-Kissinger, 8 January 1975.
[154] Quoted in Waechter, *Schmidt und Giscard*, 102.
[155] Although it had rarely managed to play this role effectively in the 1950s and 1960s. See K. Ruane and J. Ellison, 'Managing the Americans: Anthony Eden,

to the Ford administration had by 1975 largely removed the necessity for such a role, given that Schmidt and Giscard simply preferred to deal with the Americans directly. Most importantly, Giscard also managed to resolve the long-standing Franco–American conflict over how to best deal with the consequences of the oil shock.[156] Whereas previous French policy had been to deal with OPEC countries directly and often unilaterally, Giscard – an internationalist by instinct – was instead convinced that France's economic self-interest was to act in tandem with both the United States and its other European partners. Already after his very first meeting with Giscard in June 1974, for example, Schmidt told the American Ambassador that the new French leader appeared 'visibly embarrassed by the previous quarrels between Jobert and Kissinger'.[157] Eventually, the issue was resolved by an uneasy but lasting compromise at the Martinique Summit in in December 1974: France would not veto the creation of the US-inspired International Energy Agency [IEA] in the OECD; in turn, the Americans would acquiesce in Giscard's proposal for a consumer-producer conference in Paris.[158] For the first time in over a decade, France was no longer the odd man out in the transatlantic alliance.

For the Germans, the reconciliation of such long-standing Franco–American tensions offered a new opportunity for their long-standing efforts to coordinate European energy policies under a wider transatlantic umbrella.[159] The energy crisis had always posed rather different challenges to the West Europeans than it had to the United States, given the Europeans' disproportionate dependence on Middle Eastern oil imports:

Harold Macmillan and the Pursuit of "Power-by-Proxy" in the 1950s', *Contemporary British History* 18/3 (2004), 147–67.

[156] Möckli, *European Foreign Policy*, 184–300.

[157] 1/HSAA006638, Gespräch mit dem amerikanischen Botschafter, 6 June 1974.

[158] Gfeller, *Building a European Identity*, 175–9; Sargent, *Superpower Transformed*, 184–7.

[159] For the Franco–German quest to establish a European energy policy, see S. Tauer, *Störfall für die gute Nachbarschaft? Deutsche und Franzosen auf der Suche nach einer gemeinsamen Energiepolitik (1973–1980)* (Göttingen: Vandenhoeck&Ruprecht, 2012), 148–68. More generally on the oil crisis, R. Graf, *Öl und Souveränität. Petroknowledge und Energiepolitik in den USA und Westeuropa in den 1970er Jahren* (Munich: De Gruyter Oldenbourg, 2014); F. Venn, *The Oil Crisis* (Harlow: Longman, 2002); H. Türk, 'The Oil Crisis of 1973 as a Challenge to Multilateral Energy Cooperation Among Western Industrialized countries', *Historical Social Research* 39/4 (2014), 209–30; and the contemporary R. Lieber, *The Oil Decade: Conflict and Cooperation in the West* (New York, NY: Praeger, 1983).

The Changing Transatlantic Environment

whereas the United States only obtained around 15 per cent of its oil from the region, West European imports amounted to roughly 60 per cent.[160] Western Europe's structural dependency on Middle Eastern oil thus made both multilateral and European cooperation a necessity in German eyes, as they feared that the oil crisis might otherwise undermine not only Western Europe's economic growth but also its wider political stability. As Schmidt put it in conversation with Ford, the West Europeans would inevitably have to 'react negatively' to any further confrontations with OPEC countries and corresponding hikes in oil prices, since the Europeans simply 'could not stand' such a 'confrontation. They need stable prices and assured supply'.[161] Schmidt's convictions were again shared by Giscard, and the two leaders started to move in close tandem in order to establish the framework of an eventual joint European energy policy. As early as February 1975, for example, Schmidt told the French newspaper *Figaro* that he thought it 'absolutely necessary' that the EC 'achieves the formulation of a common energy policy, which has to be followed by each of the nine member-states as well as the EC as a whole'.[162] Internally, Schmidt even claimed that the establishment of such a joint European energy policy was the 'by far most important political and international task' Germany faced in the 1970s.[163] Schmidt and Giscard thus sought to utilize the EC as a vehicle to pursue what they regarded as shared European interests on the global stage.

This vision of a joint European energy policy, however, was yet again not shared by the British government. Though Britain had suffered heavily from the 1973 oil crisis in the short term, its discovery of significant amounts of North Sea oil offered infinitely brighter prospects in the long run, perhaps even making the country self-sufficient over energy at some point.[164] The British were therefore highly sceptical of the Franco–German initiative, fearing that it might trigger a pooling of supplies and therefore a loss of British control over its oil price.[165] Schmidt, for one, was sharply aware of these structural

---

[160] Venn, *Oil Crisis*, 131; 113–44.
[161] GRFL/NSA, Memoranda of Conversations, 1973–1977, Box 14, Conversation Schmidt-Ford, 27 July 1975.
[162] 1/HSAA006647, Interview des Bundeskanzlers mit der französischen Tageszeitung "Figaro", 2 February 1975.
[163] *AAPD 1975*, Doc. Nr. 173, Besprechung bei Bundeskanzler Schmidt, 23 June 1975.
[164] Venn, *Oil Crisis*, 121–2.
[165] TNA/CAB128/57, CC (75) 42nd Conclusions, 9 October 1975.

differences between the British and other European positions. 'If there is any different outlook on oil in Europe', he told Ford and Kissinger candidly in July 1975, 'it is in Great Britain, which will soon have its own supply'.[166] In an outspoken off-the-record press briefing the same month, he put over his views in slightly less diplomatic terms. 'Contrary to widely-held prejudices of bureaucrats and public opinion', he exclaimed, 'it is not the case that 8 nations have one interest in oil and France another, but rather, in the middle and long term they actually have one interest and Britain has another interest. This is how the matter stands. Everything else is a smokescreen of prestige'. It therefore had to be 'recognised behind all the smoke', Schmidt continued his rant, 'that in actual fact the Continental member states of the EC will remain dependent on oil and gas imports, while Britain will possibly become self-supporting in this field; that is a fundamental difference, which one cannot allow to be disguised by all kinds of possible stories'.[167]

Wider Differences over Europe's Role on the Global Stage

The focal point of British–German differences was the question of European representation at the upcoming consumer-producer conference, the so-called North-South Conference.[168] In order to ensure maximum West European coherence and strengthen its bargaining position, Germany as well as most other member-states wanted the EC countries to be represented under a shared Community mandate.[169] Britain, by contrast, was firmly opposed to such joint representation, given what it regarded as different national interests in the energy field. On 16 October, the British Cabinet discussed how Britain's position over energy was 'enormously strong', given its 'immensely valuable oil deposits in the North Sea, considerable supplies of natural gas, a third of the world's nuclear energy production and coal reserves lasting three hundred years'. It thus concluded that it seemed 'absurd' for Britain to

---

[166] GRFL/NSA, Memoranda of Conversations, 1973–7, Box 14, Conversation Schmidt-Ford, 27 July 1975.

[167] The record of the meeting was subsequently – and perhaps deliberately – leaked to the British. See TNA/PREM16/427, Bonn to FCO, 17 July 1975.

[168] For more detail, see Gfeller, *Building European Identity*, 171–95.

[169] B136/11807, Konferenz für Internationale Wirtschaftliche Zusammenarbeit, 25 November 1975; Brief: Europäischer Rat in Rom, 27 November 1975.

be represented 'by Luxembourg' at a conference that might turn out to be 'as important as Bretton Woods'.[170] At the subsequent Foreign Ministers Council, Callaghan correspondingly put his foot down, insisting that Britain was 'in a unique position' because it would 'produce 45–50 per cent of the EC's entire energy resources by 1980', and therefore needed to 'protect its national interests'. In response, Callaghan's counterparts reacted strongly, arguing that the EC's increased bargaining power as a unified actor should trump any such British concerns which could in any case be addressed as part of the shared mandate. The Luxembourgian Foreign Minister Gaston Thorn, for example, declared that British fears were 'exaggerated' and that this was not a question about Britain, but about the EC's future role in international politics; EC Commission President Ortoli agreed that a failure of the EC to be jointly represented at the conference would be 'a serious political defeat'.[171] These arguments closely mirrored Schmidt's own thinking, who had already written to Wilson a few days earlier that the 'vital interests of the Community' could 'only be protected if its members take a common stand and speak with one voice'.[172] Yet, Wilson would not buckle down, replying to Schmidt after Callaghan's Council experience that the 'material interests' of Britain and the other member-states were simply 'not identical', and could therefore not be 'over-ridden'.[173]

Tensions came to a head at a heated twelve-hour European Council meeting the following month, where Schmidt tackled Wilson sharply. The tense and aggressive language Schmidt used is testimony not only to the paramount importance he personally attributed to the oil question, but also to the key role the EC played in his vision of Europe's wider role on the global stage. He 'could not sufficiently underline nor over-dramatise the need for a common energy policy in Europe', Schmidt started off, continuing that he was 'not prepared to hand over the fate of the industrialised countries to oil producers'. Attacking Wilson directly, Schmidt exclaimed how the West Europeans 'had gone to great efforts to make it possible for Wilson and Mr Callaghan to make a success of renegotiation. ... However the Community was now at a cross-roads

---

[170] TNA/CAB128/57, CC (75) 43rd Conclusions, 16 October 1975.
[171] *AAPD 1975*, Doc. Nr. 309, Konferenz der Außenminister der EG-Mitgliedstaaten in Lucca, 18–19 October 1975.
[172] TNA/PREM16/863, Schmidt to Wilson, 10 October 1975.
[173] TNA/PREM16/863, Wilson to Schmidt, 21 October 1975.

and its members must do what they could to prevent the Community from falling apart'. Regarding the energy problem as 'a question of life and death', Schmidt even threatened German unilateralism. If Britain 'were to go it alone, as the weakest economy in the Community, it would be in trouble', he yelled, whereas the FRG was 'in a very strong economic situation. [German] reserves were as much as those of France, the Soviet Union and the United States put together. So long as he was Chancellor German economic strength would not be used for selfish national ends but it was always worth remembering that he could so use it. If everyone chose to paddle his own canoe the Germans could do so too'.[174] To many participants, it was a shocking intervention, striking some British observers as 'uncomfortably reminiscent of some of the attitudes of pre-war Germany'.[175] It may well have been one of the reasons why Wilson eventually backtracked and accepted Britain's representation under the shared EC mandate with only minor concessions. As he later recalled in his memoirs, the EC had shown 'an unaccustomed degree of unity – against Britain'.[176]

Though the consumer-producer conference ultimately proved rather insignificant, the tensions surrounding the mandate question nonetheless reveals how the erosion of bilateral trust triggered by the renegotiations now extended into far bigger questions of European cooperation in the international arena, and highlights the degree to which German and British perceptions of the EC's role on the global stage differed. Here, there was a major conceptual gap between Schmidt and Wilson that exposed key differences in their worldviews and visions: whereas Wilson regarded the issue of joint EC representation as a nuisance and potentially unwelcome restraint on Britain's freedom of manoeuvre, Schmidt instead saw it as a key part in his more general strategy to pursue German interests through the EC framework. And Schmidt showed little inclination to disguise these differences in public. 'I have to talk about myself for a while', Schmidt started off at the press conference immediately following the European Council, since this apparently could 'not be avoided with regard to today's results'. He then told the assembled journalists how he had 'very vividly illustrated' the potentially fatal consequences of a failure to achieve a shared EC

[174] TNA/PREM16/399, European Council Meeting Rome 1–2 December 1975.
[175] TNA/PREM16/399, Denman to Part (Department of Industry),
8 December 1975.
[176] Wilson, *Final Term*, 202.

Wider Differences over Europe's Role 97

mandate, claiming to have been responsible 'for everything that has happened until lunchtime. I have almost dictated this to the minute takers'.[177] On German television a few hours later, Schmidt denied press allegations to have screamed at Wilson but nonetheless stressed again that he had 'supported the idea of a united and common representation of the Community in the strongest possible terms'.[178] Not only did the episode thus reveal the extent of British–German differences over energy and the EC's role on the global stage, but it also allowed Schmidt to cast himself into the single-handed saviour of Europe – yet again at the expense of the British.

On the other side of the Channel, Schmidt's public castigation of Wilson worried many who had become concerned over Britain's isolation amongst its European partners. Even opposition leader Margaret Thatcher attacked Wilson heavily in the House of Commons. Wilson, she exclaimed, had subjected Britain 'to a series of humiliations' abroad, antagonising 'many friends upon whom we rely'. 'Could he not have achieved the same results', Thatcher continued without a trace of irony, by 'co-operating with our friends' instead of restoring to 'antagonistic tactics'?[179] Thatcher's line mirrored similar concerns amongst senior ministers and officials about Britain's growing isolation in both the EC and the more general patterns of West European cooperation. The Second Permanent Secretary at the Cabinet Office Roy Denman, for example, warned in December 1975 that the mandate controversy had shown how Britain's 'credit in the European bank' was 'not only low but overdrawn'.[180] This sentiment was echoed in a more substantial stocktaking of Britain's role in the EC a few weeks later, which similarly claimed that Britain should 'take a leaf out of the French book and learn how to present national self-interest as a high minded Community endeavour'.[181] Yet, this was a task that would fall to a different PM. On 16 March 1976, Wilson announced his resignation on the grounds of his age and severe physical and mental

[177] B136/7919, Pressekonferenz mit Bundeskanzler nach Abschluss des Treffens, 2 December 1975.
[178] B136/7919, ARD: Tagesschau 22:35h, 2 December 1975.
[179] Hansard, *House of Commons Debate* 4 December 1975, vol. 901 cc. 1935–6.
[180] TNA/PREM16/399, Denman to Part (Department of Industry), 13 December 1975.
[181] TNA/PREM16/863, Britain in the European Community 1976, 8 January 1976.

98   *Harold Wilson, 1974–1976*

exhaustion. Characteristically, it was a move that he had long planned in secret, but that still caught almost everybody by surprise.

Conclusions

Harold Wilson's final term as PM saw a marked erosion of Britain's stake in the British–German relationship, as well as within the wider framework of West European cooperation in the international arena. These developments were triggered primarily by the highly divisive 'renegotiation and referendum' exercise, which put Britain and Germany almost diametrically at odds with each other. Yet, the episode also illustrated some broader differences in British and German attitudes towards European integration: whereas Britain's structural disadvantages as a latecomer to the EC as well as the continuing domestic divisions over membership made the 'renegotiation and referendum' strategy seem like an almost inevitable exercise to secure the long-term goal of retraining EC membership, the Germans had by that stage already come to regard the EC as the key cornerstone of its foreign policy. This is why they perceived the 'renegotiations' as a more fundamental threat to European cooperation amidst the troubled times of the early 1970s, fuelling more general German perceptions of Britain as a somewhat dejected and ultimately unreliable partner in European politics.

While these wider structural differences in the outlooks of Britain and Germany stood at the heart of the bilateral controversies over the renegotiations, it is important not to neglect the personal role of Harold Wilson, particularly on the highest level. To be sure, Wilson was very much a product of his times and domestic environment. Never having displayed great personal enthusiasm over Europe and being acutely aware of the Labour Party's internal divisions, his approach towards the renegotiations was clearly motivated first and foremost by party-political considerations. Whilst he was clearly working towards keeping Britain inside the EC, he believed that he had to play the role of an uncommitted defender of British interests in order to achieve that goal. Yet, Wilson played his role rather too well. His inability – or unwillingness – to build a confidential rapport with Schmidt clearly intensified German suspicions over Britain's ultimate role and intentions inside the EC. Rather than using the frequent high-level encounters to illustrate his significant domestic constraints to Schmidt, and perhaps

Conclusions 99

even to devise a bilateral strategy to overcome them, Wilson's unwillingness to engage in substantive dialogue with Schmidt instead triggered a serious breakdown of mutual trust on the highest level. Not only did this allow Schmidt to use Wilson as a scapegoat in order to prop up his own European credentials in the German domestic debate, but the bilateral climate also contrasted harshly with the close and confidential relationship he developed with the newly elected Giscard d'Estaing at the very same time. Instead of working towards some sort of trilateral leadership of Western Europe as originally envisaged, Schmidt therefore came to rely primarily on the revived Franco–German relationship in the conduct of his foreign policy during the first years of his chancellorship. It was thus the combination of long-term structural differences and short-term failures at personal diplomacy that ultimately made Harold Wilson's final years such disastrous ones for the British–German relationship. And, just like during the renegotiations, it was up to the more diplomatically attuned James Callaghan to pick up the pieces.

3 | *James Callaghan, 1976–1979*

On 10 January 1979, a sun-tanned and visibly relaxed PM James Callaghan addressed the assembled press at London Heathrow airport after his return from the Caribbean island Guadeloupe, where he had just spent two days discussing nuclear and security politics with US President Jimmy Carter, the French President Giscard d'Estaing, and Helmut Schmidt. At home, however, the situation was dire. Having failed to renew Labour's social contract with the trade unions a few months earlier, Callaghan's government was faced with widespread industrial action, with the lorry drivers' strike that had started the week before now severely threatening the distribution of petrol and other essential supplies in Britain. When asked about his 'view of the mounting chaos in the country', however, Callaghan bluntly brushed off the interviewer. 'Well, that's a judgment that you are making and I promise you that, if you look at it from outside – and perhaps you're taking a rather parochial view at the moment – I don't think that other people in the world would share the view that there is mounting chaos'. 'Now', he grumbled, 'don't you think that's sufficient, after a 9 hour flight overnight . . . and no breakfast'.[1] Next day, the *Sun* dashed out its famous headline 'Crisis? What crisis?', fostering the image of a PM lacking grip and being out of touch with the British public.[2] It is now widely seen to have sealed the fate of his premiership.[3]

---

[1] TNA/PREM16/2050, Interview with the PM at Heathrow Airport after talks in Guadeloupe and Barbados, 10 January 1979.

[2] *Sun*, 11 January 1979.

[3] This, at least, is the conventional interpretation. See N. Ferguson, 'Introduction: Crisis, What Crisis? The 1970s and the Shock of the Global', in Ferguson et al., *Shock of the Global*, 1–24. For recent popular narratives along these lines, D. Sandbrook, *Seasons in the Sun: The Battle for Britain, 1974–1979* (London: Penguin, 2013); A. Beckett, *When the Lights Went Out: Britain in the Seventies* (London: Faber, 2010); A. W. Turner, *Crisis? What Crisis? Britain in the 1970s* (London: Aurum, 2009).

Callaghan's term in office may still be remembered primarily for its domestic failures,[4] but it also marked the highpoint of British–German cooperation during Schmidt's chancellorship. This was due not least to the new PM's successful utilization of high-level private diplomacy, the preferred modus vivendi of both himself and his German counterpart Schmidt. In striking contrast to his predecessor Wilson, Callaghan quickly struck up a close and confidential partnership with Schmidt, as well as with other key allies like Giscard d'Estaing or the American Presidents Gerald Ford and Jimmy Carter. Not only did the revitalization of the British–German relationship on the highest political level break the deadlock over many long-standing bilateral problems like Offset or Jet, but it also enabled an unprecedented degree of cooperation within wider multilateral frameworks, particularly within the transatlantic alliance amidst the worsening superpower relationship from 1977 onwards. Yet, Callaghan, too, proved both unable and unwilling to overcome the serious strategic gaps that drove Britain and Germany apart over European integration; and his ultimate refusal to join the EMS in 1978–9 might well be seen as the most lasting legacy of British–German relations during Schmidt's entire chancellorship. The Callaghan years thus demonstrate both the opportunities and limits of high-level diplomacy in shaping the bilateral relationship during the 1970s.

The Revival of Bilateral Cooperation

The personable, plain-speaking Callaghan was a very different character to his predecessor Wilson. With the background of an energetic trade unionist and naval officer during the 1930s and 1940s, he had won his first seat in parliament for Cardiff East in 1945, quickly acquiring a reputation as a brilliant orator and shrewd negotiator. By 1976, he had also become uniquely qualified for office in terms of ministerial experience, having held all three major positions of government as Chancellor of the Exchequer (1964–7), Home Secretary (1967–70), and Secretary of State for Foreign and Commonwealth Affairs (1974–6). Such practice now boded well for his new role as

---

[4] Even though that is now also increasingly open to dispute. For more positive verdicts, see Black et al., *Reassessing 1970s Britain*; Seldon and Hickson, *New Labour, Old Labour*; K. Morgan, *Callaghan: A Life* (Oxford: Oxford University Press, 1997); Hennessy, *Prime Minister*, 376–96.

international statesman. His time at the Foreign Office in particular had fostered strong convictions about the paramount importance of informal, personal diplomacy on the highest political level, convictions that were shared by his German counterpart Schmidt.[5] Already during his time as Foreign Secretary, he had worked hard to strike up an effective relationship with the German Chancellor, a relationship he now appeared keen to intensify as prime minister.

Apart from their obvious similarities in personal temperament and character, the Schmidt–Callaghan relationship also benefited from their remarkably similar centre-left outlook on domestic politics, in that they both prioritised combating inflation but were at the same time reluctant to upset employers and their parties' working-class base. In Britain, the final months of Wilson's premiership had already seen a slow move towards such an economic course, and Chancellor Denis Healey's April 1975 budget is now commonly seen as a major turning point in Labour's economic doctrine in that it cut public spending at a time of severely high unemployment.[6] In his first speech to the Labour Party conference as party leader in September 1976, Callaghan too famously declared that the option to 'spend your way out of a recession, and increase employment by cutting taxes and boosting Government spending ... no longer exists'.[7] Combined with a relatively strict incomes policy and some modest cuts in public spending, the Callaghan government was thus firmly set on a deflationary course at home.[8] In this strategy, it relied largely on voluntary support from the trade unions, which had been ingrained in the 'social contract' between the government and the Trade Union Congress (TUC) under Wilson. It formed the cornerstone of Callaghan's domestic policies throughout his time in office, and was not entirely dissimilar to the German concept of *Mitbestimmung* (codetermination); a concept that

---

[5] I argue this more extensively in M. Haeussler, 'A "Converted European"? James Callaghan and the "Europeanization" of British Foreign Policy in the 1970s', in G. Clemens and A. Reinfeldt (eds.), *Europeanization of Foreign Policies: International Socialization in Intergovernmental Policy Fields* (Stuttgart: Steiner Verlag, 2017), 153–66.

[6] Tomlinson, 'Economic Policy', 58–9.

[7] Labour Party, *Report of the Seventy-Fifth Annual Conference of the Labour Party* (London, 1976), 188–9. Also S. Fielding (ed.), *The Labour Party: 'Socialism' and Society since 1951* (Manchester: Manchester University Press, 1997), 101. Callaghan's speech has to be read in the context of Britain's International Monetary Fund (IMPF) application, which is discussed below.

[8] More generally on Labour's economic policies in the 1970s, see Tomlinson, 'Economic Policy', 55–69; Alt, 'Politics of Economic decline in the 1970s', 25–40.

The Revival of Bilateral Cooperation 103

gave workers a say in the management of their company and which had been a cornerstone of the SDP's economic doctrine for many years.

Indeed, Schmidt's support for Labour's domestic policies under Callaghan was as much driven by domestic electoral considerations as it was by his personal convictions. On 4 May 1976, his government passed the controversial *Mitbestimmungsgesetz* (Codetermination Act) in the German Bundestag, a law which required companies of over 2,000 employees to have workers' representatives taking up half of the supervisory board and which quickly became a major part of Schmidt's domestic legacy.[9] Economic policies and industrial relations were thus likely to feature heavily in the upcoming German national elections in October 1976, and this clearly shaped Schmidt's perceptions of the Callaghan government's economic agenda in turn. In an interview with the *Financial Times*, for example, Schmidt claimed that 'the reason for our relatively good economic performance [in Germany] has more to do with the functioning coordination between Government policy, companies and trade unions than with the idea that our managers are so much more clever or that our people are so much better workers than, for example, in Great Britain. ... However, they do not live together in a society which devotes much time, money and energy to the class-struggle'.[10] Indeed, it was thanks to Schmidt's personal initiative that members of the Bullock Committee, a committee set up in December 1975 to examine opportunities for 'industrial democracy' in Britain, were invited to take part in the British–German governmental consultations of July 1976.[11] During the press conference that followed, Schmidt was keen to stress the novelty of the approach. He would like to 'draw attention to the fifth hour of talks held in the presence of Trade Union leaders, industrial experts and industrial managers of both countries', Schmidt exclaimed; 'Probably it's a world premiere – talks between two European countries taking place in the company of management and trade unionists'.[12] Clearly, Schmidt was keen to enlist

---

[9] E. Conze, *Die Suche nach Sicherheit: Eine Geschichte der Bundesrepublik Deutschland von 1949 bis in die Gegenwart* (Munich: Siedler, 2009), 464; W. Abelshauser, *Deutsche Wirtschaftsgeschichte seit 1945* (Munich: Beck, 2004), 380–2.

[10] *Financial Times*, 13 October 1975.

[11] For evidence that this was indeed Schmidt's personal initiative, see TNA/PREM16/894, Callaghan to Schmidt, 7 July 1976. For a list of participants, B136/17106, Ab- und Zusageliste zu Abendessen, 30 June 1976.

[12] TNA/PREM16/894, Press Conference, 30 June 1976.

international support and blessing for his economic policies, not least for domestic consumption in the run-up to his own election campaign.

In this quest, Callaghan proved an eager partner, and the first encounters between the two leaders already reveal conscious efforts to support each other in their respective domestic struggles. Only a few weeks into his premiership in April 1976, for example, Callaghan rang up Helmut Schmidt to raise 'three or four points'. In the frank and open conversation that ensued, Schmidt strongly encouraged Callaghan to stay firm on his domestic course. 'I have the feeling, Jim', he said, 'that if you can renew the wage deal which you first concluded in July last year, if you can renew that for another twelve months so that the whole thing runs for 24 months, I think this is bound to get you out of the trouble'. He also did not shy away from offering his personal views on the pay deal the British government was about to conclude with the TUC, claiming that the proposed rise in wages was still too high. When Callaghan interjected that Schmidt's proposed figure of 5 per cent would have meant a cut to the standards of living 'for the second year running', Schmidt pointed out in return that this was already happening in Germany: 'All the major contracts for 1976 have now been concluded. They are at 5.2, 5.3 and 5.4, which means that after deduction of taxes and social insurance deductions the working class will to a great extent have a real loss of real income'. He even agreed that Callaghan might use these German figures in the British debate in order to prop up his own position.[13] It was only the first of many instances where Schmidt and Callaghan would stage and coordinate public displays of confidence in each other's respective policies. Indeed, in response to Schmidt's figures, Callaghan thanked Schmidt for his recent public praise of Britain's economic policies, not failing to add that 'our trade union leaders Jack Jones and co. have been wonderfully good and if you, Helmut, in any speech later on when we have concluded the agreement could pay some tribute to the much-derided British trade union leaders, that could have a psychological effect, you know'.[14] Such close and confidential cooperation over most sensitive domestic policies would have been unthinkable under Harold Wilson only a few weeks earlier.

[13] TNA/PREM16/881, Telephone Conversation Schmidt-PM, 28 April 1976.
[14] Ibid.

The IMF loan

3.1 James Callaghan enjoyed excellent personal relationships with his European partner Helmut Schmidt, 1977. Source: Photo by Roger Jackson & Peter Cade/Central Press/Hulton Archive/Getty Images.

The IMF Loan

Yet, the chronic instability of the Pound soon dampened the domestic mood in Britain. Although economic indicators had improved somewhat since the EC referendum in June 1975, with inflation dropping from its 1975 peak of 24.2 per cent to 16.5 per cent in 1976 and GDP simultaneously rising from −0.6 per cent to 2.6 per cent, international market confidence in Britain remained low.[15] Repeated speculative attacks on the Pound in financial markets triggered uncertainty and instability, not least because of the high amount of Sterling balances held outside the United Kingdom. From 4 March 1976 onward, the exchange rate of the Pound thus started to drop sharply, making it increasingly difficult for the British government to maintain its domestic spending commitments.[16] When Callaghan first raised these issues

---

[15] P. Sloman, 'Appendix 2: Statistical Tables', in B. Jackson and R. Saunders (eds.), *Making Thatcher's Britain* (Cambridge: Cambridge University Press, 2012), 271.

[16] For more detail on the origins and course of the IMF crisis, see K. Burk and A. Cairncross, *Goodbye, Great Britain: The 1976 IMF Crisis* (New Haven, CT and London: Yale University Press, 1992); K. Hickson, *The IMF Crisis of 1976*

in his telephone conversation with Schmidt in April 1976, the German Chancellor immediately volunteered to help. 'My Government so far had given monetary assistance to other countries within the EEC which meant some sacrifices for our own country but that we will also in the future do that under the provision that this is helping the European process', he declared; 'And this is really what I mean. I will get into deep trouble with my Central Bank over it when we come to such a decision but both Genscher and I are deeply determined to do so if the need does occur and we really meant what we said'.[17] Yet, the Pound continued to drop sharply: by the end of September, it had fallen from \$2 to \$1.63 in less than six months. Having run out of options to foot the bill, an application to the IMF for a major loan seemed like the only remaining possibility to the Callaghan government. On 29 September, Chancellor of the Exchequer Denis Healey therefore announced the government's intention to apply for a \$2.5 billion standby-credit. Any IMF loan, however, was likely to be conditional on serious cuts in British public expenditure and the budget, to which large parts of the Labour government including heavyweights like Tony Benn, Anthony Crosland, or Michael Foot were deeply opposed. There was thus a very real danger that the IMF application would split up the Labour government, as well as damage industrial relations in Britain beyond repair.

On the highest level, Callaghan himself was firmly convinced that the IMF loan was the only sensible option for Britain to take, but he also worried deeply about a potential split of his government over the issue. He therefore hoped to cash in on Schmidt's earlier promises of substantial German help, trying to use the German Chancellor as an intermediary to soften the IMF's position. Immediately after Schmidt's victory in the German elections on 3 October, Callaghan therefore called the German Chancellor the next day.[18] The conversation that ensued is worth quoting at some length not only because it reveals the sophisticated ways in which Callaghan courted the German Chancellor, but also

---

    and British Politics (London: Tauris Academic Studies, 2005); K. Burk, 'The Americans, the Germans, and the British: The 1976 IMF Crisis', *Twentieth Century British History* 5/3 (1994), 351–69.

[17] TNA/PREM16/881, Prime Minister's Talk with Chancellor Schmidt, 28 April 1976.

[18] Although the CDU/CSU had received the largest share of the vote, the SPD-FDP coalition was nonetheless able to stay in power with a majority of ten seats. It was a somewhat disappointing result for Schmidt nonetheless, with the SPD having lost 3.2 per cent compared to 1972.

The IMF loan 107

because it conveys a sense of a language and tone that was very different to the Wilson years:

CALLAGHAN: I rang up to say how delighted I was with your success. I would have felt very lonely if you hadn't been there and I am delighted you're going to be there. It's a great source of strength to me and encouragement that you should be there.

SCHMIDT: You are very kind, Jim, and I love that you have called – I am really glad. [...]

CALLAGHAN: I'd like to just have a gossip with you because – well, we survived our Party Conference – but it was surviving it – and fortunately we've got the unions one hundred per cent with us. And this is the main thing. But what I've failed to do, I've failed to get the Party with me. And this is of course always awkward. I've got a lot of the Party with me, but, you know, there is a bit of a sour feeling about the policies we're following. Inevitably, I can understand that. And so I'd like to have a political gossip with you. I don't want to be over dramatic. But I'd like to talk over with you how we're going to preserve our value as an ally and a partner, especially in Europe. Because these are the issues that are raised by some of our present difficulties. I think our policy is the only one that can carry us through.

SCHMIDT: I have no doubt about that.

Having established a personal rapport by consciously evoking a sense of comradery and trust by using colloquial words like 'gossip' or 'awkward', Callaghan then went on to say what the actual purpose of his call was – to get Schmidt to exercise influence in order to loosen the IMF's likely harsh conditions:

CALLAGHAN: I don't want to be forced off [my economic course] by short-term difficulties, like the fall in sterling, and so on. Because when you get these financial difficulties, which, as you know, are totally unrelated to your economic assessment of your position, these short-term speculations – then they send all these frenetic people into a paroxysm who say: "Now we must have a different policy." And what would be dredged up really would be serious for us, and it's something I would have to combat very hard and this is what I'd like to talk to you about. I think the immediate help

> we can have Helmut, if I may say so, is if the IMF can give us this loan on the basis of our existing policies which we intend to stick to, and that would be the short-term affair. But then we should need to talk about other things after that.

SCHMIDT: Yes. Could that be decided in Manila [at the annual meeting of the IMF's board of governors]?

CALLAGHAN: They have to send a team over there. But what is important in Manila is that your people should indicate, if you are free to do so and feel able to do so, that Germany feels that the existing policies are of sufficient character to enable the loan to be granted. And then the examination takes place. And it's when discouraging noises come out from big countries in Manila that the markets start to tremble again. So anything your people can say in Manila is bound to be of help.

SCHMIDT: A matter of hours, Jim, or of days?

CALLAGHAN: Oh, of days, really. We don't need the money quickly – what we need is to know that it is going to be available on the basis of our existing policies. That's really it. Because if I were forced into different policies now the whole thing would start to – well, it would look very different from what it does.

SCHMIDT: I talked about this subject with [Bundesbank President] Karl Klasen yesterday and he very much applauds your policies and also the trade unions and says they were marvellous – he had never expected it and one should do anything one could to help so I think the general attitude on our side is going to be helpful. For my own attitude, we will always be co-operative as much as we can. ... I will try to get a word out tomorrow which expresses my expectation in this stable course.[19]

Not only is this excerpt testimony to the marked change that had taken place in the personal relationship on the highest level since Wilson's departure, but it also shows how Schmidt and Callaghan consciously sought to shape and steer international as well as public opinion through personal collaboration. Encouraged by Schmidt's supportive stance, Callaghan even invited Schmidt to an informal visit to Chequers for a public demonstration of German confidence in his domestic

---

[19] TNA/PREM16/895, Telephone Conversation between the PM and Chancellor Schmidt, 4 October 1976.

The IMF loan 109

course a few days later. Schmidt readily agreed, in spite of having to intermit his post-election holiday, and suggested as a cover story that Callaghan had invited him for a private meal in order to celebrate his election victory. 'Isn't that good that you are coming over just for a little dinner party to celebrate', Callaghan replied.[20]

Schmidt's hastily arranged visit a few days later indeed constituted an important public relations success. 'Schmidt boost for Callaghan', the *Daily Telegraph*'s front-page headline read, and the *Observer* even claimed to know that Schmidt was 'determined to help Britain through the current crisis and prevent any further slide of sterling'.[21] In the House of Commons on 12 October, Callaghan used Schmidt's apparent blessing to prop up his own position, dwelling at length on their wide-ranging conversations that 'went on for three and a half hours'.[22] Over the coming months, Schmidt would continue to strongly support the Labour government in public. On both German and American television, he repeatedly praised Callaghan's 'marvellous job in bringing about that wage deal',[23] arguing that Labour was pursuing its policies with such devotion and willpower that it was hard to see why the world markets were still intent on speculating on the Pound purely for 'psychological reasons'.[24] Indeed, Schmidt's positive view of Labour's economic policy was in line with internal German assessments of the situation: a brief of the *Bundeskanzleramt*, for example, argued that the slump of the pound was triggered by 'factors outside the economic realm ... that can no longer be explained purely by differences in competitiveness and costs'.[25] According to some accounts, Schmidt even made promises to Callaghan that he might use German reserves as a guarantee sterling balances, although he quickly backtracked on the offer afterwards.[26]

[20] TNA/PREM16/895, Record of Telephone Conversation between PM and German Chancellor at 1945, 6 October 1976.
[21] *Daily Telegraph*, 11 October 1976; *Observer*, 10 October 1976.
[22] Hansard, *House of Commons Debate* 12 October 1976, vol. 917 cc. 234–7.
[23] BPA, Interview des Bundeskanzlers mit dem amerikanischen Fernsehen ABC, 18 July 1976.
[24] BPA, DFS 20 Uhr, 29 October 1976. See also BPA, Interview für Deutschlandfunk, 14 November 1976.
[25] B136/16869, Großbritannien, hier: Wirtschafts- und Zahlungsbilanzlage, 8 October 1976. This also reflects most subsequent verdicts by historians. See Burk and Cairncross, *Goodbye Great Britain*, xv, 225; Tomlinson, 'Economic Policy', 61.
[26] Unfortunately, no governmental record of the discussions could be found, probably due to the fact that this was designated as a strictly 'private' dinner. For

Indeed, professing support in public was one thing, but actually exercising influence on the negotiations was quite another. Enthused by his electoral victory and charmed by Callaghan's sweet-talk, Schmidt seems to have promised rather more than he was eventually able to deliver. Perhaps most important was the German central bank's constitutional independence from government policy, meaning that Schmidt was simply not empowered to commit Bundesbank reserves to any potential credit to Britain.[27] There were also strong internal divisions within the German government, with the Ministry of Finance appearing particularly keen to impose tough conditions on Britain and thus speaking out openly against Schmidt's much softer line.[28] Finally, Schmidt's own political authority was significantly compromised by the still ongoing coalition talks with the FDP, which revealed serious differences in the government coalition over how to deal with the FRG's federal budget and growing deficit.[29] Against this precarious background, FDP leader and Foreign Minister Hans-Dietrich Genscher was clearly taken aback by Schmidt's unilateral dealings with Callaghan, complaining in a strongly worded letter to Schmidt that he had not have been adequately informed about the talks and questioning the extent of German help allegedly promised by Schmidt.[30]

As a result, Schmidt's actual influence on the IMF negotiations was rather limited, although he did try to use his contacts with the Ford administration to mediate the hard-line American position dominated by the neoliberalists in the Treasury and Federal Reserve Chairman Arthur Burns.[31] On 23 November, for example, Schmidt strongly urged Ford for greater restraint, exclaiming that the United States 'should not go so far as to overthrow this [Callaghan's] government. There is no one else to take the reins and there may be a period of

---

subsequent recollections, see the discussion in Burk, 'IMF Crisis', 363, and Callaghan, *Time and Chance,* 431–2.

[27] Burk and Cairncross, *Goodbye Great Britain*, 66.

[28] For tensions between Schmidt and the Finance Ministry during the IMF negotiations, see ibid., 90–2.

[29] TNA/PREM16/1276, Bonn to FCO, 8 October 1976.

[30] PHSA, Großbritannien 1972–6 Band 1, Genscher to Schmidt, 18 October 1976; Genscher to Schmidt (second letter), 18 October 1976; Schmidt to Genscher, 18 October 1976.

[31] See, for example, PHSA, Großbritannien 1972–6: Band 1, Besprechung des Herrn BK mit Under-Secretary Yeo, 3 November 1976; Schmidt to Callaghan, 3 November 1976; Schmidt to Callaghan, 16 November 1976. Also, Burk and Cairncross, *Goodbye*, 37–8, 42.

The IMF loan 111

disorder which could affect us all deeply. . . . If Callaghan had to resign, that would set us back'.[32] Yet, Schmidt's repeated demarches produced few tangible results, not least because Ford had just lost the 1976 Presidential election and was thus unlikely to invest much political capital in the matter.[33] This in turn forced Schmidt to put his foot down as well, eventually telling Callaghan on the margins of the European Council on 30 November that he could offer no more help and that Britain had no option but to take the IMF route.[34]

Yet, rather more important than the actual results of Schmidt's lobbying were the effects his efforts had on the British domestic debate, given the British Cabinet's sharp internal divisions over the issue. Whereas some members like Chancellor of the Exchequer Denis Haley by and large accepted the IMF's case for wage restraint and further cuts in public expenditure, others like Tony Benn or Anthony Crosland – though approaching the issue from different angles – instead advocated alternative economic strategies, such as the introduction of import controls.[35] Callaghan himself seems to have been convinced that the IMF loan was the only sensible option available, but at the same time remained reluctant to disclose this position openly in Cabinet. Both Callaghan and Healey thus cleverly utilised Schmidt's ultimate refusal to help in order to push their Cabinet colleagues towards acceptance of the IMF's conditions. On 23 November 1976, for example, Healey claimed there was 'no hope of obtaining bilateral aid from other countries ... if negotiations with the IMF failed', whereas the cuts demanded by the IMF 'would be painful but [they] would be made with the full endorsement of the IMF and our major allies'.[36] On 1 December, Callaghan similarly claimed that the 'formal position of the United States and West German Governments was that the negotiations over the loan were for the International Monetary Fund (IMF) to handle ... it seemed that they were not prepared to bring pressure to bear on the Fund on the United Kingdom's account'.[37] Tony Benn, a key opponent of the IMF application, even

---

[32] GRFL/NSA, Memoranda of Conversations, 1973–7, Box 21, Memorandum of Conversation (Phone Call) between Schmidt and Ford, 23 November 1976.

[33] Burk and Cairncross, *Goodbye*, 112; Hickson, *IMF Crisis of 1976*, 199.

[34] Burk and Cairncross, *Goodbye*, 92.

[35] For some of flair of these heated discussions, see the records of various Cabinet meetings in TNA/CAB128/60, July–December 1976.

[36] TNA/CAB128/60, 33th Conclusions CM (76) 33, 23 November 1976.

[37] TNA/CAB128/60, 35th Conclusions CM (76) 35, 1 December 1976.

recalls how Callaghan at one point exclaimed that 'Ford and Schmidt had let him down . . . and it was the first time in his life that he felt anti-American'.[38] It was a risky gamble, but it paid off eventually: on 2 December, Cabinet agreed on the principle of accepting an agreement with the IMF, even though the precise conditions and spending cuts took another two weeks to negotiate.[39]

In the end, Callaghan thus managed to keep both Cabinet and party remarkably united over the issue, and the terms agreed with the IMF eventually turned out to be significantly less onerous than originally expected.[40] In achieving both aims, Callaghan's publicised as well as private dealings with Schmidt had played a crucial role. Afterwards, the two leaders therefore lost no time in staging their cooperation for public consumption in a joint television interview on the *ITN News at Ten* in January 1977. 'I think what has happened, thanks to the great efforts of the Chancellor', Callaghan declared, 'not only made our-selves stronger but we have also added to the stability of Europe'. Schmidt readily agreed, playing up his own contribution both at home and on the international stage: 'I had to try to find ways and means, not only with my own Cabinet and my own domestic set up, but also with the greatest of our allies, with the United States'.[41] The actual extent of high-level bilateral cooperation may have been limited, but the image projected to the respective audiences at home was clear nonetheless: Schmidt and Callaghan were united by common purpose and destiny in their domestic economic policies.

High-Level Diplomacy to Overcome Lower-Level Resistances: Offset, JET, and Domestic Terrorism

Although 1970s British–German relations had become deeply entangled in wider multilateral frameworks, there remained a couple of bilateral issues which had been largely ignored during the Heath and Wilson years. The most prominent one was the longstanding question of German Offset payments to Britain, which had first been introduced in 1954 to pay for the stationing costs of the British Army of the

---

[38] Quoted in Burk and Cairncross, *Goodbye*, 107.
[39] TNA/CAB128/60, 36th Conclusions CM (76) 36 (Limited Circulation Annex), 2 December 1976.
[40] Burk, 'IMF Crisis', 366–7.
[41] 1/HSAA006687, ITN News at Ten: Transcript, 24 January 1977.

High-Level Diplomacy 113

Rhine (BAOR) and were subject to regular reviews and adjustments.[42] After the expiration of the last Offset agreement, the British started to lobby strongly for an early renewal, hoping that a new agreement might ease its precarious fiscal situation and Labour's internal divisions over economic policy.[43] The Germans, by contrast, adopted a restrictive stance, stressing Offset's unpopularity in German domestic opinion and arguing that a fixed-sum bilateral offset agreement made little economic sense at an age of highly volatile exchange rates.[44] In February 1976, for example, Schmidt sharply brushed off the British Ambassador over the issue, exclaiming that it would be 'very difficult indeed for him to commit himself publicly to any arrangement' and that he 'did not fancy paying offset till the year 2000'.[45] The Offset issue had thus reached deadlock: the Germans insisted that they could not continue Offset in its current form; the British insisted that it was politically impossible to drop the subject altogether. This remained the state of affairs throughout 1976.[46]

Just like during the IMF negotiations, Callaghan decided to elevate the Offset question to the highest political level, deciding to personally tackle the issue at the January 1977 British–German consultations with Schmidt while circumventing most ministers and officials. Already prior to the bilateral talks, Callaghan had hinted to the British delegation that he would 'have a preliminary private word with Chancellor Schmidt on offset', asking them to stay clear of the subject 'in front of other German Ministers at dinner'.[47] In Germany too, it was evident that Schmidt himself would be in charge, with Finance Minister Apel revealingly telling his British counterpart Healey that, while he was personally opposed to a new agreement, he could 'of course be overruled by Chancellor Schmidt'.[48] In their four-eye talks, Schmidt and Callaghan indeed dashed out the cornerstones of what would

---

[42] For further background on German rearmament and BAOR in the 1940s and 1950s, see Dockrill, *West German Rearmament and Mawby, Containing Germany.*

[43] 1/HSAA006671, London Embassy to Auswärtiges Amt, 4 February 1976.

[44] TNA/PREM16/892, Notes of Meeting between PM and FRG Chancellor, 7 February 1976; *AAPD 1976*, Doc. Nr. 39, 7 February 1976.

[45] TNA/PREM16/892, Bonn to FCO, 3 February 1976.

[46] TNA/PREM16/1276, FRG Internal Scene, 21 January 1977.

[47] TNA/PREM16/1276, Visit of Chancellor Schmidt: Offset, 20 January 1977.

[48] TNA/PREM16/1277, Record of meeting between Chancellor of Exchequer Healey and Herr Apel, Minister of Finance, 24 January 1977.

eventually become the new Offset agreement a few months later. Schmidt professed his readiness to accept a final renewal of the agreement in spite of his earlier insistences to the contrary; in turn, Callaghan accepted an agreement for two years of 125 million Deutschmark per annum, significantly less than the initial British demand of 500 million. In light of the deal's likely unpopularity in Germany, with Schmidt insisting that the agreement would be seen 'as a victory for Great Britain' by his public, the two leaders agreed to keep their deal secret in light of on-going budgetary discussions in Germany; and the eventual agreement was concluded and signed only in October 1977.[49] Yet again, Schmidt's and Callaghan's high-level diplomacy had resolved a potentially highly contagious problem with minimal diplomatic friction.

This pattern was mirrored in the other major bilateral problem at the time, the location of the proposed Joint European Torus (JET). Although the EC had decided to develop and build this device for European research on nuclear fusion in 1970, it had initially left open its eventual location. Given that JET was likely to attract significant interest and resources, its eventual location thus became a highly contested issue amongst the member-states. By the mid-1970s, the two main contenders were the British town of Culham in Oxfordshire, and the German alternative Garching in Bavaria. Both governments had high domestic stakes in the question, with both Secretary of Energy Tony Benn and the British Cabinet strongly pushing Culham for 'scientific, technological, and political grounds'.[50] Unfortunately, however, Garching soon emerged as the clear favourite of the EC Research Council.[51] Yet again, Callaghan decided to raise the issue at an intimate dinner as part of the June 1976 British–German consultations in Bonn. To his great surprise, the SPD Minister for Research and Technology Hans Matthöfer spontaneously claimed in response to Callaghan's intervention that he was personally convinced that 'Culham was by far the best site', even though he would have to clear his position with Schmidt before saying so publicly. When Callaghan 'encouraged him to

---

[49] *AAPD 1977*, Doc. Nr. 10, Gespräch des BK Schmidt mit PM Callaghan in Chequers, 24 January 1977.

[50] TNA/PREM16/847, Benn to Treasury, 10 December 1975; TNA/PREM16/847, Callaghan to Benn, 11 February 1976. See also the chronology of events in TNA/PREM16/847, FCO to No. 10, 30 April 1976.

[51] TNA/PREM16/847, FCO to No. 10, 30 April 1976.

High-Level Diplomacy 115

do so there and then', Schmidt replied after some fairly confused internal discussion amongst the Germans 'that he accepted Herr Matthoefer's view, although he could not say so until after the election, since a decision in favour of Culham would cause political trouble in Bavaria, and he did not want to give the [CDU's Bavarian sister party] CSU a peg for their campaign'. Given the powerful influence of the Bavarian FDP Minister Josef Ertl in the coalition government, Schmidt also urged the British not to mention the issue to FDP leader Genscher, since he 'would fight it all the way'.[52] In this somewhat conspiratory mood, Callaghan and Schmidt then agreed to insist on certain mechanisms and criteria in the EC Research Council that would almost inevitably force a decision for Culham. To the British, it therefore seemed 'quite clear' afterwards that Schmidt had 'committed himself to Culham' at the dinner.[53]

This time, however, political and bureaucratic resistances in the aftermath of the meeting proved more profound, and were only overcome after a sustained period of bilateral and multilateral hackling.[54] Part of the reason was that the October 1976 election result had strengthened rather than resolved the intra-coalition rifts within the Schmidt government, which severely constrained Schmidt's and Matthöfer's freedom of manoeuvre as the powerful FDP ministers Ertl and Genscher continued to insist strongly on Garching.[55] This meant, as Matthöfer bluntly put it to his British counterpart Benn in January 1977, that he could not now publicly state his personal preference for Culham and 'survive politically'.[56] Tensions came to a head at the European Research Council on 29 March 1977, when Matthöfer unexpectedly dropped his support for Culham, and the British delegation in response blocked any vote on the issue.[57] It was only through yet another personal intervention by Callaghan that

[52] TNA/PREM16/847, No. 10 to FCO, 1 July 1976. At dinner, Schmidt was not briefed well on the issue and evidently confused: see the handwritten notes on the German menu cards ('Unsere sagen Garching ist das Beste', etc.), preserved in B136/17106, Programme for the Visit of His Excellency the Prime Minister of the United Kingdom of Great Britain and Northern Ireland, The Right Hon. James Callaghan, MP to the Federal Republic of Germany, 30 June 1976.
[53] TNA/PREM16/847, No. 10 to FCO, 1 July 1976.
[54] TNA/PREM16/1278, Note: JET: Research Council, 29 March 1977.
[55] 1/HSAA008741, Standort JET, hier: Ministergespräch, 13 October 1977.
[56] TNA/PREM16/1278, Note: JET: Research Council, 29 March 1977.
[57] Ibid.

things could be swayed once again. At the British–German consultations in October 1977, he offered an impassionate plea for Culham, playing heavily on his domestic constraints and wider notions of European solidarity. He had 'a hard battle to fight domestically on the EEC', he told Schmidt, and if Germany exercised its veto over Culham there would 'be strong feeling … in the UK'. Yet, he clearly 'could not force the FRG's hand; if they said, "it must be Garching", so be it'.[58] Schmidt, who had thus far refrained from taking a firm position himself, eventually gave in. 'He was not a Bavarian; if he was, he would have to fight for Garching to the last breath', Schmidt declared, before accepting to withdraw the FRG's reservation on Culham – under the condition that the planned follow-up project would not go to the United Kingdom also, and that the decision would not be taken by the Council of Foreign Ministers but by the Research Council to protect Genscher from domestic criticism.[59] Yet again, a top-level compromise between Schmidt and Callaghan, dashed off as part of the regular biannual British–German consultations, managed to break the deadlock on lower levels.

The by far most important example of close British–German collaboration under Callaghan, however, occurred in the context of the wave of extremist left-wing terrorism shaking the young Federal Republic to its very foundations during the late 1970s. In the autumn of 1977, Germany's so-called 'Red Autumn', events culminated in the kidnapping of the German industrial leader Hanns Martin Schleyer on 5 September, and the related hijacking of a Lufthansa aircraft by a terrorist subgroup of the PLO on 13 October.[60] Facing the comparable challenge of IRA terrorism at home, Callaghan's government strongly supported Schmidt in both moral and practical terms, not least because the October 1977 British–German consultations

---

[58] TNA/PREM16/1278, Record of Meeting with the Federal German Chancellor, 18 October 1977.

[59] Ibid. One important consideration for the Germans may well have been that the planned follow-up project, which was likely to be significantly bigger in scope, would now probably go to them. See B136/17107, JET und Nachfolgeprojekte, 13 October 1977.

[60] On Germany's fight against domestic terrorism in the 1970s, see K. Hanshew, *Terror and Democracy in West Germany* (Cambridge: Cambridge University Press, 2012); S. Aust, *Der Baader Meinhof Komplex* (Hamburg: Hoffmann und Campe, 1986); B. Peters, *Tödlicher Irrtum: Die Geschichte der RAF* (Berlin: Argon, 2004).

coincided with the five-day hijacking of the Lufthansa aircraft. The Germans therefore decided to turn them into a major public demonstration of international solidarity, receiving the British delegation with full military honours and national anthems.[61] Callaghan even took part in meetings of the FRG's cross-party emergency task force headed by Schmidt; partly, as Schmidt confided to Callaghan afterwards, to convince 'his own colleagues that they should stand firm against the hijackers. He himself had always believed in standing firm but some had had their doubts'.[62] The Callaghan government also provided concrete military assistance to the Germans, with two members of the British Special Air Service (SAS) assisting the Germans in their rescue preparations.[63] Indeed, the successful storming of the aircraft at Mogadishu on 18 October took place during the bilateral consultations, enabling the British delegation to witness the tense and emotional scenes in Bonn at first hand.

As a result, the October 1977 consultations triggered strong and lasting feelings of mutual solidarity and partnership. At the plenary session following the successful rescue operation, the visibly moved Schmidt told the assembled British delegates how he was 'particularly grateful for the services of the two British officers; and the British "flash bangs" which had been very successful. Nobody had been injured by them, despite the explosives on board the hijacked aircraft'.[64] Callaghan responded with suitable hyperbole, claiming that Schmidt 'had fought a battle for the whole world and had won

---

[61] TNA/PREM16/1278, Bonn to FCO, 19 October 1977.

[62] TNA/PREM16/1278, Record of Meeting with the Federal German Chancellor, 18 October 1977.

[63] Unfortunately, the file describing the precise nature of British help is still not open for public access, even though it exists: TNA/PREM16/1675, Hijacking: Lufthansa Hijacking: British Government assistance to FRG; Review of procedures for military intervention in terrorist incidents overseas, October 1977. See also T. Geiger, 'Die "Landshut" in Mogadischu: Das außenpolitische Krisenmanagement der Bundesregierung angesichts der terroristischen Herausforderung 1977', *Vierteljahreshefte für Zeitgeschichte* 57/3 (2009), 433–4. More generally on European attempts at cooperation over combating terrorism, E. Oberloskamp, 'Die Europäisierung der Terrorismusbekämpfung in den 1970er Jahren: Bundesdeutsche Akteure und Positionen', in J. Hürter (ed.), *Terrorismusbekämpfung in Westeuropa: Demokratie und Sicherheit in den 1970er und 1980er Jahren* (Berlin: De Gruyter Oldenbourg, 2015), 219–38.

[64] TNA/PREM16/1278, Record of Meeting in the Federal Chancellor's Office, 18 October 1977.

118 *James Callaghan, 1976–1979*

it'.[65] As the British Ambassador to Bonn Oliver Wright reported to the FCO afterwards, the bilateral consultations had been 'a moving experience ... for all who were privileged to share in it'.[66] Even when I interviewed the late Helmut Schmidt more than thirty years after these events, the lasting impression the episode had made on him shone through clearly. Talking about Callaghan's attitudes towards transatlantic relations, he suddenly stopped and said that he now wanted to mention something completely different. 'Without Callaghan we may well have stormed the aircraft at Mogadishu', he continued, 'but with umpteen casualties. But he provided us with an instrument that we did not have ourselves, and that the French did not have either, the so-called flashbangs ... The fact that we got away without any casualties is due to these flashbangs and to Jim Callaghan'. He paused for a short while. 'You have to write this, even if is not part of your topic. In my view this was a great achievement of Callaghan'.[67] Combined with the simultaneously concluded agreements over Offset and JET, the October 1977 consultations thus formed the tragic high point of British-German relations under Callaghan.

Still Awkward: Intra-EC Tensions over Direct Elections, Fisheries, and the Green Pound

Everything might have been well in the British–German relationship, had it not been for the recurring bilateral tensions inside the EC. When Callaghan entered 10 Downing Street as PM, British concerns over its standing inside the EC had already been mounting for some time. In January 1976, for example, the Second Permanent Secretary at the Cabinet Office Roy Denman, himself a lifelong advocate of British EC membership, had written a lengthy memorandum on the United Kingdom's future European policy.[68] 'Lord Salisbury once defined British foreign policy in terms of drifting gently downstream and fending off obstructions with a boat hook', he began. While this approach had not been 'without its advantages in the days of splendid isolation', British power now seemed 'no longer splendid and we are no longer

---

[65] Ibid. [66] TNA/PREM16/1278, Bonn to FCO, 19 October 1977.
[67] Interview with Helmut Schmidt, 23 September 2013.
[68] For ample evidence of Roy Denman's pro-EC commitment, see Denman, *Missed Chances*.

Still Awkward 119

isolated'. Thus, he called for a more proactive European policy, regarding the EC as the main 'power base for external action'.[69] It was a view that was widely mirrored within the Foreign Office, which continuously advocated using the European Community as a vehicle for British leadership and influence in the post-imperial world throughout the 1970s.[70]

Such advice also fitted in well with Callaghan's personal views, although he could hardly be suspected of being overly in favour of European integration at first sight. Indeed, as his biographer put it, Callaghan regarded the EC essentially as 'an inward-looking, parochial, protectionist grouping' for most of his political life, mirroring the generally sceptical attitude of his party for much of the 1950s and 1960s.[71] Yet, his time as Foreign Secretary under Wilson had not only made him realise the post-imperial limits of British power and the potential of joint European action on the international stage, but it had also instilled in him a greater appreciation of the essentially pragmatic and intergovernmental nature of intra-EC policy-making during that period.[72] Already in June 1975, he had thus written to Wilson that Britain's European policy after the referendum 'should be active and not passive; should give a lead in areas where our interests or our experience fit us to do so; and as there will be some institutional areas where we cannot agree with others, hope that an active policy will divert criticism'.[73] It was a vision he articulated forcefully in public in January 1976, when he addressed the Hamburg *Übersee-Club* with a speech entitled 'Building the Europe of Tomorrow'; a speech the Germans somewhat paternalistically regarded as 'an important step in Callaghan's development from an agnostic into a supporter and motor of the Community'.[74] It helped that Callaghan's approach to EC questions largely matched the views of his German counterpart Schmidt. In an interview with the BBC, for example, Schmidt praised

---

[69] TNA/PREM16/863, British Objectives in the European Community, 15 March 1976.

[70] Oliver and Allen, 'Foreign Policy', 187; G. Clemens, 'Der Beitritt Großbritanniens zu den Europäischen Gemeinschaften', in Knipping and Schönwald, *Aufbruch zum Europa der zweiten Generation*, 325–6.

[71] Morgan, *Callaghan*, 396.

[72] I argue this more extensively in Haeussler, 'A "converted European"?'.

[73] TNA/PREM16/863, Callaghan to Wilson, 13 June 1975.

[74] B136/17105, London to AA, 26 January 1976. German copy of speech in 1/ HSAA006671, Das Europa von Morgen bauen, 22 January 1976.

Callaghan as 'a very good example of what I call British pragmatism. ... He's a pragmatist, he goes on step by step, and doesn't take the third or fourth step before he has taken the first one. I think that's a very practical and promising approach. I myself am more or less of the same breed'.[75] With Callaghan's appointment as Prime Minister and the renegotiations out of the way, the scene thus seemed set for a British–German rapprochement inside the EC.

Yet, formidable structural obstacles continued to drive Britain and Germany apart over key EC issues. The notorious issue of direct elections to the EP is again a case in point. Though Wilson had ultimately lifted Britain's general reserve in July 1975, he had been unable to agree on a precise date for the elections. Schmidt, who still regarded the issue as a politically opportune and inexpensive opportunity to prop up his European credentials against his domestic rivals Genscher and Kohl,[76] therefore pressed Callaghan heavily on the matter. 'A failure to agree on direct elections now would destroy the EEC', Schmidt told Callaghan in June 1976, even though he personally remained 'opposed to giving the European Parliament any additional rights or powers ... [T]he important thing was somehow to ensure that it did not enhance what he [Schmidt] called the "enormous malign cancerous bureaucracy" in Brussels'.[77] Callaghan's hands, however, were tied by British domestic politics. Not only did the idea of a directly elected EP feed into widespread fears over a potential loss of British national sovereignty within parts of the Labour government, but the question was further complicated by the PM's delicate domestic power base: by March 1977, the Labour Party had lost its majority in the House of Commons and was only able to remain in power through a pact with the Liberals, the so-called 'Lib-Lab Pact'. The Liberals, however, made their support for direct elections conditional on the principle of

---

[75] TNA/PREM16/892, Transcript: Panorama Filmed Interview at Chequers between Michael Charlton and Helmut Schmidt, 9 February 1976.

[76] For Genscher's strong support of direct elections, see TNA/PREM16/893, Visit by Herr Genscher (brief), 24 May 1976. In July 1976, the German opposition leader Kohl even told Callaghan directly how he thought that 'once Direct Elections were implemented ... this development in itself would have so much motive force that the European Parliament would automatically acquire more powers'. See TNA/PREM16/891, Note of a Meeting between PM and Dr Helmut Kohl in House of Commons, 8 July 1976.

[77] TNA /PREM16/894, Note of conversation between the PM and FRG Chancellor after lunch in the Chancellary [sic!], 30 June 1976.

Still Awkward 121

proportional representation, a long-standing domestic aim of the party. All of this led to lengthy protracted negotiations and disputes, which meant that Britain was unable to meet the 1978 deadline and the eventual postponement of the first direct elections to June 1979.[78]

The negative effects of these disputes on British–German relations were intensified by the fact that they played out against Britain's seemingly uncompromising pursuit of national interests in many day-to day areas of EC policy-making, often caused by the structural disadvantages of Britain's late membership. One particularly notorious issue was the EC's Common Fisheries Policy, which had been set up just prior to British membership and sought to give all EC member-states equal access to fishing waters. Britain, naturally rich in fish resources, was highly opposed to the policy, but had felt forced to accept it anyway in the early 1970s as part of the membership negotiations. Tensions intensified once the EC decided to extend its fishing zone from 12 nautical miles to 200 nautical miles, as Britain became increasingly concerned over its own share.[79] Within the bilateral realm, the dispute mirrored familiar dynamics: Britain claimed it was only seeking a fair and just agreement; the Germans by contrast bemoaned that Britain pursued allegedly narrow national interests by needlessly playing them up as major 'questions of national importance (no surrender of national sovereignty)'.[80] The simultaneous bilateral dispute over the so-called 'green currencies', a fixed exchange rate mechanism set up in the early 1970s to keep agricultural support mechanisms free from the currency fluctuations, revealed a similar picture: Britain simply declined to realign the now grossly overvalued 'Green Pound', refusing to give up on one of the few technical mechanisms that actually turned out to benefit the country at the time.[81] As Foreign Secretary David Owen put it in the House of Commons, he did 'not see it as my job – both as a proponent and a strong advocate of Britain's full membership of the Community – to give up a national advantage which has been legitimately negotiated'.[82] A justified position, perhaps; but it also

---

[78] 1/HSAA006625, Innenpolitische Aspekte der Direktwahl zum Europäischen Parlament, 20 July 1977. See also George, *Awkward Partner*, 118–21; Young, *Britain and European Unity*, 122–3.

[79] Young, *Britain and European Unity*, 122.

[80] B136/17110, Beitrag zur EG-Fischereipolitik, 16 October 1978.

[81] See also commentary and additional materials in *AAPD 1977*, Doc. Nr. 10, Gespräch des BK Schmidt mit PM Callaghan in Chequers, 24 January 1977.

[82] Hansard, *House of Commons Debate* 10 January 1977, vol. 923 cc. 1077–8.

reinforced German impressions of British hard-headedness and egotism in EC politics. As an internal assessment by the *Auswärtiges Amt* complained in March 1978, Britain still seemed to regard the EC 'as a means to pursue its own interests, and not as a Community which works for the greater good of everybody'.[83]

In contrast to previous years, however, these intra-EC differences did not affect the bilateral relationship on the highest level. Part of the reason was the excellent personal rapport the two leaders had established, enabling them to communicate their domestic difficulties and reasoning in a frank and confidential manner. At times, Schmidt and Callaghan even side-lined or ignored contentious issues altogether. A particularly obscure moment occurred during Callaghan's short visit to Bonn in March 1978, where Schmidt suddenly turned on the television set in his office. Watching news reporting on their bilateral talks, Schmidt told Callaghan 'that the reporter was saying that they were discussing fish'. In response, Callaghan simply commented 'that that was splendid, and they had now discussed fish'.[84] And that was all that was talked about fish. Publicly, too, Schmidt and Callaghan went to great lengths to make sure that bilateral tensions inside the EC remained confined to lower diplomatic levels. In a joint interview on the BBC's major news programme *Panorama* in April 1978, for example, the interviewer Robin Day confronted the two leaders with an alleged statement by Genscher that Britain pursued a 'neo-Gaullist role' inside the EC. Schmidt brusquely replied that he had not heard any such comment, and then immediately turned his attention on the interviewers. 'But let me ask a question of you gentlemen', he said, 'do you really think it is good that you go on trying to prop up Government and public opinions of two countries against each other?' Callaghan quickly jumped in to help. 'No, it's not good but it's news, Helmut'. When Day interjected 'with respect' that such comments were 'a bit unfair', Callaghan replied 'No – without respect, without respect, not with respect on this. We can meet and discuss our problems for 36 hours together and we'll have different points of view and we will come to a conclusion on some of them or we will not. Then we will part, respecting each other, and knowing that our countries

---

[83] 1/HSAA008779, AA: Britisches Verhalten in der EG, 9 March 1978.
[84] TNA/PREM16/1615, Note for the Record, PM's meeting with Chancellor Schmidt at the Bundeskanzlei [sic] Bonn, 12 March 1978.

The Parting of Ways? 123

have perhaps got a different point of view'.[85] It was a convenient line to take, of course; and one that worked well in painting over bilateral disagreements in relatively minor technical areas. Yet, these tactics also disguised the much wider conceptual gulf separating the two leaders over European integration, as their much more consequential disagreements over European monetary integration show.

The Parting of Ways? The Creation of the European Monetary System

Today, the EMS, together with the creation of the European Council, stands as the most lasting achievement of 1970s European integration.[86] Introduced with much pomp and circumstance, it essentially set up an exchange rate mechanism for limiting fluctuations between EC currencies within an agreed band of 2.25 per cent. Though the technical originality of the scheme was limited and rather familiar to the EC 'snake' of the early 1970s, it is nonetheless seen as the emergence of a European fiscal identity and thus as a precursor to today's Euro currency. Britain's decision to abstain, for better or worse, would haunt both British–German relations and Britain's more general role in the European integration process for decades to come.[87]

Although Helmut Schmidt eventually became one of the EMS's main architects, his personal initiative for it was rather surprising at the time, given that he had previously appeared highly sceptical towards greater European fiscal integration.[88] Throughout his early years in power, he had insisted that greater economic convergence had to precede any attempt at monetary integration, claiming that the discrepancies

---

[85] TNA/PREM16/1655, BBC Transcript Panorama, 24 April 1978.

[86] For the creation of the EMS, see first and foremost Mourlon-Druol, *Europe Made of Money*, as well as the earlier Ludlow, *Making of the European Monetary System*. More generally on European monetary cooperation, H. James, *Making the European Monetary Union* (Cambridge, MA: Harvard University Press, 2012).

[87] Most famously of course with regard to Britain's 'Black Wednesday' in September 1992, which has shaped British debates over European integration ever since. See W. Keegan, D. Marsh, and R. Roberts, *Six Days in September: Black Wednesday, Brexit and the Making of Europe* (London: OMFIF Press, 2017).

[88] Mourlon-Druol, *Europe Made of Money*, 15–29.

between the EC member-states' economic performances could only be remedied through the coordinated pursuit of stability-oriented, deflationary policies. 'Some people seemed to think that monetary policy could make good mistakes over credit policy or mistakes over wages policy', he claimed during one session of the European Council in April 1976, 'but exchange rates were the result of the differing development of purchasing power in national economies'. If member-states 'would not be prepared to stop their printing presses from printing money', he continued his lecture, 'then there was no point in the Nine Prime Ministers talking now'.[89] Yet, Schmidt's concerns over the continuing monetary instability amongst EC countries, coupled with a growing obsession with the long-term decline of the US dollar under Nixon and Carter, seems to have triggered a profound change of mind during the early months of 1978.[90] His proposal for greater European monetary cooperation at the Copenhagen European Council on 7–8 April 1978 nonetheless came as a major surprise to most of his European counterparts.

The British PM Callaghan was one of the few assembled leaders who had in fact been consulted by Schmidt beforehand, as the German Chancellor clearly regarded British support at these early stages as vital. On 12 March 1978, with no translators or even note-takers present, Schmidt told Callaghan during a six-hour private dinner about 'an exotic idea' he had in mind. At that stage, his ideas were rather different to the EMS's eventual design. He wanted to 'create another European [Currency] snake, but of a different kind', he told Callaghan, where 'the F.R.G. and certain other members of the Community should each put half their reserves into a new currency pool, the currencies of which would be fixed against a European Unit of Account. This Unit of Account would be the currency which operated vis-a-vis the dollar, and would be the sole unit of intervention'. Schmidt's overarching motivation to guard EC currencies against recurrent dollar fluctuations clearly shone through. The pool would

---

[89] TNA/PREM16/853, Record of Meeting of the European Council at Luxembourg, 1 and 2 April 1976.

[90] Although nobody knows exactly why or when Schmidt's change of mind occurred. See Mourlon-Druol, *Made of Money*, 153; G. Thiemeyer, 'Helmut Schmidt und die Gründung des Europäischen Währungssystems 1973–1979', in Knipping and Schönwald, *Aufbruch zum Europa der zweiten Generation*, 245–68; H. Soell, *Helmut Schmidt: 1969 bis heute: Macht und Verantwortung* (Munich: DVA, 2008), 691–4.

The Parting of Ways?
125

not 'be tied to the dollar because the U.S. economy was too large and uncontrollable', he exclaimed at one point; 'the captain was not in charge, even though he was well meaning'. Concluding his remarks, Schmidt urged Callaghan to keep complete confidence, and in particular not to inform Chancellor of the Exchequer Denis Healey about their conversation.[91] It was a surprisingly vague and ambiguous proposal, which did not really become any clearer over subsequent weeks either. Even after Schmidt had formally launched his ideas at Copenhagen, an internal British meeting between Callaghan, Healey, and the Treasury official Ken Couzens complained about the 'high level of generality' and secrecy surrounding the German position. '[T]he Prime Minister should tell Chancellor Schmidt that he was destabilizing opinion by his vague hints', Healey complained; continuing that not even the German Minister of Finance Matthöfer apparently knew 'what was afoot'.[92]

The uncertainty surrounding Schmidt's ideas may have contributed to Callaghan's instinctive scepticism about Schmidt's proposal, but even more important were his lingering suspicions that it was somehow directed against the United States. At an intimate trilateral breakfast with Schmidt and Giscard at Copenhagen, Callaghan even told his counterparts bluntly that the EMS in his eyes reflected 'a turning away from the dollar and from U.S. financial policy', and made clear that he would express public scepticism if questioned.[93] Although the Germans worked actively to dispel such notions over the following weeks, Callaghan remained unconvinced, continuing to claim in internal British discussions that Schmidt's ideas were 'founded in the distrust of the United States'.[94] At the same time, however, Callaghan feared that an openly hostile attitude towards Schmidt's proposals might exclude Britain from key negotiations and thus from the inner circle of European decision-making. Thus, Britain agreed to take part in a trilateral Franco–German–British expert group to

[91] TNA/PREM16/1615, Note for the Record. Prime Minister's Meeting with Chancellor Schmidt at the Bundeskanzlerei [sic] Bonn, 12 March 1978.

[92] TNA/PREM16/1654, Note of a Meeting held in the Cabinet Room, 20 April 1978. Even the German Bundeskanzleramt claimed not to know anything specific about Schmidt's ideas, see *AAPD 1978*, Doc. Nr. 120, Überlegungen zur Verstärkung des EG-Währungssystems, 21 April 1978.

[93] TNA/PREM16/1615, Prime Minister's Discussion on 8 April with Chancellor Schmidt and President Giscard, 11 April 1978.

[94] TNA/PREM16/1654, Note of a Meeting held in the Cabinet Room, 20 April 1978.

develop Schmidt's ideas further, even though the largely non-committal and sceptical attitude of the appointed Treasury official Kenneth Couzens meant that he soon played second fiddle to his French and German counterparts Bernard Clappier and Horst Schulman.[95]

At the heart of the instinctively different British and German approaches stood bigger differences over the role of European integration in their respective national strategies. Schmidt's initiative may have partially been motivated by economic motivations, but much more important to him was the wider political imperative to reassure France and other European partners against Germany's growing economic dominance by embedding its fiscal policies firmly in a European mantle.[96] 'The more successful we are in the areas of foreign policy, economic policy, socio-economic matters, and military matters', Schmidt told a group of highly sceptical German bankers during his famous appearance at the Bundesbank council in November 1978, 'the longer it will be until Auschwitz sinks into history'.[97] By contrast, such wider strategic imperatives were lacking in Britain's European policy, making Callaghan approach Schmidt's proposals in light of more pragmatic short-term considerations. The result was that Britain saw little potential benefits in joining the scheme, given that participation was likely to trigger a significant and unwelcome devaluation of the Pound adding to the already severe political pressures on the Labour government. As Callaghan put it to Schmidt as early as April, joining the EMS would be 'a political act and with an election in 12 to 18 months it simply was not feasible for him as Prime Minister to go to the country saying that we had decided to enter the Snake again with a 20 per cent devaluation'.[98] It did not help that cabinet opinion was

---

[95] Mourlon-Druol, *Europe Made of Money*, 177–83.

[96] See in particular G. Thiemeyer, 'The European Currency System and the European Policies of Helmut Schmidt', in J. Laursen (ed.), *The Institutions and Dynamics of the European Community, 1973–83* (Baden-Baden: Nomos, 2014), 195–9; Waechter, *Helmut Schmidt und Valéry Giscard d'Estaing,* 109–23.

[97] Margaret Thatcher Foundation (henceforward: MTF), Transcript of meeting of the Bundesbank Council, Document ID: 111554, 30 November 1978, http://www.margaretthatcher.org/document/111554 (translations by Margaret Thatcher foundation) [accessed on 13 June 2018].

[98] TNA/PREM16/1655, PM's Meeting with Chancellor Schmidt at Chequers, 23 April 1978.

The Parting of Ways?   127

deeply divided too, with Tony Benn in particular speaking out strongly against the scheme. On 13 July, Benn even circulated a note to Cabinet in which he claimed that joining the EMS under Franco–German conditions would 'ruin our long-term economic future and destroy our remaining political independence'.[99] A delicate mix of long-term strategic differences and more short-term political calculations thus put Britain and Germany yet again at odds with each other over a key scheme towards European integration.

Over the following months, growing signs of British scepticism over the scheme eventually made Schmidt and Giscard decide to go ahead without Callaghan. On 23 June, they met up at Schmidt's private home in Hamburg to dash out a common position for the upcoming European Council in Bremen, followed by a joint Franco–German discussion paper on 28 June. The British were disturbed by such Franco–German bilateralism, particularly since neither Callaghan or Couzens had been invited to these discussions.[100] At the subsequent European Council, Callaghan appeared isolated and dejected, with EC Commission President Roy Jenkins recalling in his diary how Schmidt and Giscard simply left the British PM 'to wriggle on his hook ... saying that they wanted no papering over cracks where real differences existed'.[101] The Franco–German hard-line approach vis-à-vis the British only intensified over the following months, as both appeared uncompromising over British demands to include significant resource transfers in the scheme. It was not his intention 'to make the EMS palatable to the British with all kinds of concessions', Schmidt told Jenkins on 27 October, 'and then afterwards receive a rejection'.[102] To make matters worse, the hardening of the German stance over the summer of 1978 was accompanied by a profound turn in Callaghan's domestic fortunes. Labour's annual party conference on 2–6 October saw a grassroots rebellion against the Callaghan government, rejecting its proposed 5 per cent limit

[99] TNA/CAB129/203, CP (78) 80, 14 July 1978.
[100] TNA/PREM16/1634, Note of Meeting held at 10 Downing Street, 3 July 1978.
[101] Diary Entries for 6 and 7 July 1978, R. Jenkins, *European Diary 1977–1981* (London, 1989), 287, 289.
[102] '*AAPD 1978*, Doc. Nr. 329, Gespräch BK Schmidt mit Präsidenten der EG-Kommission Jenkins, 27 October 1978. See also recollection in Jenkins, *European Diary*, 331.

on wage increases and thereby threatening the very cornerstone of its domestic policies.[103] Combined with Labour's lack of an overall majority in the House of Commons and the need for a general election within the next year, Callaghan and his key confidantes eventually concluded that joining the EMS was too big a political risk. On 10 October, a cabinet subcommittee on European monetary co-operation secretly decided that it was 'clearly not in our interests to join'; a decision that was confirmed by Cabinet on 30 November and announced by Callaghan at the Brussels European Council a few days later.[104]

The fact that Britain's eventual non-participation in the EMS did not result in lasting frictions in the British–German relationship was primarily due to Callaghan's personal communications with Schmidt. In marked contrast to Wilson's handling of the renegotiations a few years earlier, Callaghan took great care to elaborate and explain his political calculations in several lengthy and confidential discussions with Schmidt, conveying the impression of being genuinely torn in his mind. At the British–German consultations in October 1978, for example, Callaghan illustrated his domestic situation in the gravest possible terms. '[I]f Great Britain makes it through this winter it has won; if not, it has lost', Callaghan exclaimed, since '[f]ighting inflation was the most important thing'. It was 'battle he would fight even at the cost of his political career. Great Britain was at cross roads. If this battle could be won, Britain would be one of Europe's economically strongest countries by 1985'.[105] Crucially, he also gave Schmidt an advance warning about Britain's eventual decision not to join prior to the official announcement. 'I don't think my position is any different from what it was when I talked to you privately', Callaghan told Schmidt on 26 November 1978; 'We've got a lot of political interest

---

[103] 1/HSAA008814, Britische Haltung zum geplanten Europäischen Währungssystem (EWS), 12 October 1978. For the impact of the 1978 conference in historical perspective, see R. Saunders '"Crisis? What crisis?" Thatcherism and the seventies', in Jackson and Saunders, *Making Thatcher's Britain*, 38–9.

[104] TNA/CAB130/1047, Minutes of meeting of Ministerial Group on European Monetary Co-Operation, 10 October 1978; TNA/CAB128/64/21, Conclusions CM (78) 41, 30 November 1978.

[105] B136/17111, Vermerk über das Gespräch des Bundeskanzlers mit PM Callaghan, 18 October 1978; 1/HSAA00814, Protokoll der deutsch-britischen Konsultationen (Plenarsitzung), 19 October 1978.

here in it but really what we are faced with is not so much the normal political opposition, but the technical doubts, and it is a combination of political opposition which could be overcome with technical doubts which is going to be the difficulty for me'. Nonetheless, he professed 'that I would like to see such a scheme established, that we shall certainly do everything we can to ensure that it is and we would like to play a part in it with certain reservations that you know about'.[106] Schmidt, in turn, professed understanding of Callaghan's situation, even defending the British position in his appearance at the Bundesbank Council. 'The Prime Minister would certainly be inclined by his political instincts to venture taking part in it all right from the start', Schmidt asserted, '[b]ut if I put myself in his position, confronted by the trade unions, confronted by the Conservatives, confronted by his own party, confronted by this trend in public and published opinion about the EC, then I would almost believe that he will come to the conclusion that he cannot fight on twelve fronts simultaneously'.[107]

Thus, while the EMS episode may not have differed in substance from previous bilateral controversies over European integration, Callaghan's and Schmidt's strong personal relationship and confidential high-level diplomacy ensured that such differences did not spill-over into other areas of bilateral cooperation this time round. As Schmidt reflected in 2013, Callaghan was an 'absolutely reliable guy, and when he said, "I'm not joining, but I won't be making you any troubles", then he stuck to it'.[108] Such personal trust and mutual confidence was a crucial prerequisite for the two leaders' simultaneous collaboration within the wider framework of the transatlantic alliance.

Callaghan, the Transatlantic Translator: Tensions over Human Rights

The election of Jimmy Carter as US President on 2 November 1976 is now widely seen as a major turning point in the post-war transatlantic relationship.[109] After a period of relative calm and benevolent

---

[106] TNA/PREM16/2049, Prime Minister's Conversation with Chancellor Schmidt, 26 November 1978.
[107] MTF, Transcript of meeting of the Bundesbank Council, 30 November 1978.
[108] Interview with Helmut Schmidt, 23 September 2013.
[109] The classic work remains R. L. Gartoff, *Détente and Confrontation: American-Soviet Relations from Nixon to Reagan, Revised Edition* (Washington, DC:

cooperation under Ford and Kissinger, Carter came to the White House with significantly different attitudes towards both transatlantic relations and the wider East–West relationship than his predecessors. Already during the election campaign, Carter and his foreign policy adviser Zbigniew Brzezinski had strongly criticized Ford and Kissinger's détente policy for its alleged indifference towards human rights abuses inside the Eastern bloc; once in office, Carter moved quickly to turn the issue of human rights into a major cornerstone of his foreign policy.[110] This reorientation of US foreign policy immediately caused concerns amongst the West Europeans, who feared that Carter's public attacks on Soviet human rights breaches might endanger the wider East–West relationship and thereby jeopardize political détente with the Eastern bloc. At the heart of these US–European differences were deeply ingrained tensions between superpower and inner-European détente since at least the early 1970s. Whereas the Americans tended to regard détente as a largely static and inherently conservative policy to fix the geostrategic Cold War order amidst the political and economic troubles of the early 1970s, the West Europeans had always harboured more dynamic conceptions of détente, hoping that an initial acceptance of the status quo would in the long run increase political, economic, and personal East-West interlinkages and thereby create interdependencies that might eventually trigger internal transformations within the Eastern bloc.[111] Carter's new approach to East–West relations now threatened to upset this delicate West European strategy.[112] Yet, even though Britain and Germany shared similar concerns over the new American President, the ways in which they sought to deal with them differed profoundly.

Brookings Institution, 1994). More recently, O. Njølstad, 'The Collapse of Superpower Détente, 1975–1980', in M. P. Leffler and O. A. Westad (eds.), *The Cambridge History of the Cold War, Vol. III: Endings* (Cambridge: Cambridge University Press, 2010), 135–55.

[110] For the evolution of Carter's human rights agenda prior to the Presidency, see P. G. Vaughan, 'Zbigniew Brzezinski and the Helsinki Final Act', in L. Nuti (ed.), *The Crisis of Détente in Europe: From Helsinki to Gorbachev, 1975–1985* (London and New York: Routledge, 2009) 11–25.

[111] J. M. Hanimäki, The Rise and Fall of Détente: American Foreign Policy and the Transformation of the Cold War (Washington, D C: Potomac Books, 2013); Sargent, *Superpower Transformed*, 59–67; Kieninger, *Dynamic Détente*; Niedhart, 'Ostpolitik: Transformation Through Communication', 14–59.

[112] Jimmy Carter Library, Atlanta, GA (henceforward: JCL/), NLC-28-10-3-2-5, Impact of US stand on human rights, 20 April 1977.

Callaghan, the Transatlantic Translator

The ruptures triggered by Carter's new course in the East–West relations were unsurprisingly felt most acutely in West Germany, since the inner-German border and the country's unique vulnerability over Berlin made the country even more susceptible to Soviet pressure than most other West Europeans. It put the West Germans in an uneasy position: while the revival of superpower tensions illustrated their continuing dependence on American protection, it also increased their determination to continue the process of East–West relaxation and détente. For Schmidt's SPD government, there was also a clear domestic dimension to all of this, since, as Schmidt's adviser Klaus von Dohnanyi told the British Ambassador in September 1977, 'it was only under the umbrella of a tolerable superpower relationship that their own Ostpolitik could thrive'.[113] Schmidt was therefore determined to continue his pursuit of inner-European détente, speaking out early and strongly against Carter's human rights rhetoric whilst also trying to cultivate Carter personally.[114] This dual-track strategy frequently resulted in conflicting messages by Schmidt, who seemed forthcoming in direct dealings with the US administration whilst publicly displaying much more critical attitudes. It was a situation that was hardly helped by the only very thinly disguised personal animosity between Schmidt and Carter.[115] On 13 July 1977, for example, Carter recorded in his diary that he 'liked Helmut Schmidt and got along with him well when we were together in London, but reports from Europe indicate there's a difference between him and me concerning our human rights effort'.[116] He put his confusion in somewhat less diplomatic terms a few months later: 'Schmidt seems to go up and down in his psychological attitude. I guess women aren't the only ones that have periods.'[117]

[113] TNA/PREM16/1278, Bonn to FCO, 2 September 1977.
[114] On Schmidt's attitudes towards Ostpolitik, see O. Bange, '"Keeping Détente alive": Inner-German Relations Under Helmut Schmidt and Erich Honecker, 1974–1982', in Nuti, *Crisis of Détente*, 230–43; D. Pick, *Brücken nach Osten: Helmut Schmidt und Polen* (Bremen: Edition Temmen, 2011); Spohr, *Global Chancellor*, 46–54.
[115] K. Wiegrefe, *Das Zerwürfnis: Helmut Schmidt, Jimmy Carter und die Krise der deutsch-amerikanischen Beziehungen* (Berlin: Propyläen, 2005).
[116] Diary entry for 13 July 1977, in J. Carter, *White House Diary* (New York: Farrar, Straus and Giroux, 2010), 69.
[117] Diary entry for 14 February 1978, in ibid., 172.

132   *James Callaghan, 1976–1979*

The British, on the other hand, were torn between rather different pressures. On the one hand, Britain's traditional attachment to the Anglo–American relationship meant that Callaghan, regarding himself as an unabashed Atlanticist, went to great lengths to build an immediate personal rapport with Carter and thus preserve the closest possible bilateral relationship.[118] As Brzezinski recalls in his memoirs, he was 'amazed [by] how quickly Callaghan succeeded in establishing himself as Carter's favorite, writing him friendly little notes, calling, talking like a genial older uncle, and lecturing Carter in a pleasant manner on the intricacies of inter-allied politics. Callaghan literally co-opted Carter in the course of a few relatively brief personal encounters'.[119] The British were also predictably keen to stage the Anglo–American relationship for public consumption, culminating in Carter's visit to Newcastle in May 1977 where he addressed enthusiastic crowds with the Geordie greeting 'Ha'way the Lads'.[120] In substance, however, Britain shared many German concerns over Carter's human rights course. Geographically much closer to the Cold War frontline than the United States, Britain not only felt more directly exposed to the Soviet Union's military threat, but it was also entangled in various long-term East–West economic contracts as part of its own détente policies. Above all, however, the British knew that their own security ultimately depended on a well-functioning transatlantic alliance, something the disputes between Carter and Schmidt now threatened to undermine.[121]

The most immediate consequence of Carter's new approach for the British–German relationship was therefore that Britain's value as a potential transatlantic intermediary between Germany and the United States increased notably, particularly on the highest level. Whereas Schmidt had previously been able to deal with key figures like Ford or Kissinger directly, his fraught relations with Carter and Brzezinski meant that he was now increasingly trying to use Callaghan in order to make his views heard in Washington. As early as January 1977, for example, Schmidt explicitly asked Callaghan to

[118] Morgan, *Callaghan*, 590, 603.
[119] Z. Brzezinski, *Power and Principle: Memoirs of the National Security Adviser 1977–1981* (New York: Farrar, Straus and Giroux, 1983), 291.
[120] Callaghan, *Time and Chance*, 481–2.
[121] Bluth, *Western Nuclear Strategy*, 235–7. For a general history of Britain's role in the Cold War, see S. Greenwood, *Britain and the Cold War 1945–91* (Basingstoke: Macmillan, 2000).

act as the spokesman for Europe during an upcoming visit to Washington, requesting that the British PM should present himself in Washington as 'Head of the European Council and to make it known that he was going as such as well as within his own rights'. He also suggested that Callaghan should discuss the agenda of his visit with EC Foreign Ministers in advance, claiming that such a united European approach stood more chance of success than 'the alternative course of several Heads of Government arranging visits, giving the impression of nine vassals being summoned to the court of King Carter'.[122] Callaghan duly obliged to Schmidt's orders, telling Carter bluntly that most EC member-states 'felt themselves too close to the Soviet Union for comfort', and that the Europeans 'had to continue to live with the Soviet Union and they were nervous about anything which might upset the existing balance'. He also suggested that 'it was wrong to give the people of Eastern Europe the hope that we could deliver more than in the event we were able to. The only country where there was a prospect of change was Poland and that was for economic and not for human rights reasons'.[123] Again, however, this was gentle criticism voiced only behind closed doors – in stark contrast to Schmidt's frequent public sneers at Carter.

Yet, the close relationship between Carter and Callaghan was no substitute for a strong US–German relationship in itself, not least given Britain's rather precarious political and economic situation at the time. Vice President Mondale, for example, was outspoken about Britain's relative uselessness to the Americans prior to Carter's first meeting with Callaghan. Although Carter would 'like' the British PM, Mondale predicted, the British government was 'in bad shape in the polls – and the spring municipal elections will be a disaster for them. . . . They want to work closely with you and see you as part of their salvation'.[124] Brzezinski held similar views, telling Carter that it was Schmidt rather than Callaghan who held the magic key to the transatlantic relationship. 'With Britain's weakness and the political challenges in France and Italy', he wrote to Carter ahead of the President's first Europe trip in May 1977, 'the strength of the Western Alliance increasingly rests on German–American relations'. A strong personal rapport between

[122] TNA/PREM16/1277, Note of a Meeting Held at Chequers, 24 January 1977.
[123] TNA/PREM16/1485, Record of Discussion between PM and US President, 10 March 1977.
[124] JCL, NLC-4–31-8-1-4, Vice President to the President, 1 February 1977.

Schmidt and Carter was thus needed, even though Brzezinski did little to disguise his personal animosity towards the German Chancellor. 'Schmidt', he claimed, was 'prone to non-stop lectures, especially on economic issues; he is not a good listener; he is stubborn and abrupt in his manner. Some say he is arrogant'.[125] Clearly, then, there remained every need for Callaghan to act as transatlantic mediator, even though his efforts could be no substitute for a strong US–German relationship as such. This applied to both major fields of transatlantic tensions at the time – macroeconomic policy and security/defence issues.

Callaghan, the Transatlantic Broker: The World Economic Summit at Bonn

Since the early 1970s, there had been simmering differences between Britain and Germany over how to best deal with the global economic downturn: whereas the British strategy focussed on state-stimulated growth and maintaining employment, the Germans instead prioritised deflationary policies and the consolidation of national budgets.[126] By the mid-1970s, these debates had come to feature prominently in high-level international diplomacy as well, particularly within the context of the now annual world economic summits.[127] Britain frequently urged Germany to reflate its economy in order to stimulate international growth and act as a so-called 'locomotive' for the world economy; the Germans, on the other side, rejected such demands just as regularly, maintaining that the long-term structural causes of the global economic crises could not be fixed by short-term reflationary measures.[128] As Schmidt put it in a speech to the German Bundestag in January 1978, it would be grossly 'overestimating the FRG's economic strength ... to turn Germany into a locomotive that could drag other countries out of the global recession alone'.[129] Carter's election, however, changed the power balance between the British and German positions on the

---

[125] JCL, NLC-25–22-7–11-0, Brzezinski to President, undated (but written in preparation for London Summit in May 1977).

[126] Lee, *Victory in Europe*, 157.

[127] Putnam and Bayne, *Hanging Together*, 36–7.

[128] B136/17108, BMWi, Bekämpfung der Arbeitslosigkeit auf internationaler Ebene, 12 October 1977.

[129] BPA, *Bulletin* 7, 20 January 1978.

3.2 James Callaghan (left) frequently had to mediate the strained relationship between the American President Jimmy Carter (centre) and Helmut Schmidt (right). Source: Photo by Evening Standard/Hulton Archive/Getty Images.

international stage markedly, since the newly elected American President too believed that a co-ordinated reflation by the US, Germany, and Japan could lift the world economy out of its depression.[130] He thus publicly and repeatedly called on the Germans to change course, much to the dismay of Schmidt. 'Any American economists who argue that the solution to our economic problems here is reflation should go back and study the problems of Europe', Schmidt was quoted in the *New York Times* as early as January 1977; 'Until then, they'd please better shut their mouths.'[131]

Behind the scenes, however, the first months of Carter's presidency saw a certain rapprochement of British–German positions, partly as a result of the change in the American position. Domestic pressure on the Schmidt government to reflate was mounting as well by that stage,

---

[130] Putnam and Bayne, *Hanging Together*, 64.
[131] *New York Times*, 24 January 1977. More generally on the Carter-Schmidt feud over the locomotive theory, von Karczewski, *Weltwirtschaft*, 283–302; Putnam and Bayne, *Hanging Together*, 63–9.

with the CDU/CSU opposition, the Federation of German Industries BDI, and even its coalition partner FDP publicly calling for tax cuts.[132] The British were acutely aware of these internal German dynamics. Already in January 1977, the German Finance Minister Hans Apel bluntly told his British counterpart Denis Healey that 'public opinion in Germany was pressing for reflation', and that the Germans would therefore 'welcome visible international pressure from European and other countries'.[133] Schmidt, in striking contrast to his public statements, similarly confided to Callaghan around the same time that it might 'be helpful ... if the British Government were to say something publicly about the need for the Germans to reflate', as long as such a statement would not be 'done in such a way as to precipitate a reaction from himself'.[134] Much like during the IMF episode, Schmidt and Callaghan therefore again tried to use their close relationship to steer and shape domestic debates.

When Germany's economic situation worsened in early 1978, Callaghan seems to have remembered these earlier hints and nudges, sensing an opportunity to reconcile US–German differences over macroeconomic policy by striking a high-level deal with himself acting as the broker. In early 1978, he therefore developed what came to be known as the plan for 'concerted action for economic growth', or the 'Five-Point Plan'. At its heart stood a compromise between American demands for the reflation of the German economy, and German demands for US fiscal discipline. By proposing the plan, Callaghan was not only able to pursue Britain's macroeconomic priorities subtly in the background, but he also carved himself a niche on the international stage. On 12 March 1978, he put the main outline of his plan to Schmidt for the first time, introducing all of its components 'without ever proposing a package as such'. But he received only a lukewarm response by Schmidt, who was in a somewhat fatalistic mood about the world economy and clearly more preoccupied with his EMS ideas. 'He did not believe in printing money', Schmidt responded to Callaghan's initiative, and in any case 'saw no solutions to the problems of German industries' in the long run. Nonetheless, he encouraged Callaghan to

---

[132] von Karczewski, *Weltwirtschaft ist unser Schicksal,* 371–6.

[133] TNA/PREM16/1277, Record of meeting between Chancellor of Exchequer Healey and Herr Apel, Minister of Finance, 24 January 1977.

[134] TNA/PREM16/1277, Note of Meeting between PM Callaghan and Chancellor Schmidt, 24 January 1977.

Callaghan, the Transatlantic Broker 137

raise the subject with Carter.[135] Having sensed a certain readiness to move behind all of Schmidt's smoke and mirrors, Callaghan then tried to enthuse Carter about the idea. 'Each nation could do something it does not like', he proposed during a subsequent visit to Washington, 'and if all would do this, then each one could. Schmidt might swallow this'. Yet, Callaghan also made clear that the success of any compromise would depend on American action over the dollar, urging Carter not to 'regard the problem of the dollar simply as a matter for a domestic crusade'. Finally, he suggested to wrap up the whole package deal in time for the upcoming world economic summit in Bonn in July 1978, believing that Schmidt's role as host would increase German readiness to make concessions.[136]

Over the next few months, Callaghan worked tirelessly to bridge the substantial differences between the American and German positions, as well as to improve the personal relationship between Schmidt and Carter. It was not an easy task: their recent fallout over the neutron bomb, discussed more extensively below, had just dealt a shattering blow to the personal trust between the two leaders from which their relationship never fully recovered. Callaghan thus devoted most of his energy to mediating these personal differences, continuously explaining to both sides their very different temperaments and political preoccupations. On 17 April 1978, for example, Callaghan phoned up Carter to explain some of the deeper reasons behind Schmidt's seemingly erratic diplomatic behaviour.

CALLAGHAN: I'm not sure whether – when you talk to Helmut – whether you really get his opinion or not. They are the largest and most important economy in Europe. They are likely to get stronger still, and he feels very much that Europe has got to organise itself more, because the American economy will be running separately and the dollar we don't know what's going to happen and so on. And I think you've got to get alongside Helmut, not you personally necessarily, but your people have really got to know what they're thinking there. It's a very odd situation because they've got a coalition government, Genscher and Helmut aren't necessarily on the same wavelength, the Bundesbank has an independence of its

---

[135] TNA/PREM16/1615, PM's meeting with Chancellor Schmidt, 12 March 1978.
[136] JCL, NLC-23-23-8-13-9, Summary of President's Meeting with UK PM Callaghan, 23 March 1978.

138 *James Callaghan, 1976–1979*

own and isn't necessarily told what Helmut is thinking, but I believe myself that I'm not sure that you're getting the real depth of Helmut's views.

CARTER: I'm not either. Because when I talk to Helmut either in person and privately when I talk to him on the telephone or when we exchange communications by dispatch or private sealed letter, we have a very good meeting of the minds and when he raises a question I answer it, and he comes back and says that's a very good answer, I'm satisfied it [sic]. But I've continued ever since I've been in office to hear privately or among other people that Helmut expresses deep concerns about our policy or our relationship with the FRG, and I think you've put your finger on an important aspect of it that I've not been able to solve myself.

CALLAGHAN: No. Well, it's very difficult to solve if he won't tell you what he is really thinking. But my understanding of his thoughts is that he believes that the American economy cannot go on expanding, that the dollar is going to get into serious trouble, and we ought to try to insulate ourselves from it as much as possible ...

CARTER: ... when he comes let myself be more brief on this subject than I would ordinarily and try to get Helmut to be frank. He has an ability to speak very bluntly and frankly when he is so motivated, without embarrassment. Why he has any reticence in talking to me I don't quite comprehend. But I'll try to break down that reserve or that apparent language communication barrier when he comes and I'll take advantage of this conversation to move on him.

CALLAGHAN: I wonder if it would be a good idea if you were to suggest that you had perhaps [Chairman of the Federal Reserve] Miller with you and that he might bring privately either Emminger, the Governor of his Central Bank, or whoever he wants to bring, you know.

CARTER: Yes, we could. He'll only be here a short time. We might even arrange a luncheon meeting as we did when you were here just very briefly and have a very tiny group of people in on both sides.

CALLAGHAN: Yes I think it would, I really do. I think if you have a tiny group in and really get him to talk. You see he knows about international finance, he understands it, he was a Minister of Finance himself, he cares about it and he believes American policy is all wrong. Now as long as that persists there's going to be trouble. ... What he is concerned about, and indeed a lot of people are concerned about, is the external value of the dollar. That is a most difficult technical problem. If you could reduce your balance of payments deficit by some energy measures I think that would have a very healthy effect on the way that Helmut and others think about it.

CARTER: Well, so do I. Well Jim thank you very much. It is valuable for me to have you.[137]

This conversation is worth quoting at some length since it reveals some of the sophisticated ways in which Callaghan performed his role as transatlantic interlocutor. Not only did he create a sense of comradery and friendship, enabling Carter to let off some steam and talk honestly about his feelings of irritation with Schmidt, but he then also stepped in to explain the domestic pressures behind Schmidt's confusing and often contradictory behaviour. Finally, he volunteered some concrete suggestions over how to improve the Carter–Schmidt relationship, sounding out the possibilities for his Five-Point plan. This was high-level diplomacy at its finest, fostering a climate of mutual trust and achieving real progress as a result.

Having sensed Carter's eventual readiness to act on the dollar and energy, Callaghan went back to Schmidt a few days later. He now played a rather different role, patiently sitting through Schmidt's ramblings over how Europe's economic problems were 'structural' and needed 'something more and quite different from a half per cent increase in "growth" brought about by tax cuts designed to benefit housewives'. Then, however, he subtly pressed Schmidt on what the Germans actually expected in substance from the American side. The answer was unambiguous. He 'would be prepared to pay a very high price if the United States, to remove its deficit, took action on energy and inflation', Schmidt exclaimed according to the British record; such a move might even enable the Germans to commit themselves 'to decisions which were in all other respects "errors"'. Carter, Schmidt continued, simply 'would have to make the American

---

[137] TNA/PREM16/1616, PM's Telephone Conversation with President Carter, 17 April 1978.

consumer pay a lot more for his gas at the pump and only by so doing would everybody see that he was serious ... If President Carter would only do that, he would go on his knees and praise God'.[138] This was the information Callaghan needed. Afterwards, he informed Carter's chief economic adviser Henry Owen that Schmidt had 'explicitly' told him that 'if President Carter would act on inflation and energy, then he [Schmidt] would act (notwithstanding his lack of intellectual conviction) on stimulating the FRG economy'.[139]

In due course, Callaghan's Five-Point plan would form the basis of the eventual US–German compromise reached at the Bonn world economic summit in July 1978, in which the United States agreed to raise its oil prices to world levels by the end of 1980 and the FRG in turn committed itself to reflationary measures of around 1 per cent of its GNP.[140] Callaghan continued to play the role of the honest broker throughout, even staging the precise choreography of the summit's proceedings.[141] Thus, while the successful outcome of the summit was celebrated as a major diplomatic achievement by Schmidt and Carter at the time, it had been Callaghan who had played the most crucial role as transatlantic broker and mediator behind the scenes. It was one of the few occasions in 1970s international politics were Britain managed to fulfil its self-attributed role as transatlantic bridge between Europe and the United States, thereby also subtly pursuing its own objectives and punching above its diplomatic weight.[142] These dynamics were mirrored in the field of security and defence, where Callaghan again proved the key facilitator of a US–German

---

[138] TNA/PREM16/1655, PM's Meeting with Chancellor Schmidt at Chequers, 23 April 1978.

[139] S. G. Galpern (ed.), *Foreign Relations of the United States [henceforward: FRUS], Nixon-Ford Administrations 1969–1976, Energy 1974–1980, Volume XXXVII* (Washington DC: United States Government Printing Office, 2012), Doc. Nr. 149, Memorandum from Henry Owen to President Carter, 11 May 1978.

[140] MTF, Bonn G7 Communiqué (The Bonn Declaration), 17 July 1978: http://www.margaretthatcher.org/document/111544 [accessed on 13 June 2018]. On Callaghan's blueprint, see also Putnam and Bayne, *Hanging Together*, 78.

[141] *AAPD 1978*, Doc. Nr. 220, Gespräch BK Schmidt mit PM Callaghan, 15 July 1978.

[142] For an interesting study of the mindset of British foreign-policy making elites in this regard, see M. D. Kandiah et al., '"At the Top Table": British Elites' Perceptions of the UK's International Position, 1950–91', in J. W. Young, E. G. H. Pedaliu, and M. Kandiah (eds.), *Britain in Global Politics Volume 2: From Churchill to Blair* (Basingstoke: Macmillan, 2013) 179–97.

compromise over some of the major strategic questions confronting the transatlantic alliance in the late 1970s.

Callaghan, the Transatlantic Mediator: The Shaping of NATO's Dual-Track Decision

The transatlantic alliance had experienced cyclical patterns of harmony and despair ever since its creation in the late 1940s. At the heart of these recurring tensions were the structural asymmetries of power between the United States and Western Europe, as well as their different geostrategic positions vis-à-vis the Soviet Union. In the 1960s, European doubts over the credibility of the American security guarantee as well as simultaneous US fears over an autonomous Europe had eventually resulted in NATO's strategy of 'flexible response' and the Harmel Report of 1967. To retain credibility, however, NATO required sufficient military deterrence vis-à-vis the Soviet Union on all military levels: the nuclear-strategic level between the superpowers, the level of tactical-nuclear weapons in Europe, and the conventional level. Only with a rough balance of power in all areas, so the dogma went, was NATO able to ensure an appropriate response to all levels of military escalation.

By the late 1970s, however, the Soviet build-up of a new generation of *SS-20* intermediate-range ballistic missiles threatened to upset this delicate balance in the field of tactical-nuclear weapons in Europe, the level of so-called Theatre Nuclear Forces (TNF). Not only did NATO lack adequate tactical-nuclear deterrents, but the *SS-20s* were also not included in either the Strategic Arms Limitation Talks II (SALTII) or the Mutual and Balanced Force Reduction talks (MBFR), since they were non-conventional nuclear weapons that were able to strike Western Europe but not the United States. Many members of NATO therefore saw the danger of an emerging Soviet superiority in the tactical-nuclear TNF field, and feared the emergence of a so-called 'grey area' in Europe not covered by either arms limitation treaties or sufficiently strong NATO deterrence.[143]

---

[143] For recent studies of the genesis of NATO's dual-track decision see Spohr, 'Conflict and Cooperation in Intra-Alliance Nuclear Politics', 39–89; L. Nuti, 'The Origins of the 1979 Dual Track Decision – A Survey', in Nuti, *Crisis of Détente*, 57–71.

142

James Callaghan, 1976–1979

The potential dangers of the Soviet threat were felt most acutely in West Germany. Not only was the FRG the most exposed and thus most threatened country within the transatlantic alliance, but the Germans also feared that the Soviet lead in the TNF field might eventually lead to a US 'de-coupling' from Western Europe and thereby make them susceptible to Soviet blackmail in case of a limited nuclear attack.[144] Such German concerns were aggravated further by the fact that, in contrast to France and Britain, the FRG did not have independent nuclear capabilities acting as deterrents on their own, which made them feel even more vulnerable and exposed. Having spent much of the 1960s studying nuclear strategy, Schmidt appeared particularly concerned about the situation, given his almost dogmatic belief in the need for a balance of power on all military levels.[145] In his famous speech at the London-based *International Institute for Strategic Studies* in October 1977, Schmidt therefore warned strongly about the emerging gap in the TNF field. Any arms control agreement confined solely to the superpowers would 'inevitably impair the security of the West European members', Schmidt argued, unless one removed 'the disparities in military power in Europe in parallel to the SALT negotiations'.[146] He found a most receptive audience amongst British attendees. Given France's continuing self-exclusion from the military wing of NATO,[147] Britain, as the only nuclear-armed European member of NATO, almost inevitably had to take the lead in shaping the West European response to the Soviet threat, given both its own geostrategic vulnerability to a Soviet *SS-20* attack and the fact that its own security ultimately depended on the transatlantic alliance as well.[148] Over the following months, Britain and Germany thus lead the way in shaping NATO's policy on sub-strategic nuclear weapons in

---

[144] For German concerns over the continuing validity of NATO's doctrine in the 1970s, see the still excellent H. Haftendorn, 'Das doppelte Mißverständnis: zur Vorgeschichte des NATO-Doppelbeschlusses', *Vierteljahreshefte für Zeitgeschichte* 33 (1954), 244–87.

[145] For the evolution of Schmidt's military-strategic thought, see Spohr, *Global Chancellor*, 60–84.

[146] H. Schmidt, 'The 1977 Alastair Buchan Memorial Lecture', *Survival*, 20/1 (1978), 2–10. Also, the various drafts in PHSA, EA 20.10.-15.11.1977.

[147] Although Giscard himself did become informally involved in shaping NATO strategy on the highest level; Waechter, *Schmidt und Giscard*, 124–34.

[148] For further background on the increasing commonality of British and German views on the issue, see Bluth, *Western Nuclear Strategy*, 201–37.

Callaghan, the Transatlantic Mediator 143

Europe, particularly within the frameworks of the Nuclear Planning Group (NPG) and the newly created High Level Group (HLG).[149]

The British and German desire to collaborate closely within the transatlantic alliance was strengthened by their growing doubts over US leadership.[150] In April 1978, Carter's unilateral decision to cancel the production of the so-called neutron bomb, a highly controversial new weapon which both the British and the Germans had supported only very reluctantly, was seen as a major diplomatic affront to the West Europeans, as well as confirmation of Carter's ultimate unreliability. While the British and German public reactions were rather different, with Schmidt making little attempt to conceal his anger in the German *Bundestag* whilst Callaghan merely told the House of Commons that the issue had been 'a political matter for the President alone to decide', the two leaders were nonetheless united in their dismay over the US handling of the issue.[151] Behind closed doors, both Bonn and London stressed the grave consequences of Carter's decision on the climate of transatlantic cooperation and trust in strongest terms. While the British were 'utterly candid in their desire to be helpful', the American Embassy in London reported, they had nonetheless 'underscored the disastrous impact the decision will have on the President's credibility and hence leadership of the western world'.[152] Although the British would back the US 'whatever you decide', the Embassy added in another despatch a few days later, the 'complete reversal of our apparent intentions' was 'bound to shake allied confidence in our constancy and our military and political resolve'.[153]

The transatlantic fallout over the 'neutron bomb' intensified West European resolve to take the underlying TNF problem into their own hands.[154] In marked contrast to questions of European integration, the

---

[149] Spohr, 'Conflict and Cooperation', 50–9, 88; Bluth, *Western Nuclear Strategy* 201–37; 303.

[150] For recent studies of the transatlantic controversies surrounding the neutron bomb, see Spohr, 'Neutron Bomb', 259–85; with a tighter focus on Britain, M. Elli, 'Callaghan, the British Government and the N-Bomb Controversy', *Cold War History*, 15/3 (2015), 321–39.

[151] BPA, *Bulletin* 34, 14 April 1978; Hansard, *House of Commons Debate* 11 April 1978, vol. 947 cc. 1177.

[152] JCL, ZBC, Subject File, Container 22, Inderfurth to Dr Brzezinski, 1 April 1978.

[153] JCL, ZBC, Subject File, Container 22, London to Brzezinski, 4 April 1978.

[154] Spohr, 'Neutron Bomb', 279.

FRG depended heavily on British support on the matter, given not least its still semi-sovereign status and lack of an independent nuclear capability themselves. Partly as a result of his personal preoccupation with nuclear strategic questions, Schmidt was particularly determined to keep the TNF issue on the bilateral agenda, and frequently sought to get Callaghan on his side. A few weeks after the 'neutron bomb' controversy, he again told the British PM how 'European security interests were not being taken care of in the field of intra-European weapons'.[155] The transatlantic alliance thus needed to address the issue as soon as possible, Schmidt claimed, given the uncertainty surrounding the future Soviet leadership after Brezhnev. 'Brezhnev knows that his political life is coming to an end and sees his task as wanting to stabilise peace', he continued, whereas others in the Politburo 'were not too keen'. Therefore, Schmidt urged Callaghan that NATO 'should exploit the situation while he is there – fix and stabilise it'.[156] The British PM, however, was rather less enthusiastic. Not only did the British fear that potential arms control negotiations over TNF might impact on their own independent nuclear deterrent, but they also did not fully share Schmidt's obsession with the Soviet SS-20s, believing that they constituted primarily a political-psychological rather than a new strategic-military threat.[157]

Yet again, a frank high-level exchange between Schmidt and Callaghan during the October 1978 British-German consultations triggered the eventual rapprochement of their positions, with Schmidt using his excellent personal rapport with Callaghan to dramatically illustrate his personal concerns over the FRG's exposed and vulnerable position. '[H]e thought that strategic thinking in the UK and in France was apt to be prejudiced by the fact that both countries possessed nuclear weapons', Schmidt started off. The Germans did not have a comparable counterweight to the Soviet threat, which meant that they would eventually have to 'go begging' to their British or American partners 'and ask them to produce a counter-threat'. Such a request,

---

[155] PREM16/1655, Record of Conversation between PM and Schmidt, 24 April 1978.

[156] PREM16/1655, Record of PM's Meeting with Chancellor Schmidt at Chequers, 24 April 1978.

[157] For the evolution of British attitudes during 1978, see Okamoto, 'Britain, European Security and the Cold War', 254, 261–4; Bluth, *Britain, Germany, and Western Nuclear Strategy*, 217, 234.

Schmidt concluded, 'would only be met in the last extremity of a crisis, perhaps only after Soviet nuclear weapons had already been launched. The old question of 1938 would be resurrected: "Europe or Danzig?"'.[158] When Callaghan still refused to accept Schmidt's reasoning, stressing the American and British resolve to protect the FRG and highlighting the role of British troops on German soil, Schmidt volunteered what would in due course become the essence of NATO's dual-track decision. 'Turning to the question of a potential Western bargaining chip in the grey areas', Schmidt replied, 'the West could create an option of producing and deploying equivalent weapons and could then offer to give up this option in return for a reduction by the Soviet Union in the weapons they already had. This would be an option for the Americans, rather than for the British, to create'. Callaghan responded favourably, adding that if the UK was 'going to have cruise missiles it made no difference if they were American ones'.[159] The two leaders then agreed that the issue should be discussed further in a wider NATO framework, and instructed a group of British and German officials to jointly prepare a detailed assessment of the problem for subsequent discussion at heads of government level.[160]

Such discussions were conducted a few weeks later at the Guadeloupe summit in January 1979, an informal meeting of Schmidt, Giscard, Callaghan, and Carter to discuss wider nuclear-strategic questions.[161] Yet again, Callaghan's role proved vital in mediating and eventually overcoming the differences between Carter and Schmidt, and his earlier bilateral talks with Schmidt now enabled him to play that role effectively. The British PM intervened early to calm the heat, claiming that his talks with Schmidt a few weeks ago had made him realise the extent of German concerns, and had illustrated to him the need to 'reassure the Federal Republic of Germany which was the most threatened country' about the continuing viability of NATO's flexible response doctrine. At the same time, he also pushed Schmidt gently away from his preference on arms control negotiations towards an

---

[158] TNA/PREM16/1984, Conversation between PM and Chancellor Schmidt in Bonn, 19 October 1978.
[159] Ibid.
[160] See chronology in TNA/PREM16/2049, Hunt to PM, 6 November 1979.
[161] For a recent study of the Guadeloupe summit, see Spohr, 'Guadeloupe', 167–92; Spohr, *Global Chancellor*, 94–101.

eventual acceptance of a possible deployment of new US tactical-nuclear weapons in Germany.[162] This mediating role proved crucial in brokering the US–German compromise at Guadeloupe, resulting in what would eventually become the essence of NATO's dual-track decision: to pursue arms control negotiations and the modernization of NATO's tactical-nuclear weaponry simultaneously and in parallel.[163] In the aftermath of the summit, Callaghan then tried to ensure that all sides would stick to the compromise. After an Anglo–American meeting in March 1979, for example, he phoned Schmidt to tell him how he had emphasised strongly 'the British-German agreement to treat TNF modernization and arms control as two parallel and not, as the US had originally intended, as two separate processes', suggesting that 'the Germans and the British should solve these questions bilaterally first in order to express their common stance more clearly'.[164] By that stage, however, the precarious domestic situation Callaghan found upon his return from Guadeloupe had caught up with him. At the May 1979 general election, Callaghan's government was defeated decisively, with the Conservatives winning 44 per cent of the popular vote, and a majority of 43 seats. It would fall to Callaghan's rather less consensus-oriented successor Margaret Thatcher to shape the British-German relationship for much of the following decade.

Conclusions

After his own fall from office in 1982, the *Financial Times* asked Helmut Schmidt about his future plans. After some dithering, Schmidt replied to the surprise of the interviewer that he 'would like to play the role of Mr Jim Callaghan'. The former British PM, Schmidt elaborated, was 'a strong character. A dependable human being'.[165] Indeed, the strong personal relationship between Schmidt and

---

[162] TNA/PREM16/2050, Four-Power Discussions in Guadeloupe: Second Session, 5 January 1979.

[163] TNA/PREM16/2050, Four-Power Discussions in Guadeloupe: Third Session, 6 January 1979.

[164] 1/HSAA006593, Vermerk über Telefongespräch BK mit PM Callaghan, 6 March 1979.

[165] *Financial Times*, 16 December 1982.

Conclusions 147

Callaghan had been the defining characteristic of the British–German relationship from 1976 to 1979. It not only helped them overcome many long-standing bilateral disputes, such as the question of Offset payments or the location of JET, but it also fostered an atmosphere of purposeful bilateral cooperation and harmony which both leaders utilised successfully in their respective domestic struggles. In the wider international arena too, the close high-level cooperation between Callaghan and Schmidt helped resolve many contentious areas in the wider multilateral setting of the transatlantic alliance, with the British PM playing a crucial role as arbiter and mediator between Schmidt and Carter. Indeed, Callaghan's premiership was one of the few occasions where Britain actually managed to succeed in its long-standing diplomatic strategy to exercise international influence through multilateral cooperation, particularly as regards the Anglo-American relationship. This was due not least to Schmidt's own troubled relationship with Carter after 1977, which – coupled with the FRG's dependence on the Western alliance in terms of its own security and defence – meant that Britain's value to Germany as a transatlantic interlocutor increased as a result.

Yet, even Callaghan's excellent diplomatic skills and his hard-headed realism over Britain's limited post-war influence were ultimately insufficient to overcome the wider strategic gap that separated Britain and Germany over European integration. The British refusal to join the EMS is a case in point. Whereas Schmidt consciously sought to utilise the EC to better protect the West Europeans against what he regarded reckless American policies, Callaghan instinctively rejected such ideas, lacking Schmidt's long-standing personal convictions about the necessity of European integration as the very foundation of Western Europe's role in the post-war world. Faced with a largely hostile domestic environment and not seeing any particular economic advantages in EMS membership, Callaghan thus opted for looser and more *ad-hoc* mechanisms of informal cooperation in European and transatlantic frameworks. Yet, whereas the economic crisis following the second oil shock evaporated many short-term achievements of Callaghan's informal multilateral diplomacy such as the policies agreed at the Bonn summit of 1978, the EMS was there to stay, and continued to compromise the British–German relationship well into the 1990s and beyond. Ironically, then, Callaghan's years in office thus marked the most significant departure between British and German national strategies throughout Schmidt's chancellorship, even though their close high-level relationship ensured that the short-term consequences of this strategic departure remained fairly minimal and did not impact other areas of bilateral relations, as it had previously done under Wilson and would do again under the premiership of Margaret Thatcher.

4 | *Margaret Thatcher, 1979–1982*

When Helmut Schmidt published his memoirs in 1990, the former Chancellor decided to open his sixty-two-page chapter on Britain with the graphic description of a particularly memorable European Council meeting in Dublin in November 1979. At stake was the issue of Britain's disproportionately high net contributions to the EC budget, an issue that the new PM Margaret Thatcher had forcefully put on the European agenda quickly after her election earlier that year. As Schmidt recalls:

The atmosphere was cool, almost frosty. The talks had been going on for some time without a result, the right to speak had been handed over several times. Now, the new British PM Margaret Thatcher spoke for the umpteenth time ... She kept herself brief: "I want my money back, and I want it now!" She said it with vigour in her voice, and it sounded a bit shrill. No readiness for any give-and-take could be detected ... After Margaret Thatcher had said for the third time that she wanted her money back – she actually said, "my money", – we postponed the whole issue. We did not want to be treated for hours as if we were enemies of Great Britain.[1]

Writing around the time of German reunification, Schmidt's vivid recollection of Thatcher's performance surely struck a familiar chord with many contemporary observers: after all, her fall from office in November 1990 had been triggered not least by her thinly disguised personal hostility towards the intensification of the European integration process and virulent opposition against German reunification.[2]

---

[1] Schmidt, *Die Deutschen und ihre Nachbarn*, 91.

[2] In July 1990, two episodes revealed these dynamics to the wider public: first, the leak of the protocol of the famous 'Chequers seminar', which Thatcher had convened in March 1990 to discuss the German 'national character' with some eminent British historians; second, Trade Secretary Nicolas Ridley's interview with *The Spectator*, where he described the proposals for European economic and monetary union as a 'German racket designed to take over the whole of Europe'. See *The Spectator* 14 July 1990. For the record of Thatcher's Chequers seminar,

149

It thus took little imagination at the time to recognise Schmidt's depiction of Thatcher as an eternally Eurosceptic and Germanophobe, an image that had after all also been consciously cultivated by Thatcher herself after her time in office.[3] 'During my lifetime most of the problems the world has faced have come ... from mainland Europe', she famously wrote in one of her last publications, 'and the solutions from outside it'.[4]

Looking back at the time of Thatcher's election in May 1979, however, it seems surprising that the European issue would come to occupy such prominence in the British–German relationship during her time in office. After all, the Conservatives had fought their campaign on an avowedly pro-European platform, proclaiming a sharp break with the European policies of the previous Callaghan government. Thatcher herself was not known for holding particularly strong views on the EC either: though not emotionally attached to the European integration project like her Conservative predecessor Edward Heath, she nonetheless accepted its political and economic advantages to Britain and appeared unequivocal about her support of British membership. Within only a few months, however, British–German tensions inside the EC had again come to dominate the bilateral relationship almost completely, largely due to Thatcher's personal preoccupation with what came to be known as the British budgetary question. These intra-EC tensions eventually came to overshadow the unprecedented extent of bilateral cooperation outside the realm of EC politics that was taking

---

'Appendix: The PM's Seminar on Germany', 24 March 1990, in Her Majesty's Stationary Office (ed.), *Documents on British Policy Overseas, Series III Vol. VII: German Unification 1989–1990* (London: Routledge, 2010), 502–9. For the sometimes drastically diverging recollections of key participants, G. Urban, *Diplomacy and Disillusion At the Court of Margaret Thatcher; An Insider's View* (London: Tauris, 1996); T. Garton Ash, *History of the Present* (London: Penguin, 2001); N. Stone, 'Cold War: Germany? Maggie was absolutely right', *The Sunday Times*, 23 September 1996. For more general takes on British attitudes towards German reunification, see J. Bullard, 'Great Britain and German Unification', in Noakes et al., *Britain and Germany in Europe*, 219–30; L. Kettenacker, 'Britain and German Unification, 1989/1990', in Larres and Meehan, *Uneasy Allies*, 99–126.

[3] For an insightful survey of the growing identification of Thatcher with Euroscepticism during the final years of her premiership and beyond, see in particular A. Gamble, 'Europe and America', in Jackson and Saunders, *Making Thatcher's Britain*, 218–33.

[4] M. Thatcher, *Statecraft: Strategies for a Changing World* (London: William Collins, 2002), 320.

place at the same time, as both Britain and Germany sought to foster a distinct West European response to the resurgence of Cold War tensions over NATO's dual-track decision and the Afghanistan and Poland crises of the early 1980s. The early Thatcher years thus saw Britain move closer towards Europe in its foreign policy than ever before; yet this British–German rapprochement was overshadowed almost completely by the vocal and virulent disputes over the EC budget taking place at the same time. It is this contradiction that stands at the heart of British–German relations under Schmidt and Thatcher.

Initial Perceptions and the Drawing of Battle Lines over the British Budget Question

Margaret Thatcher's election as PM signalled a watershed in British politics. After decades of largely consensus-orientated domestic politics, the Thatcher government projected a radical break with the past, embarking upon far-reaching fiscal and economic reforms that centred on tightening public expenditure and the curbing of trade union powers.[5] Her government also professed to be firmly set on playing a more positive and constructive role inside the EC. Its election manifesto had claimed that the Conservatives would 'work honestly and genuinely with our partners in the European Community', playing 'a leading and constructive role in the Community's efforts to tackle the many problems which it faces'.[6] This unreserved commitment to EC membership was seen to reflect Thatcher's personal views at the time. Though never emotionally attached to the European project like her Conservative predecessor Edward Heath, Thatcher nonetheless regarded the EC as a major building block of the post-war European order, not least as part of the West's defence against the Soviet threat.[7]

---

[5] For recent historical evaluations of the Thatcher years, see Jackson and Saunders, *Making Thatcher's Britain*, as well as the biographies by C. Moore, *Margaret Thatcher: The Authorised Biography, Vol. I: Not for Turning* (London: Penguin, 2013); C. Moore, *Margaret Thatcher: The Authorised Biography, Vol. II: Everything She Wants* (London: Penguin, 2015).

[6] Conservative Party, 'Conservative General Election Manifesto', 11 April 1979. Accessed through the MTF, Thatcher Archive: www.margaretthatcher.org/document/110858 [accessed on 13 June 2018].

[7] R. Vinen, 'Thatcherism and the Cold War', in Jackson and Saunders, *Making Thatcher's Britain*, 209. More generally, P. Sharp, *Thatcher's Diplomacy: The Revival of British Foreign Policy* (Basingstoke: Macmillan, 1997).

During the 1975 referendum, she had campaigned unreservedly in favour of continuing membership, culminating in her participation at an all-night candlelight vigil where she wore a brightly coloured jumper displaying various European flags – according to the *Daily Express* proving that it was 'Europe or bust for her'.[8] Though Thatcher shared some of the Callaghan government's concerns over Britain's budget contributions, such criticisms had never translated into opposition to the principle of British membership during her time as opposition leader. As she put it in an interview with the *US News & World Report* in 1977, 'You don't pull down the whole house merely because you don't like the decorations in the sitting room'.[9]

In Germany, it was therefore expected that the Thatcher government's European policy would be more closely aligned with West German priorities than the previous Labour government had been.[10] Schmidt, who had attributed most previous problems in intra-EC decision-making processes primarily to Callaghan's difficulties with Labour's left wing, clearly believed that the new government would be easier to deal with, even though it was just as likely to bargain hard for its specific national interests. As he told German journalists in an off-the-record discussion in May 1979, he expected the Thatcher government to 'be smarter than the previous government in its relationship with Europe ... not basically different, but smarter in its presentation'.[11] The Germans placed particularly strong hopes on the appointment of the highly experienced Lord Carrington as Foreign Secretary, who had served in every Conservative government since 1951 and had already cooperated extensively with Schmidt during his time as Secretary of Defence from 1970 to 1974. The German *Auswärtiges Amt* therefore regarded Carrington as a major stabilising force inside an otherwise largely inexperienced government. Not only was Carrington 'pragmatic' and 'German-friendly', as the Germans claimed internally, but he also seemed 'very open-minded in European questions'.[12] Even the *New York Times* suggested that Britain's European partners should anticipate 'a better relationship with the

---

[8] *Daily Express*, 5 June 1975.
[9] *US News & World Report 1977*, 12 September 1977.
[10] 1/HSAA006737, Brief: Deutsch-Britische Konsultationen, 9 May 1979.
[11] 1/HSAA006737, Gespräch BK mit deutschen Korrespondenten in London, 11 May 1979.
[12] 1/HSAA006737, Brief: Deutsch-Britische Konsultationen, 9 May 1979.

Initial Perceptions 153

Conservative Margaret Thatcher than they had with Labor. Since 1956, the Tories have been stronger Europeanists than Labor and not so keen on the "special relationship" with the United States'.[13]

The British–German consultations on 10–11 May 1979, merely a week after Thatcher's election, largely confirmed these positive impressions. The British government in particular appeared determined to strike up a strong bilateral relationship, not least because of fears that it might otherwise find itself permanently side-lined against the Franco–German axis. Key to this, as Cabinet Secretary John Hunt briefed the new PM, was to establish a strong personal connection with Schmidt from the very beginning, given the German Chancellor's close relationship with Giscard and his more general preference for informal high-level diplomacy.[14] Thatcher heeded Hunt's advice. In her first personal talk with Schmidt, the two leaders embarked upon a wide-ranging and substantive *tour d'horizon* that covered all major issues of international relations and economics. Yet, a moment of friction occurred when Thatcher raised her concerns over Britain's disproportionately high contributions to the EC budget.[15] It was the issue that would do more than anything else to undermine British attempts to forge a stronger British–German relationship throughout Thatcher's first term.

Britain's contributions to the EC budget had been a serious problem in Britain's relationship with its European partners ever since its accession to the EC in 1973.[16] Its root cause were long-term structural discrepancies caused by Britain's different trading and agricultural patterns: Britain traditionally imported high quantities of foods and other goods from non-EC countries, for which levies and taxes now went directly into the EC budget under the EC's 'own resources' principle, whereas it had a comparatively small and efficient agricultural sector, into which around 70–75 per cent of EC expenditure went

[13] *The New York Times Magazine*, 26 August 1979.

[14] TNA/PREM19/58, Note: Meeting with Chancellor Schmidt, 4 May 1979.

[15] TNA/PREM19/58, Record of the PM's Discussion with the Chancellor of the Federal Republic of Germany, Herr Schmidt, at 10 Downing Street, 10 May 1979; TNA/PREM19/58, Record of the PM's discussions with Chancellor Schmidt in plenary session, 11 May 1979; 1/HSAA006737, Vermerk über das Gespräch des BK mit PM Thatcher, 10 May 1979.

[16] For a recent historical overview of the British budgetary problem during Thatcher's first term, see Ludlow, *Roy Jenkins*, 207–224; Moore, *The Lady Is Not for Turning*, 485–95.

at the time. Simply put, the result was that Britain was contributing more to the EC budget than it got out of it. It was a problem that had already featured prominently in the accession negotiations in the early 1970s, but that had eventually been side-lined by then PM Edward Heath, who thought it pivotal to accept all EC rules and regulations in order to achieve the overarching strategic goal of membership. Once inside the EC, so he hoped, the situation could still be remedied by restructuring the EC's budget from within, and in any case, the Commission had promised to find an 'equitable solution' if such an 'unacceptable situation' to Britain ever arose.[17] Throughout the 1970s, transitional requirements had thus far eased Britain's situation, although the issue had already resurfaced briefly during the 1974–5 renegotiations. With the transitionary period now running out, however, the Thatcher government was soon to be confronted with the full burden of Britain's budget contributions. 'Despite having the third lowest GNP per head in the Community', it calculated in May 1979, 'we are at present … either the largest or the second largest (after Germany) net contributor to the Community Budget'.[18] According to estimates of the European Commission, the total British contribution to the EC budget now amounted to 20 per cent, whereas it received only 5 per cent of CAP expenditure in return.[19] At least to the British, it thus seemed clear that the so-called 'unacceptable situation' had arisen.

While the issue would have resurfaced in any case, it was Thatcher's personal initiative that gave the issue such prominence in both the British–German relationship and the more general agenda of the EC.[20] Thatcher felt strongly that this was a thoroughly unjust situation to Britain which had to be remedied as soon as possible. It was, as her biographer Hugo Young put it, a problem that suited 'her angular mind

---

[17] The Commission's promise was also the legal basis on which the Thatcher government now centred its demands. See TNA/PREM19/472, The Community undertaking to remedy unacceptable situations, 15 March 1980. For the budget issue during the accession talks in the early 1970s, see D. Furby, 'The Revival and Success of Britain's Second Application for Membership of the EC 1968–71', unpublished PhD thesis (Queen Mary University of London, 2009), esp. 232–75.

[18] TNA /PREM19/58, EEC Resource Transfers and Convergence, 9 May 1979.

[19] Ludlow, *Jenkins*, 208–9.

[20] For the extent of Thatcher's personal agenda-setting on the issue, see S. Wall, *A Stranger in Europe: Britain and the EU from Thatcher to Blair* (Oxford: Oxford University Press, 2008), 5–7; Moore, *The Lady Is Not for Turning*, 485–95.

Initial Perceptions   155

and her instinct for aggression. . . . There would be a winner and a loser, and only the winner would have justice on her side'.[21] As a result, Thatcher intervened early to push the budget problem to the centre of her government's agenda. Reviewing briefing papers for the British–German consultations in May 1979, Thatcher complained heavily about the 'wordy generalisations' on the EC budget, putting on record that she wanted to make quick progress 'towards remedying a thoroughly unsatisfactory situation'.[22] Given that Germany was the only other net contributor to the EC budget at the time, the British placed great hopes in the Federal Republic as a potential major ally. During the Thatcher government's very first Cabinet meeting on 10 May 1979, it was decided that the upcoming British–German talks should be used not only to 'underline the Government's European commitment', but also 'to stress that ... we should need German help over our legitimate interests on fisheries, the Community Budget and the Common Agricultural Policy'.[23] Again, Britain's somewhat transactional approach towards EC questions can be seen in Thatcher's position: while she intellectually accepted the strategic advantages of British EC membership, she nonetheless lacked the strong emotive attachment to the post-war European integration process that her European counterparts like Schmidt and Giscard displayed so regularly. She thus saw no contradiction between fighting hard over the British budget contribution and being wholeheartedly in favour of British EC membership: to the contrary, Thatcher believed that solving the budget problem was a precondition to enable the United Kingdom to play its full part inside the EC in the first place.

Yet, strong German help for the British cause was unlikely to be forthcoming. Though the Germans sympathised with the political problem of Britain's disproportionately high budget contributions, there was formidable structural opposition to any solution in several key departments. Predictably most hostile was the Ministry of Finance, given that the FRG was likely to shoulder most of the additional financial burden of any potential solution, and it thus adopted a non-compromising attitude. 'Just because Great Britain could not seize the hoped for advantages of the Common Market', it claimed in an internal

---

[21] Young, *Blessed Plot*, 313.
[22] TNA/PREM19/58, PREM to FCO, 8 May 1979.
[23] TNA/CAB128/66, CC (79) 1st Conclusions, 10 May 1979.

briefing paper, 'it cannot constantly demand a correction of the common basis of the treaty'.[24] The FRG Ministry for Agriculture shared this restrictive attitude, given that the German agricultural sector was twice the size of the UK's and many German farmers benefitted substantially from the CAP.[25] Indeed, German agricultural spokesmen in Brussels had long since acquired a reputation for sturdily defending farmers' interests; a hard-headed defence of German interests embodied by the FDP's powerful Bavarian Minister of Agriculture Josef Ertl.[26] Most important in German eyes, however, were the formidable international obstacles to any settlement, given that many member-states benefitted substantially from the EC's current financing system and thus displayed little appetite for reform. France in particular strongly opposed British demands, with President Giscard d'Estaing's position being additionally constrained by France's powerful agricultural lobby in light of upcoming Presidential elections.[27] The Germans thus feared that British demands would provoke a major intra-EC crisis threatening the Community's internal cohesion. This made Germany an unlikely arbiter between Britain and the rest of the Community, given its long-standing strategic aim to ensure the EC's stability and unity even at some short-term political or economic cost.

Schmidt's and Thatcher's first discussions of the budget problem in May 1979 already revealed Britain's and Germany's very different approaches to the problem. Thatcher, having spotted the political potency of the issue early on, sought to impress on Schmidt the sincerity of British demands in no uncertain terms. Britain was 'very concerned about the state of the UK's relations with Europe', she started off, exclaiming that her government would 'in no way lack determination to change what was unjust or unreasonable'. Taken aback by

[24] 1/HSAA006731, Gesprächsvorlage: 13.Europäischer Rat, 9 March 1979.
[25] TNA/PREM19/58, UK and German interests in the CAP, 10 May 1979. For general background on the CAP (and the FRG's often hypocritical attitude towards it), see K. K. Patel (ed.), *Fertile Ground for Europe?: The History of European Integration and the Common Agricultural Policy Since 1945* (Baden-Baden: Nomos, 2009).
[26] Ibid. Ertl was a powerful figure within the FDP and therefore seen as crucial in holding the SPD-FDP coalition together. See also Matthöfer's remarks to that extent in TNA/PREM19/58, Note of a discussion between the Chancellor of the Exchequer and the Minister of Finance of the Federal Republic of Germany, 11 May 1979.
[27] Ludlow, *Jenkins*, 213–14.

High-Level Diplomacy as Catalyst 157

Thatcher's surprisingly confrontational approach, Schmidt responded in kind. Germany too had 'real concerns' over Britain's role inside the EC, he claimed, and there was 'a certain tendency in the Community to lapse back into nationalistic attitudes'. Fearing yet another repetition of previous clashes between Britain and other EC member-states, he urged Thatcher to approach the budget issue from a more consensual and communitarian angle, arguing that nothing could be achieved in the Community by simply 'bang[ing] on the table'.[28] During the subsequent plenary session of the bilateral talks, Schmidt issued an even starker warning, urging the British delegation to 'take account of the psychological impression which would be created in the Community if it was thought that the UK wished to embark on a further renegotiation of her terms of entry to the EEC'.[29] In essence, these exchanges already set up the key dynamics that would put Britain and Germany at odds over the following months: whereas Schmidt wanted to avoid a major row and preserve the EC's general rules and mechanisms, Thatcher instead was anxious to ensure a substantive improvement of Britain's position whatever the political cost in Britain's relations with its EC partners. As she later reflected in her memoirs, the importance of the budget issue seemed such that it required 'the use of diplomatic tactics which many people thought less than diplomatic'.[30]

High-Level Diplomacy as Catalyst for Bilateral Tensions

Over the following months, British and German positions gradually hardened, reflected not least in Thatcher's and Schmidt' increasingly antagonistic high-level diplomacy. At the June 1979 European Council, Thatcher's demand of a 'broad balance' in Britain's budget contributions and aggressive lobbying for her case had left a bitter aftertaste with many of her counterparts. To Thatcher, it seemed like the battle lines had finally been drawn. It 'had proved very difficult to get the other Member States to recognise that the United Kingdom had been badly treated over the Community Budget', she told Cabinet afterwards, and Britain 'faced a real battle if we were to secure an

---

[28] TNA/PREM19/58, No. 10 Record of Conversation (MT-Chancellor Schmidt), 10 May 1979.
[29] TNA/PREM19/58, Record of PM's Discussions with Chancellor Schmidt in plenary session, 11 May 1979.
[30] Thatcher, *Downing Street Years*, 60.

adequate response from the rest of the Community'.[31] This confrontational attitude was fuelled further by widespread British impressions that the other EC member-states were not taking Britain's demands seriously enough. In Cabinet, for example, the Chancellor of the Exchequer Geoffrey Howe claimed that there was 'no disposition' amongst other EC member-states 'to recognise how substantial and urgent' the problem was, and that 'an extremely tough negotiation was therefore in prospect'.[32] Such sabre-rattling both reflected and aggravated public opinion: a survey in November 1979 showed that 55 per cent of those polled thought that Thatcher's demand of a broad balance was 'about right', and 40 per cent even claimed that Britain should leave the EC altogether if Thatcher did not secure an acceptable reduction of Britain's budget contributions.[33] On the other side of the Channel, however, the hardening of the British position only served to intensify fears of a prolonged intra-EC crisis. While the Germans generally accepted Britain's grievances as legitimate, they were nonetheless appalled by the confrontational way in which it went about securing its demands. The demand of a 'broad balance' in particular was regarded as being incompatible with the EC's political imperatives and general system of expenditure, and the British emphasis on the 'justice' of its case seemed to ignore the fact that most other member-states actually benefitted heavily from the EC's system of financing.[34]

The talks between Schmidt and Thatcher at the British–German consultations of 30–31 October 1979 illustrate how far the gap between British and German positions had widened over the summer. Thatcher started off by linking the budget question to her radical domestic reform agenda, which faced quite significant backlashes at the time. The British government 'was having to cut expenditure on a number of socially important programmes: for example, spending on housing would be reduced by £700 m in 1980 and the education programme by over £300 m', she emphasised; and public opposition to these cuts 'was made much stronger when people saw an outflow of £1,000 m' to the EC. In light of such domestic pressures, Thatcher ruled out any

---

[31] TNA/CAB128/66, CC (79) 8th Conclusions, 5 July 1979.
[32] TNA/CAB128/66, CC (79) 17th Conclusions, 18 October 1979.
[33] Margaret Thatcher Archive, Churchill College, Cambridge (henceforward: THCR), 2-11-9-14, ITN Opinion Poll, 28 November 1979.
[34] B136/17112, Problem der Britischen Nettobelastung, 23 October 1979.

High-Level Diplomacy as Catalyst   159

compromise. It was 'essential that Britain should get satisfaction', she continued, 'There could be no half measures. There had to be a broad balance'.[35] Confronted by such a maximalist approach, Schmidt responded by trying to impress on Thatcher the formidable obstacles to any solution in their second meeting after lunch. 'It was not so much a question of what was fair and unfair', he claimed, 'but of adopting the right psychological approach ... the other Governments would need to be able to show that they had got something out of whatever changes were agreed: they had their publics and Parliaments to think about as well'. When Thatcher appeared unmoved, Schmidt responded brusquely. '[I]f Britain failed to persuade her friends she would have to leave the Community', he exclaimed, and if the British attitude was 'one of "take-it-or-leave-it", the other members might well say leave it'. Crucially, he added that Germany 'could not and would not fight with the French on the question'.[36]

It was a frank and candid exchange, but one that exacerbated rather than diminished tensions. Having previously lobbied other EC member-states to take British demands seriously,[37] Schmidt became openly critical of the British approach in the aftermath of the meeting. 'PM Thatcher has shown no readiness for compromises whatsoever', he told the Dutch PM van Agt on 7 November 1979, predicting a major 'clash' at the upcoming European Council at Dublin.[38] Thatcher's hard-line position also stimulated some early doubts over Britain's more general commitment to its European partners. A few weeks later Schmidt unburdened himself for over an hour to the British Ambassador to Germany at a post-dinner conversation. 'Britain's performance in the Community to date ever since we [Britain] had joined seven years ago had disappointed all her friends', Schmidt proclaimed according to the

---

[35] TNA/PREM19/59, Record of discussion between PM Thatcher and Chancellor Schmidt (11.15h), 31 October 1979.

[36] TNA/PREM19/59, Record of discussion between PM and Chancellor Schmidt (15.30h), 31 October 1979. Also, *AAPD 1979*, Doc. Nr. 314, Gespräch des Bundeskanzlers Schmidt mit Premierministerin Thatcher, 31 October 1979.

[37] See, for example, Schmidt's various conversations with the French PM Barre or the Italian PM Cossiga. *AAPD 1979*, Doc. Nr. 157, Gespräch des BK Schmidt mit Ministerpräsident Barre, 1 June 1979; *AAPD 1979*, Doc. Nr. 284, Gespräch des BK Schmidt mit Ministerpräsident Barre, 1 October 1979; *AAPD 1979*, Doc. Nr. 288, Gespräch BK Schmidt mit Ministerpräsident Cossiga, 9 October 1979.

[38] *AAPD 1979*, Doc. Nr. 322, Telefongespräch des BK Schmidt mit Ministerpräsident van Agt, 7 November 1979.

British record, adding that Britain had 'no vision of what we wanted the Community to be. Instead we had spent six years or more haggling like Italians for a little bit here and a little bit there. This was no way for a country like Britain to act'.[39] It was a narrative that would become very familiar over subsequent months, but Schmidt's calculated ramblings failed to have any mediating effects in Britain. Prior to the European Council at Dublin on 29–30 November 1979, the British cabinet agreed that Thatcher 'should not settle ... unless we were offered something very close to what we had asked for', even if this meant provoking a major row between the EC leaders. 'There could be no doubt that the Community would face a crisis', Thatcher concluded belligerently, 'which our partners would welcome no more than we should, if this problem were not speedily resolved'.[40]

The diplomatic fallout at the subsequent Council thus came to no surprise to either the British or the Germans. Adopting a hard-line position from the very beginning, Thatcher insisted on achieving a broad balance throughout the discussions – partly because of the way in which domestic pressures had by that stage built up in Britain, but primarily because she felt so strongly about the issue herself.[41] In response, the other EC leaders stressed that any additional expenses to help Britain had to be economically 'justifiable' to their own publics, and that the EC's own resources principle could not be touched. The German record afterwards described the basic dynamics at the Council as an 'antagonism between Thatcher and the other members'.[42] As Commission President Roy Jenkins recalled in his diary, Schmidt got 'frightfully bored and pretended ... to go to sleep', and the Danish PM Jorgensen 'at times behav[ed] like a little street urchin calling out insults'.[43] When Thatcher rejected a Franco–German offer to modify the 1975 'corrective mechanism' which would have

---

[39] TNA/PREM19/762, Bonn to Carrington, 20 November 1979.

[40] TNA/CAB128/66, CC (79), 23rd Conclusions, 28 November 1979.

[41] Unfortunately, Thatcher's handwritten speech notes and a short German debrief are the only records available from this particular Council, since the British apparently did not produce one of their usually very detailed records this time. See THCR1/17/58, Speech to Dublin Council, 30 November 1979; *AAPD 1979*, Doc. Nr. 362, Runderlass des Vortragenden Legationsrats I. Klasse Ellerkmann, 5 December 1979.

[42] *AAPD 1979*, Doc. Nr. 362, Runderlass des Vortragenden Legationsrats I. Klasse Ellerkmann, 5 December 1979.

[43] Diary Entry for 29 November 1979, in Jenkins, *European Diary*, 529.

The Conflation of the Budget Issue 161

amounted to a reduction of roughly a third of Britain's budget contribution,[44] Schmidt and Giscard even refused to discuss the issue again unless Thatcher indicated her eventual readiness to compromise, which she did only grudgingly and after repeated urgings by Carrington.[45] Afterwards, she belligerently told the press that accepting 'a third of a loaf when you are asking for a whole loaf' was 'no settlement of a problem', and that Britain was 'not asking for a penny piece of Community money' but only 'for a very large amount of our own money back'.[46] At a subsequent Cabinet meeting, Thatcher even suggested that Britain might now have to withhold parts of the UK's budget contribution, or engage 'in systematic obstruction' to impress the seriousness of its demands on its EC partners.[47] In Germany, by contrast, Thatcher was portrayed as isolated and out-of-touch, with the headline of the *Süddeutsche Zeitung* reading 'Dublin like Dunkirk'.[48] By the end of 1979, the British budgetary question had propelled from what could have been a seemingly minor readjustment to EC financing mechanisms into a major disruption of the British–German relationship; triggered not least by Thatcher's uncompromising high-level diplomacy with Schmidt.

The Conflation of the Budget Issue and the Afghanistan Crisis

The virulent rows over the budget also triggered more general German doubts over Britain's commitment to cooperation with its West European allies in non-EC matters as well. Though the Conservatives had been unambiguous about their pro-EC stance during their election campaign, the new PM Margaret Thatcher was known to be a prominent advocate of the Anglo-American 'special' relationship, as well as somebody who appeared significantly more sceptical about détente than her counterparts Giscard d'Estaing and Schmidt. Indeed, Thatcher came into office with the firm conviction that the West was in

[44] *AAPD 1979*, Doc. Nr. 362, Runderlass des Vortragenden Legationsrats I. Klasse Ellerkmann, 5 December 1979.
[45] Diary Entry for 30 November 1979, in Jenkins, *European Diary*, 531.
[46] TNA/PREM19/52, Transcript of press conference given by PM Thatcher, 30 November 1979.
[47] TNA/CAB128/66, CC (79) 24th Conclusions, 6 December 1979.
[48] *Süddeutsche Zeitung*, 1 December 1979. For more press coverage, see TNA/PREM19/52, Bonn to FCO, 1 December 1979.

retreat against a resurgent Soviet Union, and that détente had contributed significantly to the seemingly shifting power balance between East and West.[49] 'By the late 1970s', she reflected hyperbolically in her memoirs, 'the US, Britain and our European allies were faced by a Soviet Union [in an] aggressive phase. We were neither psychologically, nor militarily, nor economically in the shape to resist it'.[50] In Washington, the Carter administration welcomed Thatcher's stronger rhetoric, but it was not blind to the structural pressures drawing Britain into the European camp either. In internal evaluations of Thatcher's election victory, the Americans estimated that Thatcher, though taking 'a more sceptical view of détente' and advocating the 'strongest possible' transatlantic relationship, was at the same time likely to 'cooperate more closely with Europe' than the previous Callaghan government had done.[51] These US views matched initial German estimations that Britain would probably steer a middle course between the United States and the West Europeans in East–West relations.[52]

On 25 December 1979, the Soviet invasion of Afghanistan put the new British government's position in the transatlantic alliance to the test, exposing underlying rifts not only between the United States and Europe but also between the West European allies themselves.[53] Initial reactions differed starkly. The American President Jimmy Carter unilaterally called for tough economic sanctions against the Soviet Union

---

[49] Moore, *Not For Turning*, 495–9. For Thatcher's attachment to the Anglo–American relationship more generally, see Gamble, 'Europe and America', 218–33; Vinen, 'Thatcherism and the Cold War', 199–217. An excellent new revisionist interpretation is R. Aldous, *Reagan and Thatcher* (London: W.W. Norton & Company, 2012).

[50] Thatcher, *Downing Street Years*, 9.

[51] JCL, NLC-6-77-2-8-1, Thoughts on Thatcher: Foreign Policy Implications of the Tory Triumph, undated.

[52] 1/HSAA006737, Brief: Deutsch-britische Konsultationen, 9 May 1979.

[53] For the growing literature on the Afghanistan crisis, see G. Grasselli, *British and American Responses to the Soviet Invasion of Afghanistan* (Aldershot: Dartmouth, 1996); A. Bresselau von Bressensdorf, *Frieden durch Kommunikation: Das System Genscher und die Entspannungspolitik im Zweiten Kalten Krieg 1979–1982/83* (Munich: De Gruyter Oldenbourg, 2015), 99–195; Spohr, *Global Chancellor*, 110–22; D. J. Lahey, 'The Thatcher Government's Response to the Soviet Invasion of Afghanistan, 1979–1980', *Cold War History* 13 (2013), 21–42; N. E. Sarantakes, *Dropping the Torch: Jimmy Carter, the Olympic Boycott and the Cold War* (New York, NY and Cambridge: Cambridge University Press, 2011).

The Conflation of the Budget Issue

163

in a television address on 4 January 1980, including a ban on technology exports and a grain embargo.[54] This was supported vigorously by the incensed Margaret Thatcher, who similarly condemned the Soviet invasion sharply and offered rigorous diplomatic support to the United States.[55] By contrast, the reactions of other West European states were more restrained. The Germans in particular were caught between the conflicting needs of wanting to preserve inner-European détente on the one hand, and having to display solidarity with the United States on the other.[56] They therefore resorted to a wait-and-see strategy, only announcing their own positions after trying to reach unanimous agreement with their allies in multilateral consultations. The French reaction was predictably more robust: dismayed by Carter's unilateral announcement of the sanctions and traditionally sceptical towards concerted actions under US leadership, France simply refused to follow the American call and stated publicly that the Afghanistan issue should not jeopardise the more general process of East–West détente.[57]

Over the following weeks, the American proposal for a potential Western boycott of the 1980 Moscow Olympics put these different positions into the public limelight. Thatcher, who told Foreign Secretary Carrington that a Western withdrawal from the games was the one action that would 'hurt the Soviet Government most', lobbied strongly for the boycott, even asking Cabinet to consider the issue prior to Carter's public announcement.[58] But the Germans were less than enthusiastic: not only did they believe that the boycott threat had little diplomatic value in that it left the Soviets no room for manoeuvre short of complete withdrawal, but Carter's unilateral announcement had also aroused familiar fears that German interests were yet again

---

[54] Jimmy Carter, Address to the Nation on the Soviet Invasion of Afghanistan, 4 January 1980: www.presidency.ucsb.edu/ws/?pid=32911 [accessed on 13 June 2018].

[55] Lahey, 'Thatcher Government's Response', 21–2.

[56] B136/17114, AA: Die sowjetische Intervention in Afghanistan und ihre Auswirkungen auf das Ost-West-Verhältnis, 21 February 1980; B136/17114, Wirtschaftssanktionen gegenüber der Sowjetunion, 21 November 1980.

[57] *AAPD 1980*, Doc. Nr., 11, Französische Haltung zum sowjetischen Einmarsch in Afghanistan, 12 January 1980.

[58] TNA/PREM19/135, Record of Conversation Thatcher–Carrington, 8 January 1980; TNA/CAB128/67, CC (80) 2nd Conclusions, 17 January 1980. See also P. Corthorn, 'The Cold War and British Debates over the Boycott of the 1980 Moscow Olympics', *Cold War History*, 13/1 (2013), 43–66; Lahey, 'Thatcher Government's Response', 36–9.

overlooked and ignored by the US.[59] The French position was again more straight-forward: France would continue to pursue its policies towards the Soviet Union independently as a sovereign nation, Paris declared in the aftermath of Carter's announcement, and therefore planned to attend the Olympic games as part of its more general efforts towards the relaxation of East–West tensions and détente.[60]

Over subsequent months, these debates took an ironic turn: the political autonomy of Britain's Olympic committee meant that British athletes ultimately ended up attending the Olympics against their governments' recommendation, whereas American and German athletes heeded their governments' advice and stayed at home. In early 1980, however, the diplomatic confusion and disarray following Carter's proposal further exacerbated the sense of crises already hanging over the British–German relationship as a result of the budget problem in early 1980. From the German perspective, the two crises seemed intimately connected, in that the intra-EC disputes were seen to reflect a more general British lack of commitment to its West European partners. It was therefore feared that the budget question could jeopardize the more general cohesiveness and unity of the West Europeans on the wider international stage. If the 'lingering crisis' over the budget question continued, a German assessment of the situation concluded in late January 1980, then Britain might eventually 'play the Atlantic card and move closer to the United States. Denmark and perhaps the Netherlands might follow – not a good omen for the Community's cohesion'.[61] These views by German officials were shared by Schmidt himself, who feared that an Anglo–French rift over the budget might exacerbate Britain and France's more general differences over Afghanistan and the East–West relationship. Already in October 1979, Schmidt had warned Thatcher that 'a clash between the United Kingdom and France' over the budget had to be avoided by all means 'in view of the present world situation. If ever the Community broke up, the

---

[59] For example, Schmidt complained heavily in an off-the-record discussion with journalists that he had received only seven hours advance notice on the announcement of the boycott. See PHSA/EA, 17.1.-21.2.1980, Hintergrundgespräch (Off-The-Record) mit Chefredakteuren, 24 January 1980. For the general German position, B136/17114, Olympische Sommerspiele 1980 in Moskau, February 1980 (no exact date given).

[60] Bresselau von Bressensdorf, *Frieden durch Kommunikation*, 127.

[61] 1/HSAA008882, Brief: Besuch Roy Jenkins, 29 January 1980.

The Conflation of the Budget Issue

Soviet Union would pick its members off piece-meal'.[62] Afghanistan now added a sense of urgency to such fears. As he candidly put it to the German President Carstens in February 1980, the danger of a prolonged crisis over Afghanistan was that Western Europe might eventually 'fall apart' on the opposite ends of London and Paris.[63]

Although aware of such German concerns, the British rejected any interlinkage between the budget issue and other areas of bilateral cooperation, treating them as two completely unrelated and separate issues. If anything, they saw the Afghanistan crisis as strengthening their hand over the budget. As Lord Privy Seal Ian Gilmour reported to Cabinet after his tour of European capitals in January 1980, everybody on the Continent seemed 'anxious, in light of the worsening of East–West relations, to get the Community budget out of the way as soon as possible'.[64] This was widely seen as a major opportunity to impress on Britain's EC partners the seriousness of the budget problem. Even Foreign Secretary Carrington did not shy away from occasional attempts at blackmailing the Germans on the matter, telling Genscher on 27 February 1980 how the budget crises might eventually lead to a British withdrawal from the EC. In such a situation, Carrington mused, Britain would find it 'difficult to continue with our contribution to NATO, or with BOAR. We would simply not have the money, and would find ourselves on a downward escalator. We would then be talking, not just of a bust-up of the EEC, but of the NATO alliance too. The only gainer would be the Soviet Union'.[65] But such British threats only served to antagonise the Germans further, who regarded Britain's continuing hard-line position on the budget as a cynical prioritisation of what they still regarded as a minor issue in domestic politics at a time of resurgent East–West crises. Schmidt, for example, told Carrington in a similar conversation that the 'global consequences' of the UK leaving the EC because of the budget question were simply 'too big a risk' to even be contemplated, and the British should therefore just 'leave it alone' if no solution could be found.[66]

---

[62] TNA/PREM19/59, Record of discussion between PM and Chancellor Schmidt (11.15h), 31 October 1979.

[63] 1/HSAA008888, Ihr Gespräch mit dem Bundespräsidenten, 13 February 1980.

[64] TNA/CAB128/66, CC (80) 3rd Conclusions, 24 January 1980.

[65] TNA/FCO98/882, Lord Carrington's meeting with Genscher, 27 February 1980.

[66] TNA/FCO98/882, Record of Meeting between Carrington and Schmidt, 26 February 1980.

By early 1980, the dual crises over Afghanistan and the budget had thus become highly conflated from a German perspective, resulting in a damning verdict on Britain's more general attitudes towards its West European partners. This applies in particular to Schmidt, whose judgement on Britain was also affected by his now frequently gloomy and fatalistic outlook on the world situation. During his February 1980 meeting with Carrington, for example, the British delegation noted how Schmidt had spent much of it 'complaining about President Carter' whom he described as completely 'unpredictable', and Carrington himself appeared struck afterwards by 'how ill-briefed the Chancellor seemed'.[67] As the British told the Americans afterwards, Schmidt had appeared 'reasonable and constructive on the surface, but surging with "Teutonic fumes" beneath'.[68] It matched the impressions of EC Commission President Roy Jenkins, who had seen Schmidt two weeks earlier and similarly described him as 'in a worried and discursive mood'. Schmidt, as Jenkins told Carrington afterwards, had 'spoken in pessimistic, almost apocalyptic, terms' about the world situation, claiming that there was 'a smell of 1914 in the air' and 'at least a 20% chance of another world war'.[69] The widespread impression of Schmidt in early 1980 was thus one of an increasingly erratic and somewhat morose German Chancellor, some of which observers attributed to a deterioration of Schmidt's health.[70] Indeed, we now know that Schmidt frequently fainted at the time as a result of serious thyroid and heart problems; problems that were partially remedied when he was fitted a pacemaker in October 1981.[71]

All of this may well have affected his personal judgement of Britain, as Schmidt had by now concluded that the budget issue was merely one symptom of a more general British reluctance to cooperate fully with its West European partners. The main expression of these views can be found in Schmidt's repeated urgings for Britain to join the EMS, which he still regarded as the key building bloc of a strong and more independent

[67] TNA/CAB193/271/2, Secretary of State's Meeting with Chancellor Schmidt, 25 February 1980.
[68] JCL, NSA, Brzezinski Material, President's Daily Report File, Box 14, Situation Room to Brzezinski, 29 February 1980.
[69] TNA/CAB193/271/2, Secretary of State's Discussion with the President of the European Commission, 6 February 1980.
[70] JCL, NSA, Brzezinski Material, President's Daily Report File, Box 14, Situation Room to Brzezinski, 29 February 1980.
[71] *New York Times*, 14 October 1981; *Der Spiegel*, 19 October 1981.

Western Europe on the global stage. After his February 1980 meeting with Schmidt, for example, Commission President Jenkins told Carrington how the German Chancellor had appeared 'critical of the British Government's European policies generally' by suggesting that Britain's 'failure' to join the EMS illustrated that they were 'not at the heart committed Europeans'.[72] It was a line Schmidt repeated in a subsequent conversation with Carrington. The British simply 'could not conceive of their currency being tied to that of other countries', he ranted; it showed that Britain 'had an insular monetary policy, and a psychological problem about the EMS'.[73] Schmidt's apparent exasperation with the British at the time stretched far beyond EC matters: when Carrington told him that the autonomy of the British Olympic Committee meant that Britain would likely be attending the 1980 Moscow Games against the government's recommendation, Schmidt grimly replied that 'this served [the British] right for coming out too quickly in support of the Americans'.[74] Less than a year after Thatcher's election, Britain's stake in the bilateral relationship seemed alarmingly low, set against the background of a dramatically worsening East–West climate.

Bilateral Rapprochement over Afghanistan

While bilateral tensions over the EC budget clearly affected Schmidt's judgement on British attitudes towards the Afghanistan crisis, at the heart of British–German differences were the two countries' conflicting political and strategical outlooks on East–West détente. This is particularly evident at the highest diplomatic level, where Schmidt's desire to preserve inner-European détente against a worsening superpower relationship collided with Thatcher's more assertive stance against the Soviet Union. In late February 1980, the two leaders clashed heavily over the appropriate European response to Afghanistan in a long and candid personal discussion. The meeting started with Schmidt going on yet another lengthy rant about Carter's unreliability and unpredictability. The United States 'would not always be able to find sufficient people who were prepared to clap their hands on hearing the latest

---

[72] TNA/CAB193/271/2, Secretary of State's Discussion with the President of the European Commission, 6 February 1980.
[73] TNA/FCO98/882, Record of Meeting between Carrington and Schmidt, 26 February 1980.
[74] Ibid.

American policy decisions on the radio', he exclaimed, and the strategy of 'punishing the Russians' was an 'erroneous idea'. In his eyes, the 'need for the Russians to save face had to be borne in mind. There should be no pinpricking and no sabre rattling'. The Olympic boycott was a 'pinprick', and he also 'deeply resented' the line the US administration had taken on the issue of economic sanctions.[75] Thatcher, in turn, strongly defended American actions, emphasising her personal conviction that the Olympic boycott was 'the best way to bring home to the Soviet people the gravity of what had occurred'. She also shifted the blame for the West's haphazard crisis management to the West Europeans, professing to have been 'bitterly disappointed by the slowness with which the other members of the Nine had acted' in devising a common European response.[76] It was a frank exchange of views that may have served to clear the air somewhat, but it clearly did not signify any bilateral rapprochement.

In substance, however, the British position was actually much closer to the German one than it appeared on the surface, as Thatcher's personal instincts stood at odds with the structural realities of Britain's geostrategic and economic anchoring in Western Europe. As early as 10 January 1980, various members of the British Cabinet urged Thatcher for caution in her public anti-Soviet rhetoric, highlighting how Britain was 'much more exposed than her main allies to serious economic damage resulting from sanctions or other political measures affecting international trade'.[77] There was also some deeply ingrained intellectual opposition to the principle of economic sanctions in Whitehall, given both Britain's recent experiences with Rhodesia and its more long-term history as a global trading nation with a GNP share of overseas trade still amounting to 30 per cent.[78] But even more important was the inescapable truth that Britain's own security ultimately depended on the strength and vitality of the transatlantic alliance, which made the British fear an open rift between the United States and other West Europeans like Germany. Thatcher's strong public support of the American position was widely seen to aggravate such tensions. Less than three weeks after the Soviet invasion, for example, the British Ambassador to Paris warned in a diplomatic dispatch about

[75] TNA/PREM19/472, Partial Record of a Meeting between PM and Chancellor of FRG, 25 February 1980.
[76] Ibid.   [77] TNA/CAB128/67, CC (80) 1st Conclusions, 10 January 1980.
[78] Lahey, 'Thatcher Government's Response', 28–9.

Bilateral Rapprochement over Afghanistan   169

the growing gap 'between Britain on the one hand and France and Germany on the other', pointing out that it offered the French an unwelcome opportunity 'to argue that Britain is inherently un-European and always lines up first with the USA'.[79]

As Foreign Secretary, Lord Carrington was more sensitive towards these dynamics than Thatcher, and as a result consciously sought to foster a joint West European position on Afghanistan from the very beginning of the crisis by effectively utilising bilateral and multilateral consultation mechanisms including EPC.[80] In January 1980, Carrington thus embarked upon a wide-ranging tour of the Middle East, in line with European efforts to focus on the non-aligned countries as part of the Euro-Arab dialogue.[81] His motives were twofold: to realign the European strategy more closely with that of the United States, and to prop up British influence in European policy-making more generally by balancing France's policy of independence with a British strategy of dialogue and multilateralism. This mirrored the efforts of the German Foreign Minister Genscher, who similarly sought to keep open channels of communication with the Eastern bloc and divert US calls for economic sanctions.[82] British activism towards fostering a joint European position on lower diplomatic levels did not escape German attention. As the *Bundeskanzleramt* observed in February 1980, Britain's 'readiness to work together' with the West European allies had been 'confirmed again and again during EPC meetings', with Carrington in particular having turned into 'a champion of a joint European position'.[83] Even Washington noted the emergence of such an increasingly homogenous European position, albeit with much dismay. The West Europeans 'have in effect, done nothing in their bilateral relations with the Soviets to show their displeasure and concern over the invasion of Afghanistan', Carter's

[79] TNA/PREM19/135, Paris to FCO, 10 January 1980.
[80] For one of Carrington's first efforts, see TNA/PREM19/135, Carrington message to French and German foreign ministers, 7 January 1980. See also the strategic advice by the Paris Embassy to that effect, TNA/PREM19/135, Paris to FCO, 10 January 1980.
[81] For Carrington's report of his tour, see TNA/PREM19/135, Minute: Afghanistan, 19 January 1980.
[82] For an excellent analysis of the interplay between Carrington and Genscher, see Bresselau von Bressensdorf, *Frieden durch Kommunikation*, 139–42.
[83] B136/17114, Elemente für ein Gespräch über die britische Stellung in Westeuropa, 21 February 1980.

National Security Adviser Brzezinski complained in March 1980, noting that Schmidt had now made clear that he would do 'nothing other than stiffen COCOM [the Coordinating Committee for Multilateral Export Controls]' and reluctantly support the Olympic boycott. Yet, Brzezinski also added that '[n]o other European will do more than Schmidt, and most will do less'.[84] This also applied to Britain. While the United Kingdom had 'taken a strong public lead in the crisis', Brzezinski wrote to Carter, it had resisted 'any of our proposals which would cost money and recently through its Afghanistan neutralization proposal, the UK has been distancing itself more from the US and seeking to return to the EC fold'.[85]

By March 1980, Britain and Germany had thus eventually managed to come up with a coordinated position on Afghanistan, even though this had been the result of a shaky and uneven process. Yet, the bilateral rapprochement driven largely by the foreign ministers Carrington and Genscher eventually filtered through to the highest level as well. During the British–German consultations in March 1980, Thatcher and Schmidt suddenly found themselves in almost complete agreement over Afghanistan, even rejecting Carter's call for a special NATO summit by sending identical letters to the US President afterwards.[86] Apart from Thatcher's growing appreciation of the political and economic constraints on Britain's international position, the frequent British–German ministerial and official contacts clearly helped shape British views. In Washington, for example, Deputy National Security Adviser David Aaron mused that the Europeans seemed to have a 'distinct advantage over us in that they now meet quite frequently and regularly', one result being that 'even Maggie Thatcher [was] drifting toward the ambivalent continental European position on Afghanistan'.[87]

The closeness of British and German positions, however, was little noticed outside the inner circle of diplomats and experts, not least because of the very different public representations of the transatlantic relationship in both countries. Whereas Thatcher continued to

[84] JCL, NLC-17-131-4-2-2, Brzezinski to President, 18 March 1980.
[85] JCL, NLC-23-8-6-10-1, Brzezinski to President, 17 March 1980.
[86] TNA/PREM19/472, Record of a discussion between PM and FRG Chancellor, 27 March 1980; JCL, NLC-132-122-9-8-2, Schmidt to Carter, 27 March 1980; Thatcher to Carter, 27 March 1980.
[87] JCL, NLC-133-218-4-27-9, Aaron to President, 5 April 1980.

Bilateral Rapprochement over Afghanistan 171

emphasise her personal attachment to the Anglo–American relationship in strong terms, Schmidt had by now acquired a reputation for being US President Carter's most vocal European critic, culminating in a famously hostile US–German bilateral on the margins of the G7 meeting in June 1980.[88] The contrast with Britain could hardly have been greater: whereas the British were supportive of US policies in public but critical behind closed doors, almost the reverse was the case in Germany. Indeed, Schmidt's erratic handling of Carter triggered frequent complaints by some German ministers and officials who feared the negative impact of Schmidt's personal diplomacy on the wider transatlantic relationship. 'Margaret Thatcher makes loud noises of support for Carter – but she doesn't come through for him like we do', a German source allegedly close to Schmidt complained in the *US News & World Report* in July 1980:

While we went along on sanctions against Iran, the British diluted their sanctions. Mrs. Thatcher also cheered Carter on the Olympics boycott. But the British and the French athletes will be going to Moscow while our athletes, like the Americans, will be staying at home. Then people in Washington started to get hysterical about our Chancellor going to Moscow. What you Americans should remember is this: We are still the best boys in your class.[89]

But if some Germans were annoyed by the alleged lack of US appreciation for their support, the British were even more disheartened by the lack of recognition their constructive and proactive role within EPC received from the other West Europeans. Whatever British efforts to foster a joint European position on Afghanistan behind the scenes, the public perception was still one of a joint Franco–German lead. Indeed, when the EPC launched its widely noticed 'neutralization'

---

[88] The American record describes how Schmidt at one point 'responded that one should be prepared to be criticised and that "I can fight." Brzezinski responded that the fight can be reciprocal and that there are those on the U.S. side who know how to do that too', an exchange after which Carter indicated 'with the wave of his hand . . . that he thought it would be better to cool the situation'. Carter later annotated that the record was 'accurate enough', and that 'Helmut's ok now – for a while'. Copy in MTA, Carter-Schmidt memcon, 21 June 1980: www.margaretthatcher.org/document/110482 [accessed on 13 June 2018]. See also Carter's diary entries for 20–1 June 1980, in Carter, *White House Diary*, 439, and Brzezinski, *Power and Principle*, 309–10.

[89] *U.S. News & World Report*, 7 July 1980. Copy in LoC, Manuscript Division, Henry Brandon Papers, Box 34: Reference File.

proposal on Afghanistan on 19 February 1980 that was largely due to Carrington's initiative, the British Foreign Secretary afterwards even had to deny rumours that the proposal had actually been put forward by Schmidt and Giscard in the first place.[90] Behind the scenes, France had indeed become concerned that British activism might jeopardize their own leadership role of the European bloc. It thus sought to delay and obstruct many of Carrington's more ambitious proposals, starting already during and immediately after the EPC's Rome Meeting in February 1980.[91] In turn, the Germans – reluctantly but perhaps inevitably – concluded that no European scheme would succeed without French backing, and thus frequently fell in line with the French position. On 26 February 1980, for example, Carrington and Genscher had agreed to press ahead quickly with a joint proposal in EPC, only for the British to find out a few days later that the Germans had changed course and were now supporting the French position.[92] The British were outraged by the German diplomatic snub, and the FCO suggested to tell the Germans in no uncertain terms that 'tripartite consultation becomes less valuable if one of the Three is not warned in advance that the other two have concerted a different line in private'.[93]

Quite apart from Franco–German duplicity, however, the episode also reveals the strong intellectual interlinkage between the two seemingly separate issues of the EC budget and much bigger questions of Europe's role in the international arena. Britain's diplomatic behaviour over the EC budget question, as seen above, had strongly reinforced lingering German doubts over Britain's more general commitment to genuine cooperation with its European partners, and these shaped German perceptions of British behaviour within the transatlantic alliance as well, in spite of British efforts to separate the two arenas as much as possible. Only occasionally did British foreign policy-makers grasp the interlinkage of these two areas of bilateral cooperation in German mindsets. Perhaps most attuned to the German position was the head of the FCO's West European department David Gladstone, who had spent four years as First Secretary at the British Embassy in Bonn during the

---

[90] *Der Spiegel*, 25 February 1980.
[91] *AAPD 1980*, Doc. Nr. 57, 93. Politisches Komitee am 12/13.2. sowie 37. Ministertreffen am 19.2. in Rom, 21 February 1980.
[92] TNA/FCO98/946, Braithwaite to Maitland, Tripartite Consultations, 3 March 1980.
[93] TNA/FCO98/946, Fithert to Fergusson, 29 February 1980; ibid.

1960s and later served as Political Adviser and Head of Chancery in Berlin from 1976 to 1979. 'At present the Germans frankly regard us as still insufficiently committed to the Community', he commented on the EPC episode, and these feelings were 'bound, if only subconsciously, to rub off on their attitude towards our membership of the inner circle'. France and Germany had been 'through fire together on more than one occasion', he concluded, and 'neither Schmidt nor Giscard will accept us as full partners until we have been through a little fire too: that is no doubt one consideration underlying Schmidt's repeated attempts to persuade us to prove our manhood by joining the EMS'.[94] Indeed, Britain and Germany may have mended forces over Afghanistan, but they remained at loggerheads over the budget issue. This was bound to influence the more general diplomatic climate and effectiveness of the bilateral relationship, at least from the German perspective.

Continuing Divisions over the Budget

The early months of 1980 may have seen British–German rapprochement within the transatlantic alliance, but both sides continued to stick to their maximalist positions over the EC budget. In February 1980, Thatcher raised the stakes even further by publicly musing in a television interview that Britain might be forced to withhold its contributions to the EC budget if no deal could be done — a statement that was widely noted and picked up by the German press.[95] Neither was there any rapprochement on the highest level, as Schmidt's and Thatcher's talks on the budget in February 1980 again revealed a familiar picture: Schmidt urged Thatcher to approach the issue more consensually and from a communitarian viewpoint, perhaps by tying the issue to CAP reform or drawing up a package deal with steel and fisheries; Thatcher, in turn, wondered 'whether the difficulty lay in the failure of anyone so far to come up with the right scheme for solving the problem or whether it was a question of the unwillingness of the other members to pay the bill'.[96] At the press conference

[94] TNA/FCO98/946, Gladstone to Fergusson, Tripartite Consultations, 4 March 1980.
[95] THCR 5-2-7, German Reaction to Thatcher Panorama Interview, 29 February 1980.
[96] TNA/PREM19/223, Partial record of discussion between PM and Schmidt, 25 February 1980.

afterwards, Schmidt described the meeting as 'frank' rather than friendly, a comment that was quickly picked up by both the British and German press and which forced Thatcher to stress in Cabinet that the discussions had actually been 'successful . . . contrary to newspaper reports'.[97]

By March 1980, there was thus a clear sense of crisis hanging over the bilateral relationship. At the British–German consultations, the two leaders again clashed heavily over the issue. 'The feeling that the UK was not getting an equitable deal was getting stronger and stronger', Thatcher exclaimed in her talks with Schmidt, pointing out that 120 Conservative backbenchers had just signed a motion for withholding Britain's VAT contribution if a deal could not be done. Schmidt, in turn, kept insisting that any deal would involve real financial sacrifices from other member-states, and that Britain therefore had to signal its eventual readiness to compromise, whatever the intellectual merits of the UK's case. It would simply be 'impossible', he told Thatcher, 'for any of the other Heads of Government, especially himself and President Giscard, to return home empty-handed, saying that they had agreed to pay more to the Community budget in order to help Britain. There had to be a semblance of a quid pro quo'.[98] Towards the end of the meeting, he almost pleaded with Thatcher that all member-states should be able to leave 'the battle scene with an equal feeling of dissatisfaction. If that did not happen and one country was able to emerge claiming a victory, the compromise that had been achieved would not be workable'. But Thatcher remained unwavering, claiming that she was 'not so certain that the other members of the Community really grasped her difficulty'. Nonetheless, there was some indication of slight movements in the British position, with Thatcher signalling a certain readiness to be a 'small net contributor' and claiming that the desire to solve all problems on their own merits did not preclude them 'being solved within the same time scale'.[99]

Thatcher herself may have appeared uncompromising, but there was clearly some movement on lower diplomatic levels. Already in January 1980, EC Commission President Roy Jenkins had suggested

---

[97] TNA/CAB128/67, CC (80) 8th Conclusions, 28 February 1980; *The Times*, 26 February 1980.

[98] TNA/PREM19/225, Meeting between PM and Chancellor Schmidt, 28 March 1980.

[99] Ibid.

Continuing Divisions over the Budget 175

in conversation with Schmidt that one solution might be to circumvent Thatcher by working primarily with Carrington, hoping that the Foreign Secretary might be more attuned to the political realities within the EC than his PM.[100] Lord Privy Seal Ian Gilmour too appeared eager to foster some compromise, hinting in conversation with the German Finance Minister Hans Matthöfer as early as January 1980 that Britain might be prepared to remain a small net contributor to the EC budget.[101] In Germany, the State Secretary for EC affairs Klaus von Dohnanyi similarly seemed anxious to make progress, meeting up repeatedly with his British counterparts and suggesting various technical mechanisms and possibilities.[102] Yet, the budget issue remained primarily a political one and could only be solved with personal authority on the highest level. 'The French', von Dohnanyi told Carrington and Gilmour in February 1980, 'were, in the last analysis, prepared to risk a row in the Community (not least for political reasons at home) rather than settle for a figure which came anywhere near meeting UK demands'. The problem had thus 'moved into the realm of pure politics, and in particular French and British domestic politics'.[103] It mirrored the line of Foreign Minister Genscher, who plainly told Carrington a few weeks later that the British 'were up against a political reality over the budget. There was also a French reality – the President could only be re-elected with the support of the farmers; and a German reality too – the farmers were also significant there'. Whatever Britain's justified concerns over the CAP, the fact remained that 'no alternative policy existed, however illogical the CAP seemed'.[104] Even the British Ambassador to Bonn Oliver Wright now openly begged Thatcher for moderation. The Germans 'do not need convincing of the justice of our case', he wrote on 24 March, but they did 'need to be deprived of the

---

[100] 1/HSAA008882, Vermerk Gespräch BK mit Jenkins, 31 January 1980; Diary Entries for 31 January and 5 February 1980 in Jenkins, *European Diary*, 565, 567.

[101] TNA/CAB193/270/1, Record of meeting between Lord Privy Seal and FRG Committee of European State Secretaries, 18 January 1980; Record of Meeting between Lord Privy Seal and FRG Finance Minister, 1 January 1980.

[102] TNA/CAB193/270/1, Briefing Paper: Visit by Lord Privy Seal to Bonn, 17 January 1980.

[103] TNA/CAB193/271/2, UK/EC Budgetary Contribution: Dinner with Von Dohnanyi, 26 February 1980.

[104] TNA/FCO33/4416, Note: The Secretary of State's talks with Genscher on 28 March – the Community Budget, 31 March 1980.

4.1 The row over Britain's contributions to the European Commission budget dominated the complicated relationship between Helmut Schmidt (right) and Margaret Thatcher (left). Source: Photo by Régis BOSSU/Sygma via Getty Images.

argument that we are pursuing it in terms so absolute as to preclude any sort of realistic bargain ... The German complaint is that we have seriously overplayed our hand with regard to the political realities'.[105]

By March 1980, it seemed clear that any budget deal could only be based on a high-political compromise between Thatcher and her European counterparts. Yet, Thatcher remained unwavering in her hardline position, even though internal opposition was mounting. During a heated Cabinet meeting preparing the upcoming European Council in Luxembourg, Carrington argued strongly for a package solution including concessions over other controversial issues such as CAP prices, sheep meat, fish, and energy. 'Although we had resisted any link between our budget problem and other current issues', he argued, 'it was clear that the other member states would not be able to justify a substantial concession ... unless they were able to take something home themselves'. But other voices were less accommodating. The Chancellor of the Exchequer Geoffrey Howe, for example, demanded that Thatcher should

[105] TNA/PREM19/472, Bonn to FCO, 24 March 1980.

Continuing Divisions over the Budget

'be armed by the Cabinet with the fullest authority, including the discretion to threaten to withhold our contributions [to the EC budget] if a solution were not found'. After an intense and somewhat confused discussion, the Cabinet decided on a British position that almost amounted to squaring the circle: at the European Council, Thatcher and Carrington 'would have the authority of the Cabinet to use their discretion, depending on the degree of progress towards a settlement, and taking account of the views expressed in the discussion at this meeting of the Cabinet, to decide whether and in what terms to make it clear that the Government would be obliged to consider withholding some part of our net contribution, if a satisfactory settlement was not reached at the European Council in June'. At the same time, however, they should 'also make it clear that the Government was and would remain fully committed to membership of the European Community and had no intention whatever of coming out of it'.[106]

Whatever such professions of British benevolence, the Germans had by now come to regard Britain's uncompromising pursuit of the budget question as reflective of the country's more general scepticism towards the EC, particularly on the highest level. Increasingly doubtful over Thatcher's motives and ultimate intentions, they therefore again joined ranks with France and closely coordinated their respective positions in advance of the Council. Both Schmidt and Giscard were determined to get the issue out of the way in light of the dramatically worsened international situation since Dublin, fearing that a prolonged intra-EC crisis might jeopardize the West Europeans' ability to act in other areas as well.[107] 'The current international situation is reminiscent of the situation in 1914 in many respects', Schmidt told EC Council President Cossiga on 26 April 1980, and it was thus 'all the more important to solve all the disputes in the Community soon in light of the global political situation'.[108]

Supported by the Italian EC Presidency, Schmidt and Giscard therefore came up with a dramatically improved temporary compromise

[106] TNA/CAB128/67, CC (80) 12th Conclusions, 20 March 1980. The Secretary of Trade John Nott also argued for a hardline approach in a note circulated to Cabinet in advance of the meeting. See TNA/CAB128/67, Secretary of Trade to PM Thatcher, 7 March 1980.

[107] *AAPD 1980*, Doc. Nr. 64, Telefongespräch des Bundeskanzlers Schmidt mit Staatspräsident Giscard d'Estaing, 29 February 1980.

[108] *AAPD 1980*, Doc. Nr. 132, Gespräch des Bundeskanzlers Schmidt mit Ministerpräsident Cossiga in Hamburg, 26 April 1980.

formula at the May 1980 European Council in Luxembourg, offering Britain a rebate of around £760 million for two years, tied to a promise of a more long-term general reform of the EC's financing structures. Yet, though this offer amounted to a reduction of around two thirds of Britain's net contributions and thus almost double to the initial offer from Dublin, Thatcher again decided that it was not enough, much to the dismay of Carrington and most British officials.[109] Back in Britain, the subsequent Cabinet discussion revealed the serious internal divides that had by now emerged over the question. Thatcher put the blame for the Council's failure firmly on France and Germany, claiming that Giscard's proposals had been 'considerably less attractive' than the ones the French had floated prior to the Council, and that the FRG's failure to help Britain stemmed primarily from its 'preoccupation' with its own contributions. Carrington, by contrast, offered a rather different picture of the proceedings, with only thinly disguised criticism of Thatcher's line. The Council had been 'a missed opportunity', he claimed, and Schmidt's proposal had actually been 'double the authority he had had from his Cabinet and that, if it had been accepted by us, he might have been faced with the resignation of his Finance Minister. Others were feeling sour and upset'. Painting the picture of an almost completely isolated Britain, Carrington thus concluded that 'the prospects of resuming negotiations on the same basis were not very bright'.[110] Indeed, the Germans publicly withdrew their offer in the aftermath of the Council, with Schmidt making it 'vigorously' clear to Thatcher that he would not move any further.[111] The new German position was now one of studied apathy. As Oliver Wright reported from Bonn, Schmidt had 'switched off' completely, and there was 'no guidance ... coming down from Schmidt to the negotiating departments'.[112]

Faced with such high-level failure, the much smoother machineries of lower-level British–German cooperation kicked in once again to draw up a mutually acceptable face-saving device, and the Council of EC Foreign Ministers meeting on 29–30 May 1980 was instructed to find a short-term temporary solution to the budget question. On the

---

[109] See the recollection in Jenkins's diary entry for 28 April 1980 in Jenkins, *European Diary*, 593.

[110] TNA/CAB128/67, CC (80) 18th Conclusions, 1 May 1980.

[111] B136/17493, Vemerk über Ihr Gespräch mit PM Thatcher, 9 May 1980.

[112] TNA/CAB193/272/1, Bonn to FCO, 28 May 1980.

British side, Carrington and Gilmour adopted a much more conciliatory attitude vis-à-vis their European counterparts than their PM had done; on the German side, von Dohnanyi took centre stage because of Genscher's – perhaps deliberate – absence from the meeting. With help from the Commission and Italian Foreign Minister Colombo, von Dohnanyi thus ended up playing a key role in brokering the eventual solution in a twenty-four-hour mammoth session, going far beyond his brief and clearly outstepped his personal authority (which, according to the British delegation, in any case consisted only of the fact that Schmidt knew 'what he is doing and has not objected to it').[113] The final agreement amounted largely to the same numbers as the Luxemburg offer, a reduction of the British EC contribution of around £1.570 million over the period 1980 to 1981. The crucial difference was that this temporary deal now included the assurance of a similar solution for a third year if no permanent solution of the problem could be found in the meantime.[114]

Though it was evident that this was close to the maximum that could have been achieved, Thatcher remained highly critical of the compromise. Back in Britain, as Stephen Wall recalls, she gave Gilmour and Carrington an extremely hostile reception, treating them 'as if they were schoolboys who had failed to produce their homework to the standard required' and only accepting the deal after threats of resignation by both of them.[115] As Carrington justified the deal to Cabinet the following day, it was 'the maximum we could get short of provoking a major crisis that would weaken still further the Community's capacity to cope with world events as well as its own internal problems'.[116] In the House of Commons, Ian Gilmour was similarly at pains to defend the settlement against Labour's prominent Eurosceptic Peter Shore. 'In a negotiation as complex as this, no one party can expect to get everything that he wants and to concede nothing', Gilmour said, and 'there should be no belittling of the concessions that our partners

[113] TNA/CAB193/272/1, Bonn to FCO, 28 May 1980.
[114] For records and recollections of the meeting, see Ludlow, *Jenkins*, 222–4; I. Gilmour, *Dancing with Dogma: Britain Under Thatcherism* (London: Simon&Schuster, 1992), 238–41; P. Carrington, *Reflecting on Things Past: The Memoirs of Lord Carrington* (London: Collins, 1988), 322; Jenkins, *European Diary*, 603–6.
[115] Wall, *Stranger in Europe*, 7. See also Jenkins, *European Diary*, 607; Young, *Britain and European Unity*, 131.
[116] TNA/CAB128/67, CC (80) 21st Conclusions, 2 June 1980.

180 *Margaret Thatcher, 1979–1982*

are making at a time when, whatever the impact on them of the Community budget, the general economic background is unfavourable'.[117] Indeed, Carrington's and Gilmour's line seems to have mirrored the British public's growing exasperation over Thatcher's hard line stance: *The Times*, for example, claimed that Thatcher had needlessly 'antagonized her partners and stirred up British opinion against the Community in a way that was neither wise nor necessary'.[118]

Yet, the temporary deal also came at significant cost to the Germans, increasing their net contribution to the EC budget from 1.2 to 1.7 billion ECUs in 1981 while the British contribution decreased from 2.1 to 0.7 billion.[119] It was a heavy price to pay not least in light of the FRG's recent economic downturn following the second oil shock of 1979, as a result of which its GNP had fallen from 4.1 per cent in 1979 to a mere 0.9 per cent in 1980.[120] The deal there-fore fed into a serious rift in the SPD-FDP coalition in the run-up to the 1980 national elections: whereas the SPD's Minister of Finance Hans Matthöfer openly spoke out against the agreement, anxious to demon-strate the party's fiscal responsibility to potential voters, the FDP's Foreign Minister Genscher instead welcomed the deal in light of its wider significance for the FRG's foreign policy and the stability of the EC.[121] At the decisive Cabinet meeting which lasted almost ten hours, Chancellor Schmidt eventually sided with Genscher, even though the government had to make special provisions in the FRG's budget of altogether 1.7 billion Deutschmark.[122] To Schmidt, the political importance of the EC's coherence and stability yet again proved

[117] Hansard, *House of Commons Debate* 2 June 1980, vol. 985 cc. 1046.
[118] *The Times*, 3 June 1980.
[119] These estimations were borne out by subsequent numbers. See B136/17116, EG-Finanzstruktur, 10 April 1981.
[120] Bundeszentrale für Politische Bildung [BPB], Wirtschaftliche Entwicklung in der Bundesrepublik, 4 April 2002: www.bpb.de/izpb/9748/wirtschaftliche-en twicklung-in-der-bundesrepublik [accessed on 13 June 2018].
[121] Matthöfer's opposition even made the front page of the *Sunday Express* in a piece entitled 'German blow to Market peace deal'. See *Sunday Express*, 1 June 1980. More generally, An, 'British–German Relations in the EC/EU', 102.
[122] Bundesarchiv, Kabinettsprotokolle der Bundesregierung online, 181. Kabinettssitzung am Mittwoch, dem 4. Juni 1980: www.bundesarchiv.de/coc oon/barch/0000/k/k1980k/kap1_1/kap2_23/index.html [accessed on 13 June 2018].

decisive in determining his final position. As he told the subsequent meeting of the SPD's chief executive council, the FRG's fiscal sacrifice to accommodate Britain's budget demands had been necessary to secure 'the maintenance of détente and economic stability' in Europe.[123] Yet again, the long-term political importance Schmidt attached to the perseverance of the European integration process led to sacrifices of short-term domestic and economic goals.

But Britain also paid a high price for the eventual deal in that it found itself once again side-lined inside the EC by a revived Franco–German axis, much to the dismay of many who had hoped for a stronger British voice in Europe under Thatcher. In August 1980, for example, Cabinet Secretary Robert Armstrong wrote a wide-ranging memorandum in which he claimed that Britain was 'more and more tending to find, not just in the Community but also in wider international gatherings ... that the French and Germans have got together in advance to work out a common line; and that this practice greatly enhances their ability to get their way'. He therefore urged Thatcher to make a top-level initia- tive to strengthen Britain's bilateral relationships with France and Germany, in order for Britain to continue 'to play a significant part in shaping the world we live in'. If Britain failed to strengthen its relation- ships with its European allies, he predicted gloomily, it would 'end up bleating more or less ineffectively from the sidelines, like the Italians and Canadians today'.[124] Yet, the potential success of any top-level initiative was severely compromised by Schmidt's profound personal disappointment with Thatcher's budget crusade; a bitterness that now stretched far beyond the realm of intra-EC politics. During Oliver Wright's farewell call on Schmidt in February 1981, the outgoing Ambassador was treated to yet another forceful *tour d'horizon* of Schmidt's views. 'Britain was really indifferent to what was happening on the Continent', Schmidt started off, claiming that 'the instinctive reaction of any British government was to say that whatever suited the American Administration suited Britain'. In Schmidt's eyes, Britain was now 'no more than a half-hearted member of the European Community ... without any ideas or concept of what we wanted Europe to become'.[125] It was an outburst that gave some sense of the

[123] 1/HSAA006320, SPD Präsidiumssitzung, 2 June 1980.
[124] TNA/PREM19/756, Note: Relations with Allies, 14 August 1980.
[125] TNA/PREM19/762, Farewell Call on the Chancellor, 17 February 1981.

182   *Margaret Thatcher, 1979–1982*

extent to which intra-EC tensions had by now come to overshadow many other areas of British–German cooperation – not least within the transatlantic alliance.

British–German Cooperation over NATO's Dual-Track Decision

Ronald Reagan's election as 40th President of the United States on 4 November 1980 was widely seen at the time to mark a sharp break from the previous Carter administration, as well as a sea-change for the transatlantic alliance more generally.[126] Reagan's repeated public rejections of détente, which he famously described as a Soviet 'one-way street' during his first press conference as President, was of particular concern to the West Europeans.[127] Though the shift towards a more confrontational American strategy in East–West relations had already been visible during the Carter years,[128] Reagan's forceful rhetoric nonetheless posed new challenges to the West Europeans, not least in light of rapidly growing peace movements in many countries. In response, the West Europeans cooperated closely in order to preserve the state of inner-European détente against an increasingly adversarial superpower relationship during Reagan's first term in office.

As the two most important West European members of NATO, Britain and Germany were bound to play an important role in impressing European viewpoints and strategic concerns onto the new administration in Washington. Trying to avoid a repetition of the transatlantic disarray over Afghanistan, Britain and Germany sought to harmonise their respective approaches from the start. Though initial

[126] N. P. Ludlow, 'The Unnoticed Apogee of Atlanticism? US-Western European Relations During the Early Reagan Era', in K. K. Patel and K. Weisbrode (eds.), *European Integration and the Atlantic Community in the 1980s* (Cambridge: Cambridge University Press, 2014), 17–38.
[127] R. Reagan, 'The President's News Conference', 29 January 1981. In *Public Papers of the Presidents of the United States: Ronald Reagan 1981* (Washington, DC, 1982), 57.
[128] O. Njølstad, 'The Carter Legacy: Entering the Second Era of the Cold War', in O. Njølstad (ed.), *The Last Decade of the Cold War: From Conflict Escalation to Conflict Transformation* (London and New York: Frank Cass, 2004), 196; B. J. Auten, *Carter's Conversion: The Hardening of American Defense Policy* (Columbia: University of Missouri Press, 2009). The classic work remains Garthoff, *Détente and Confrontation*.

British and German perceptions of the new American President different somewhat, with Thatcher being significantly more attuned to Reagan's anti-Communist rhetoric and economic doctrine than Schmidt, both sides hoped for greater predictability and clarity from the new US administration, something they felt had been sorely missing under Carter.[129] Only a few days after Reagan's election, Schmidt and Thatcher therefore discussed candidly how to improve the quality of transatlantic consultations. The alliance needed 'two things which went together – leadership from the United States and much more consultation', Schmidt asserted; and Thatcher agreed that it was important to explain to Reagan 'the complexity of relationships within the Alliance and the fact that all its members saw NATO from different perspectives'. Interestingly, Thatcher also volunteered her view that 'there would often be occasions where it would be desirable for the three European allies to consult together first before approaching the Americans' in order to arrive at a more coherent West European position.[130] After a quick trip to Washington a few days later, Schmidt almost enthusiastically told Thatcher over the phone that Reagan had 'made it very clear' that he wanted closer transatlantic cooperation.[131]

The most immediate area of British and German concerns was the implementation of NATO's dual-rack decision of 12 December 1979. In response to the Soviet build-up of SS-20s missiles, NATO had resolved to deploy 572 Pershing II and Ground-Launched Cruising Missiles (GLCMs) in Western Europe by 1983 if simultaneously pursued arms control negotiations had failed to deliver an agreement by then. Largely following Callaghan's earlier footsteps at Guadeloupe, Thatcher soon emerged as the most solid and consistent West European supporter of the dual-track strategy. Believing that effective deterrence ultimately depended on the credibility of threats, she regarded the

---

[129] Although the Thatcher-Reagan myth of their special relationship has recently come under some scrutiny by historians. See Aldous, *The Difficult Relationship*. For Schmidt's relationship with Reagan, Spohr, *Global Chancellor*, 121–3.

[130] TNA/PREM19/471, Note of a Conversation over Dinner, 16 November 1980. See also the German protocol, B136/17115, Gespräche BK mit PM Thatcher und AM Carrington, 17 November 1980.

[131] TNA/PREM19/471, PM's Telephone Conversation with Chancellor Schmidt, 23 November 1980.

dual-track decision as a major step towards restoring NATO's military lead over the Soviet Union and thus towards restoring Western strength in the superpower conflict.[132] As a result, the British PM had already cooperated closely with Schmidt in the run-up of the December 1979 decision, lobbying wavering governments in Italy and the Netherlands to fall in line with the dual-track strategy in spite of growing domestic opposition.[133] Thatcher also offered Schmidt more direct help with his own domestic difficulties: in September 1979, Britain accepted the deployment of an additional sixteen GLCMs to keep down the final number of GLCMs based in Germany.[134] Such British support was vital for Schmidt to demonstrate to both his government and the wider German public that the FRG was not isolated and disproportionately exposed on the issue, but that the dual-track decision had strong support of the entire NATO alliance.[135]

Yet, Reagan's forceful rhetoric threatened the appearance of such transatlantic unity, bolstering public perceptions that the new American President was a warmonger with little interest in arms control negotiations. His 'nuclear cowboy' image fuelled rapidly growing numbers of peace movements all across Western Europe, serving as an ideal unifier for the often highly heterogenous groups held together by a somewhat diffuse mix of anti-nuclear sentiment, pacifism, and anti-Americanism.[136] These developments did not go unnoticed in the United States, where Secretary of State Al Haig noted four months into the new administration that US and European politics were

---

[132] Thatcher, *Downing Street Years*, 239–42.

[133] For evidence of such British–German coordination of their lobbying efforts even on the highest level, see TNA/PREM19/15, Extract from discussions between PM and Chancellor Schmidt, 31 October 1979; R. van Dijk, '"A mass psychosis": The Netherlands and NATO's dual-track decision, 1978–1979', *Cold War History* 12/3 (2012), 381–405.

[134] TNA/PREM19/15, Note: United States Ground Launched Cruise Missiles in the United Kingdom, 20 September 1979.

[135] See, for example, notes to this effect for an important Cabinet meeting on the issue, B136/17112, Vermerk für die Kabinettsitzung, 6 November 1979.

[136] For the 'Reagan effect' and the German peace movement, H. Nehring and B. Ziemann, 'Do All Paths Lead to Moscow?', *Cold War History*, 12/1 (2012), 1–24; P. Gassert, 'Did Transatlantic Drift Help European Integration? The Euromissiles Crisis, the Strategic Defense Initiative, and the Quest for Political Cooperation', in Patel and Weisbrode, *European Integration and the Atlantic Community*, 165.

'largely out of phase, with environmentalism, anti-nuclear sentiment, and a hunger for disarmament on the rise in many Allied countries'.[137] The European backlash was strongest in West Germany, where Schmidt's unwavering support for the dual-track decision not only threatened his government's domestic support but also compromised his personal standing within the party. By 1981, large fractions of the SPD – particularly at the grassroots level – had come to share many concerns of the peace movement, and key SPD figures like Erhard Eppler, Egon Bahr, and at times even Willy Brandt appeared openly sceptical or even hostile towards Schmidt's course.[138]

In Britain, Schmidt's domestic difficulties were watched with growing concern, occasionally even stimulating doubts over Germany's more general reliability in the East–West conflict. Thatcher, whose childhood experience of the Second World War had instilled in her deeply seated suspicions over Germany, did not even shy away from voicing her personal concerns to some of her European counterparts at times.[139] In a telephone conversation with Giscard d'Estaing in November 1980, for example, she mused how 'Helmut's views on the East/West question were a little bit different' from those of other European leaders, with Giscard predicting in response that 'the stability of the relations between Germany and the United States will not be a reality in the years to come as it was five or ten years ago'.[140] She was even more outspoken with Giscard's successor François Mitterrand, telling him on the margins of the European Council in June 1981 how the Germans 'tended to hold views different from her neighbours ... because of the FRG's common frontier with a Communist country', and that the Germans 'were lucky to have Herr Schmidt as Chancellor, given his unique position both inside and outside the country'.

---

[137] Ronald Reagan Presidential Library, Simi Valley, CA [henceforward: RRL/], National Security Council (NSC), Meeting Files, NSC0008, Haig to President, 29 April 1981.

[138] For the SPD's debate over the dual-track decision, see in particular J. Hansen, *Abschied vom Kalten Krieg? Die Sozialdemokraten und der Nachrüstungsstreit (1977–1987)* (Berlin and Boston: De Gruyter Oldenbourg, 2016).

[139] Though such lingering suspicions over Germany would become much more pronounced in the later stages of her premiership, particularly around German reunification and the end of the Cold War. See Young, *This Blessed Plot*, 306–74.

[140] TNA/ PREM19/760, PM's Telephone Conversation with President Giscard, 13 November 1980.

Mitterrand seems to have shared Thatcher's concerns, professing in response that Schmidt 'might not last for longer than a few months unless TNF negotiations could be started' and that he 'admired Schmidt as one of the rare Germans he knew who had the courage to stand up to the Soviet Union'.[141] Such latent doubts over Germany's future were at the heart of British attempts to help Schmidt with his precarious domestic situation over the dual-track decision.

Finely attuned to such West European suspicions and increasingly unable to make his own voice heard in Washington, Schmidt started to use Thatcher as a transatlantic intermediary to impress German viewpoints on the new American administration. Prior to Thatcher's first visit to Reagan in February 1981, Schmidt asked her to tell the Americans that they could rely on him over the dual-track decision. 'I would stick to that decision and make it stick', he insisted to Thatcher, '[b]ut please in order to make it stick I have to be sure that the United States ... would stick to the words of that decision. Number one to the deployment of such weapons in Europe and number two to the invitation and the will of the West towards the Soviet Union to negotiate mutual balance – ceilings – or whatever you call them. Both are necessary and the Americans must not give the impression to the European public ... that the second half of the decision does not really matter and what matters is just the first half. This would make it very, very difficult to get this "swallowed" domestically'.[142] Such pleas remained a constant feature of Schmidt's dealings with Thatcher during the final years of his chancellorship. At the British–German consultations in March 1982, for example, he again illustrated his domestic situation graphically. 'Many people were honestly disturbed by American speeches about a pre-war situation, about the possibility of limited nuclear war in Europe and the need to make greater defence efforts', he exclaimed, continuing that 'Germany was a divided country ... He had to be careful not to give the German people the impression that the West was seeking to inject steel and concrete into the iron curtain ... Germany was the only country in Western Europe that had denied itself nuclear ambitions. It was the principal battle

[141] TNA/PREM19/462, Record of a meeting between the PM and President Mitterrand at the French residence, Luxembourg, 30 June 1981.
[142] TNA/PREM19/762, Record of Telephone Conversation between PM and Chancellor Schmidt, 24 February 1981.

ground. There were great dangers in emphasising world tensions. A balanced policy was necessary'.[143]

Such dramatic interventions surely amplified Thatcher's concerns over the anti-nuclear wave in Europe, given that Britain's own security ultimately depended on the stability and effectiveness of the transatlantic alliance. The combination of her personal convictions and Schmidt's warnings thus turned Thatcher into an ardent defender of the West European position on the dual-track decision in Washington. In various conversations and letters during the early 1980s, she stressed in strongest terms the need for genuine US efforts at arms control negotiations in light of West European public opinion.[144] As early as February 1981, for example, the Americans noted how Thatcher continuously sought to reaffirm the US commitment to arms control negotiations in order 'to prevent a split with Allies and counter domestic pressures from the Labour Party and Schmidt's SPD'.[145] Such pleas fell on receptive ears within the US State Department, where Secretary of State Al Haig frequently urged for a start of TNF arms control negotiations in order to preserve Allied unity.[146] 'The British remain our most reliable Ally', he wrote in a memorandum to Reagan in April 1981, and 'the French by far the most robust. However, both Mrs Thatcher and Giscard are deeply concerned that we take into account the situation in the FRG. Mrs Thatcher almost pleaded with me in London that we take care not to isolate Chancellor Schmidt, whom she described as "a really good friend of the U.S."'.[147] But other members of the Reagan administration were less receptive towards West European views. Next to Haig's note, for example, Reagan's hawkish National Security Advisor Richard Allen scribbled: 'Who cares? State does, but why?'. It was, Allen continued, '[n]ot our job to keep Schmidt in power – or any of the others ... STATE is too concerned on saving European governments and lets that become

[143] TNA/PREM19/764, Record of Conversation between PM and Chancellor (noon), 19 March 1982.
[144] Aldous, *Difficult Relationship*, 39.
[145] RRL/NSC, Executive Secretariat, VIP Visits RAC Box 1, US–UK–West European Relations, 13 February 1981.
[146] Evident not least in Haig's repeated interventions during various National Security Council Meetings, for example RRL/NSC, Executive Secretariat, Meeting Files, NSC0008, Meeting Notes, 30 April 1981.
[147] RRL/NSC, Executive Secretariat, Meeting Files, NSC0008, Haig to President, 29 April 1981.

overriding concern in setting US policy ... Someone at State misses fact trend in Europe is to the right. Alternative, in case of Germany, is not Willy Brandt or anyone like him!'[148] Secretary of Defense Weinberger too professed in a National Security Council meeting around the same time to be 'weary of defining our policy on what Schmidt wants. Our policy should be leadership – not anticipating what our Allies will say and setting our policy on that'.[149]

In spite of repeated bilateral efforts, the ultimate successes of British–German efforts to influence US policy were therefore mixed. Though Reagan's announcement of the so-called 'zero option' on 18 November 1981 might be seen partly as a response to European concerns, it did little to calm the mounting domestic opposition in West Germany. The final months of Schmidt's chancellorship saw repeated mass demonstrations in Bonn and elsewhere; triggering perceptions of domestic instability that were further intensified by the SPD's growing internal divisions. Indeed, it would ultimately fall to Schmidt's conservative successor Helmut Kohl to push through the deployment of Pershing II missiles in Germany in December 1983. British–German cooperation may therefore not have saved Schmidt's domestic fortunes, but it nonetheless contributed to preserving the shaky transatlantic consensus and West European positions against at times heavy US opposition.

The Resurfacing of the EC Budget Issue and Differences over the Falklands

Britain and Germany may have cooperated closely over the implementation of the dual-track decision, but they remained as far apart as ever inside the EC. Though the budget issue had been put temporarily on hold by the May 1980 compromise, Britain continued to disagree with most other EC member-states over many other long-standing problems like steel and fisheries. These intra-EC tensions continued to jeopardize the British–German relationship on the highest political level too, with Schmidt and Thatcher again clashing heavily at the Maastricht European Council on 23–4 March 1981. Soon afterwards, Schmidt

---

[148] Handwritten comments on ibid.
[149] RRL/NSC, Executive Secretariat, Meeting Files, NSC00016, Record of Meeting, 6 July 1981.

The Resurfacing of the EC Budget Issue 189

spent an hour with the newly appointed British Ambassador to Bonn Jack Taylor to reiterate his now familiar complaints over Britain's role in Europe. 'If things went on as present', he proclaimed, there was a danger that the EC 'would end up as a free trade area with each country pursuing its national interests'.[150] By now, Schmidt had even come to blame Britain's antagonistic diplomacy for the more general sense of stagnation and standstill hanging over the EC at the time, mirroring dire assessments of German officials who frequently complained about Britain's confrontative style inside EC bodies.[151]

Schmidt's exasperation with intra-EC politics was strengthened by the more general sense of European weakness in the early 1980s. In Germany, Schmidt's domestic fortunes had turned rapidly after the national elections on 5 October 1980. Though he had convincingly seen off the chancellorship challenge from CSU heavyweight Franz-Josef Strauss, the governing coalition's victory was largely due to the junior partner FDP's strong performance, whereas the SPD had suffered significant losses.[152] It was a result that intensified the on-going intra-coalition rifts over economic policy, with the SPD insisting on the continuation of social reforms while the FDP was moving towards a more free-market approach.[153] All of this took a toll on Schmidt personally, who had conducted the final television debate with high fever and finished the campaign in a state of severe physical exhaustion.[154] In Britain also, the situation looked bad, with few signs of Thatcher's radical reform programme paying off in the short term: in 1980, GDP had shrunk by 2 per cent, an economic contraction that had also stimulated a correspondingly sharp rise in unemployment.[155] Such troubles were accompanied by a growing polarization of the political scene, with the Labour Party embarking upon a sharp left-wing course including threats to withdraw from the EC and

---

[150] TNA/PREM19/762, Bonn to FCO, 7 April 1981.

[151] For German criticisms of the British approach, see, for example, PHSA, Band 5: Frankreich 1981-82, Beitrag zur Lage und zu einigen Zukunftsperspektiven der Gemeinschaft, 31 March 1981.

[152] TNA/PREM19/471, Bonn to FCO, 3 November 1980.

[153] TNA/PREM19/763, Bonn to FCO, 5 May 1981.

[154] TNA/PREM19/471, Chancellor Schmidt's Health, 29 October 1980. See also the famous *Der Spiegel* cover story 'Der Herzkranke Kanzler', *Der Spiegel* 43 (1981), 19 October 1981.

[155] B. Jackson and R. Saunders, 'Introduction: Varieties of Thatcherism', in Jackson and Saunders, *Making Thatcher's Britain*, 5–6. RRL/NSC, Executive Secretariat, Trip File, RAC Box 1, British Politics, 18 June 1981.

190   *Margaret Thatcher, 1979–1982*

NATO under its newly elected leader Michael Foot.[156] Even Britain's key allies started to appear doubtful over the country's future course and reliability. In July 1981, the American Ambassador to London described the British political scene as 'inward-looking and self-absorbed', predicting a period where the US 'shall have difficulty counting fully on our usually staunchest ally'.[157] It largely mirrored Schmidt's own views. 'The Conservatives have led to nothing', he told US Ambassador Burns in December 1981, and 'Labor is completely rotten'.[158] Already a few months earlier, Schmidt had ranted in an off-the-record conversation with journalists how Thatcher's economic policies were a complete failure, and that Britain had still not realized that it had actually lost rather than won the Second World War.[159] In so doing, the German Chancellor – consciously or not – echoed simultaneous domestic debates in Britain about the impact of the Second World War in shaping the country's post-war political and economic evolution.[160]

The domestic turmoil in both countries meant that there was little hope for British–German collaboration when the British EC budget problem resurfaced in early 1981. The Germans concluded quickly that they simply could not accept any increases in their own contribution if the British sum was 'practically capped' and all other members were 'more or less on the receiving end'.[161] This was also the line Schmidt took in conversation with the newly appointed EC Commission President Gaston Thorn in June 1981. 'The Federal Republic cannot agree to a cap on the British contribution without the German contribution being capped too', he argued, pointing out that the FRG now had 'the biggest trade deficit of all industrial states (ca. 30 billion *Deutschmark*); 6 billion out of which went into the EC and a similar amount to development aid'.[162] German reluctance to accommodate British demands was strengthened further by the election of François

---

[156] For German reactions to the 1979 Labour Party conference, see TNA/FCO33/ 3985, Bonn to FCO, 12 October 1979.

[157] RRL/NSC, Country File Box 20: United Kingdom, Britain Drifts, 31 July 1981.

[158] RRL/NSC, Country File Box 14: Germany [FRG], Burns to State Department, 8 December 1981.

[159] PHSA/EA, 11.9.-27.10.1981, Hintergrundgespräch BK Schmidt mit Chefredakteuren, 11 September 1981.

[160] See, for example, Barnett, *Audit of War*.

[161] B136/17116, EG-Finanzstruktur, 10 April 1981.

[162] 1/HSAA008953, Vermerk über Gespräch BK mit Kommissionspräsident Thorn, 25 June 1981.

The Resurfacing of the EC Budget Issue

Mitterrand as French President in May 1981. True to his long-held conviction that Germany's partnership with France formed the cornerstone of any successful German foreign policy whoever the personalities in power, Schmidt was anxious to preserve the substance of the Franco–German relationship, and was therefore unlikely to break ranks with the new French President over the EC budget.[163] Instead, he hoped to work with Mitterrand in order to improve West European cohesiveness and unity within the wider transatlantic framework. Already during his very first meeting with Mitterrand as President on 24 May 1981, the two leaders thus found themselves in agreement that Thatcher – in Schmidt's words – supported the EC 'not with her heart, only with her mind', and that the British still regarded the EC 'as the scapegoat for economic, social and union difficulties in their own country'. Partly in response to Britain's budget demands, they then decided to harmonize French and German EC policies bilaterally over the summer.[164]

As a result, the British found themselves yet again rebuffed by a coordinated Franco–German position over the budget. Mitterrand flatly refused to even consider British demands, telling Thatcher bluntly how her demand of a broad balance would 'render the European Community a nullity', and that it was 'important to remember the distance which separated Britain and France on this concept'.[165] Afterwards, Mitterrand told Schmidt in private conversation that Thatcher's position essentially amounted to a 'renouncement of the Community' as a whole, and the two leaders again agreed that their finance ministers should pre-coordinate French and German positions prior to any future discussions.[166] Thatcher found herself confronted

---

[163] On the continuity of Franco–German relations from Giscard to Mitterrand, see H. Miard-Delacroix, 'Ungebrochene Kontinuität. François Mitterrand und die deutschen Kanzler Helmut Schmidt und Helmut Kohl, 1981–1984', *Vierteljahrshefte für Zeitgeschichte*, 47/4 (October 1999), 539–58.

[164] *AAPD 1981*, Doc. Nr. 153, Gespräch des Bundeskanzlers Schmidt mit Staatspräsident Mitterrand in Paris, 24 May 1981. See also 1/HSAA006771, Ihre Gespräche mit Präsident Mitterrand, 25 May 1981.

[165] TNA/PREM19/470, Record of Conversation between PM and President Mitterrand, 10 September 1981.

[166] *AAPD 1981*, Doc. Nr. 290, Gespräch des Bundeskanzlers Schmidt mit Staatspräsident Mitterrand in Latche, 8 October 1981. For the actual Franco-German preparations 1/HSAA009922, Gespräch BM Matthöfer und ST Schulmann mit dem französischen Wirtschafts- und Finanzminister Delors, 27 October 1981.

with similar arguments during a visit to Bonn a few weeks later. Germany simply 'could not pay more', Schmidt told her, stressing that 'Germany had not experienced a comparable economic downturn since the end of the war'. Any additional German contribution was therefore unthinkable.[167] Apart from the serious international and domestic obstacles towards any agreement, Schmidt and Mitterrand were also dismayed that Thatcher had yet again sought to turn the issue into one of fairness and justice. It was very unfortunate that 'one is talking about basic principles in the question of Britain's budget contributions', Mitterrand described the British position to Schmidt in March 1982, since these were 'stupid, non-acceptable principles. It would be much easier if the English [sic] told us that they needed money ... He would prefer to talk completely pragmatically without raising questions of principle, because these principles were not acceptable to the Community'.[168] Schmidt agreed with Mitterrand. At the subsequent British–German consultations in March 1982, he brushed off Thatcher by claiming that 'the pity was that the United Kingdom had joined the Community 10–12 years too late. It was very difficult to change now the rules that were established at the creation of the Community, especially as those rules brought substantial benefits to some members'.[169] Afterwards, he reported back to Mitterrand how he had been very clear to Thatcher that Britain should accept the EC's financial regulations as the historical reality of twenty-five-year-old contracts.[170] It eventually fell to Schmidt's successor Helmut Kohl and Mitterrand to resolve the British budgetary question in June 1984.[171]

By 1982, Britain's inability to penetrate the Franco–German axis inside the EC had indeed triggered a more general decline of British influence in European politics. Schmidt in particular was intent on keeping the Franco–German relationship firmly at the very centre of his foreign policy, with Britain playing a supporting role at best. As he

---

[167] 1/HSAA008968, Vermerk über Ihr Gespräch mit PM Thatcher, 18 November 1981.

[168] *AAPD 1982*, Doc. Nr. 84, Telefongespräch mit Präsident Mitterrand, 18 March 1982.

[169] TNA/PREM19/764, Note of Discussion over Lunch at Chequers, 19 March 1982.

[170] PHSA, EA, Frankreich, Band 6 – 1982-1987, Dolmetscheraufzeichnung: Gespräch BK mit Mitterrand unter vier Augen, 1 April 1982.

[171] Young, *Britain and European Unity*, 130–9.

The Resurfacing of the EC Budget Issue 193

somewhat condescendingly asserted in conversation with Mitterrand in June 1982, Britain 'could get used to the thought of belonging to the Continent only with difficulty ... because of their centuries-long traditions' as a global power. The result was that Europe had 'to be led from Paris and Bonn', otherwise it would 'fall apart or crumble away'.[172] The comparative decline of Britain's importance in Schmidt's worldview could be witnessed even in the symbolic representations of the respective bilateral relationships: whereas Schmidt's visit to Mitterand's residence in Latche in October 1981 and Mitterrand's return visit to Schmidt's private home in Hamburg in May 1982 both received a great deal of public attention,[173] the Germans put rather less effort into the medial staging of the British–German relationship. In March 1982, Schmidt treated the regular bilateral consultations at Chequers almost as a mini-holiday: he asked for the evening dinner of the consultations to be moved forward so that he could spend more time with his London-based daughter, and requested a helicopter ride for a private visit to the now retired James Callaghan, who had invited him for lunch the next day.[174] The helicopter ride in particular caused consternation in Britain, with the hospitality department complaining afterwards that 'an apparently private visit' was not usually a sufficient reason for the use of highly expensive special aircraft.[175] A minor and likely unintentional diplomatic snub, perhaps; but it does shed some light on Britain's low standing in Schmidt's eyes at the time. In public perceptions too, Britain was increasingly portrayed as being left behind by the resurgent Franco–German axis. 'Schmidt cannot lift a teacup in Bonn without saucers rattling in Washington', *The Times* moaned in December 1981, but one 'rarely finds the names of Margaret Thatcher or Lord Carrington ... As Europe counts for more and more, Britain seems to count for less and less'.[176]

In Britain, such portrayals of its apparently diminished influence fed into by now familiar concerns over its future international role, but at

---

[172] *AAPD 1982*, Doc Nr. 196, Gespräch des Bundeskanzlers Schmidt mit Staatspräsident Mitterrand in Brüssel, 29 June 1982.

[173] *AAPD 1981*, Doc. Nr. 290, Gespräch des Bundeskanzlers Schmidt mit Staatspräsident Mitterrand in Latche, 8 October 1981; *AAPD 1982*, Doc. Nr. 84, Gespräch des Bundeskanzlers Schmidt mit Staatspräsident Mitterrand in Hamburg, 14 May 1982.

[174] TNA/PREM19/764, FCO to No10, 11 March 1982.

[175] TNA/FCO33/5658, Government Hospitality to FCO, 26 March 1982.

[176] *The Times*, 2 December 1981.

194 *Margaret Thatcher, 1979–1982*

times it also stimulated genuine anger about what some regarded as deliberate German misrepresentations of Britain's commitment to European cooperation. In April 1981, for example, an internal FCO report complained that Schmidt now frequently 'talked himself into a mood of personal disenchantment towards Britain' because of its EC policies, whilst the close bilateral cooperation in security and defence issues apparently did not occupy 'such a central position in his personal picture of British–German relations as they do in that of his colleagues in the government or in ours'.[177] These observations closely mirrored perceptions by the British Embassy in Bonn. At his farewell call to Schmidt in February 1981, the outgoing Ambassador Oliver Wright even decided to tackle Schmidt head-on over the matter. '[T]he Germans had consistently undervalued the British contribution to the safety of Berlin and to our joint defence in NATO', he started off, stressing how 'in all politico-military matters – TNF modernisation, arms control, MBFR – there was an almost total identity of view between Britain and the Federal Republic'. He also refuted Schmidt's almost continuous allegations of Britain's lack of commitment to the European cause. 'In joining the European Community, we had committed our fate as a nation with that of our European partners', Wright went on, 'We saw things from a European perspective … We wanted Europe to play a larger role in world affairs. Lord Carrington had taken the lead in promoting political cooperation. If political cooperation failed to get the administrative infrastructure it needed, it would not be because of British obstruction'.[178]

During the final months of Schmidt's chancellorship, the controversies surrounding the Falklands War from April to June 1982 again revealed the correlation between intra-EC tensions over issues like the budget and more general notions of European solidarity in the minds of German policy-makers like Schmidt.[179] Although all EC member-states initially supported Britain strongly by imposing heavy economic

---

[177] TNA/FCO46/2602, FCO Steering Brief [draft], 30 April 1981. See also similar complaints in TNA/FCO46/2603, FCO to UK Delegation NATO Brussels, 29 September 1981; TNA/FCO46/2603, Summary Record of meeting held at British Embassy Bonn, 5 August 1981.

[178] TNA:PRO/PREM19/762, Farewell Call on the Chancellor, 17 February 1981.

[179] For more detail, see M. Schönwald, 'Der Falkland-Konflikt und die Europäische Gemeinschaft', in F. Knipping and M. Schönwald (eds.), *Aufbruch zum Europa der zweiten Generation: Die europäische Einigung 1969–1984* (Trier: Wissenschaftlicher Verlag, 2004), 165–86.

The Resurfacing of the EC Budget Issue

sanctions on Argentina, they were also concerned by the aggressive way in which Thatcher handled the conflict, concerns that were aggravated by military actions like the British sinking of the Argentina navy cruiser Belgrano on 2 May 1982. In various conversations at the time, Schmidt and Mitterrand discussed how to best mediate the British stance, fearing that prolonged hostilities between Argentina and the EC might jeopardize South American alignments in the Cold War conflict. 'The only winner of the conflict thus far', Schmidt commented grimly on 14 May 1982, 'was the Soviet Union'.[180]

Schmidt and Mitterrand were even more annoyed that the British did not seem to reciprocate what both regarded as a great display of European solidarity over the Falklands with a more forthcoming attitude over the budget, or over the more specific question of agricultural food prices hanging over the EC at the time. The British, Mitterrand claimed, should show a 'greater sense of proportion', otherwise their 'too rigid position on agricultural prices and the financial compensation issue' might eventually leave them 'isolated' over the Falklands.[181] Indeed, when Britain rejected the offer of a rebate around 800 million ECUs and simultaneously tried to block the decision on CAP prices in the Agricultural Council by invoking the Luxembourg compromise, the other EC members simply claimed that the issue was not one of vital national interest and thus overruled the British by majority voting.[182] The result was that Britain's intra-EC haggling and bigger questions of European solidarity remained highly conflated in Schmidt's mind. In July 1982, he complained to the new British Ambassador Taylor about the 'enormous economic sacrifices' Germany had undertaken with the economic sanctions on Argentina, citing shipment orders of around 4 billion Deutschmark. These sanctions, Schmidt vented, had been taken 'out of solidarity', but neither he nor Mitterrand were 'convinced' whether Britain valued such support of its European partners sufficiently.[183] Even in the case of a military conflict like the Falklands, intra-EC troubles had by 1982 come to overshadow other

---

[180] *AAPD 1982*, Doc Nr. 150, Gespräch des Bundeskanzlers Schmidt mit Staatspräsident Mitterrand in Hamburg, 14 May 1982.
[181] Ibid.
[182] *AAPD 1982*, Doc. Nr. 165, Telefonat Schmidt-Thatcher, 25 May 1982. For the developments in the agricultural council, see Anmerkung 7.
[183] *AAPD 1982*, Doc. Nr. 211, Gespräch des Bundeskanzlers Schmidt mit dem britischen Botschafter Taylor, 14 July 1982.

areas of European relations almost completely. The irony was that, within the transatlantic alliance, Britain and Germany simultaneously cooperated more closely than ever before in order to foster a joint West European position vis-à-vis the Americans.

Reaganomics and Poland: The Emergence of a Joint British–German Cold War Stance

While the most immediate source of transatlantic tensions during Reagan's first months in office had been the fate of NATO's dual-track decision, the period also saw more general West European concerns over the US administration's new course. In the macroeconomic field, Reagan's pursuit of tight monetary policies combined with heavy spending soon led to a sharp increase of the US deficit, stimulating a corresponding surge in US interest rates and large influx of worldwide capital into the United States. With the US share of the global GNP still at almost 25 per cent and the currency market's reliance on the US dollar, this policy was bound to have serious consequences for the global economic order. For the West Europeans, it meant that their own interest rates rose dramatically, compounding the already present recessionary tendencies triggered by the second oil shock in 1979.[184]

With structural dependencies on the American dollar driving the West Europeans closer together, Britain and Germany intervened early to impress their concerns on the new US administration. Schmidt emerged once more as the US's most vocal European critic, graphically illustrating to Reagan in May 1981 how the allegedly optimistic mood in the United States contrasted harshly with European pessimism. 'I have a feeling that you will succeed', he told Reagan, 'but please remember that what you do has consequences. There can be political destabilization as a result. You don't read much about stability in Thatcher's government, but I can assure you that it is not all that stable ... Mitterrand had campaigned on a promise to do away with unemployment, but he can't. There will be deep dis-

---

[184] For an excellent overview of these dynamics, see D. Basosi, 'The European Community and International Reaganomics, 1981–1985', in Patel and Weisbrode, *European Integration and the Atlantic Community*, 133–53.

Reaganomics and Poland 197

appointment about Mitterrand soon. This can spread to Italy'.[185] When the Reagan administration appeared to pay little attention to such complaints over subsequent months, West European statements turned increasingly sour. In personal conversation with Schmidt in February 1982, for example, Mitterrand burst out that 'even if the US wants to pursue "suicidal" economic policies, this did not mean they had the right to "kill" West European countries as well'.[186] Schmidt too instructed US Ambassador Burns in February 1982 simply to 'inform' the American President that 'he considers his budgetary policy disastrous for Europe, that he feels sure that the enormous U.S. budget deficits will keep interest rates at a very high level in the United States, that those high American interest rates are causing an outflow of capital from Europe to the United States, that the European economies are faltering as a consequence, and that a severe worldwide economic depression will inevitably take place if the U.S. does not revise its budgetary plans'. Schmidt also asked Burns to stress that 'the heads of other European governments ... share his views'.[187]

Indeed, the long line of West European critics of US macroeconomic policies once again included Britain. Whatever the differences in their personal economic philosophies, Schmidt and Thatcher were united by their dismay over the apparent American disregard of European concerns, sharing feelings of resentment and powerlessness over Western Europe's structural dependency on the United States. 'Even if the economic policies of the British and German Governments were successful', Schmidt ranted at the British–German consultations in October 1981, 'they would nonetheless be "infected" by what was happening in the United States', adding that he 'did not believe that the United States Administration understood that when they decided on domestic United States economic policy, they were also deciding the economic fate of the world'. Thatcher, true to her monetarist convictions and obsession with fiscal discipline, was quick to agree with the

---

[185] RLL/NSC, Country File Box 14: Germany (FRG), Memorandum of Conversation, 21 May 1981. For early public criticism of Reagan's policies, see PHSA, EA, 29.6.-10.9.1981, Hintergrundgespräch BK Schmidt mit Mrs. Flora Lewis und Mr. Vinocur von New York Times, 7 July 1981.

[186] *AAPD 1982*, Doc. Nr. 63, Gespräch des Bundeskanzlers Schmidt mit Staatspräsident Mitterrand in Paris, 24 February 1982.

[187] RLL/NSC, Country File Box 14: Germany (FRG), Bonn to State Department, 17 February 1982.

German Chancellor's castigation of Reagan's deficit spending, adding that 'a big deficit made not for boom but for a big depression'.[188] A few months later, Schmidt and Thatcher even tried to devise common strategies to influence the Americans, with Thatcher insisting that Reagan needed to 'be persuaded of the need to change American economic policy for the sake both of the United States and of her allies like the Federal Republic and the United Kingdom'. More precisely, they hoped to install George Shultz, well-known to Schmidt because of their shared stints as finance ministers in the early 1970s, as a transatlantic intermediary to get European concerns greater airing in Washington.[189] Yet again, Schmidt resorted to Thatcher as a potential bridgebuilder, partly as a result of his own inability to influence decision-makers in Washington. As he told the British Ambassador Taylor somewhat resignedly, Reagan 'would not be willing to learn from any political leader in Europe except for Thatcher ... she is the only one that Reagan might listen to. It is therefore even more urgent than before to represent Europe's economic interests through PM Thatcher'.[190]

In June 1982, Schmidt and Thatcher indeed took the lead in trying to impress West European concerns on President Reagan at the Versailles G7 summit. Both leaders pressed Reagan strongly on reducing the US deficit and interest rates, with Thatcher quoting John Maynard Keynes to the effect that 'deficits cannot help structural unemployment'.[191] Schmidt too criticised Reagan directly, claiming that the United States had 'a leading role and nobody could take it from them. The other countries at the Summit could not dissociate themselves from American capital markets and American interest rates'. When Reagan responded that even a drop in US interest rates would be 'no panacea' and that he in any case was working towards progressively reducing the US budget deficit 'with a view to its eventual

---

[188] TNA/PREM19/766, Federal Chancellor and the PM, 18 November 1981; 1/ HSAA008968, Vermerk über das Vier-Augen-Gespräch des BK mit PM Thatcher, 18 November 1981.

[189] TNA/PREM19/764, Note of Meeting between PM and Schmidt, 19 March 1982. Shultz indeed joined the Reagan administration in July 1982, although as Secretary of State.

[190] *AAPD 1982*, Doc. Nr. 211, Gespräch des Bundeskanzlers Schmidt mit dem britischen Botschafter Taylor, 14 July 1982.

[191] MTF, G7: US Treasury Secretary Record of Conversation (Session 2), 5 June 1982: www.margaretthatcher.org/document/137273 [accessed on 13 June 2018].

Reaganomics and Poland 199

elimination', Schmidt replied grimly that he 'betted his hat that President Reagan would not achieve that'.[192] After the session, Thatcher seemed almost as agitated as the German Chancellor, boasting to Schmidt in a brief chat on the margins how 'she had tackled President Reagan about the US deficit'.[193] Yet again, however, the similarity of British and German views was largely invisible to the public. As Schmidt complained in an off-the-record discussion, Thatcher only voiced her criticisms behind closed doors and continued to profess support of Reagan's macroeconomic course in public.[194]

British criticisms of Reaganomics may have been muted, but the extent of British and German cooperation amidst the transatlantic disarray following the declaration of martial law in Poland on 13 December 1981 was plain for everybody to see.[195] The initial differences in US and West European reactions were largely the result of the long-term discrepancies and in-built contradictions between superpower and inner-European détente since the early 1970s. Whereas US strategy had primarily aimed at preserving and consolidating the status quo in superpower relations, inner-European détente by contrast had at least partially been based on the assumption that the creation of long-term political linkages and economic interdependencies between Eastern and Western Europe might gradually lead to internal transformations and corresponding reconciliation.[196] The role of East–West trade had also acquired rather different political importance in the

---

[192] TNA/PREM19/725, Versailles Economic Summit: First Plenary Session, 9.45 am, 5 June 1982; TNA/PREM19/725, Versailles Economic Summit: Third Plenary Session, 9.45 am 6 June 1982.

[193] TNA/PREM19/724, Record of Meeting held between PM and Chancellor Schmidt at Versailles, 5 June 1982. See also Schmidt's and Thatcher's similar discussions on the margins of the European Council the following month, PHSA, EG Tagung Europäischer Rat, Band 2 1979–82, Vermerk: Europäischer Rat 28/29 Juni 1982, 30 June 1982.

[194] PHSA, EA 26.2.-1.4.1982, Informationsgespräch des Bundeskanzlers mit Chefredakteuren, 23 March 1982. For the factual similarities, as well as rhetorical differences, between Schmidt's and Thatcher's criticisms of Reagan's economic policies, see Basosi, 'The European Community and International Reaganomics', 149.

[195] For general background, see H. Sjursen, *The United States, Western Europe and the Polish Crisis: International Relations in the Second Cold War* (Basingstoke: Macmillan, 2003); with a tighter focus on Schmidt and Germany, Pick, *Brücken nach Osten*, 97–122.

[196] Young, 'Western Europe and the End of the Cold War', 291–4; Kieninger, *Dynamic Détente; Sargent, Superpower Transformed*, 59–67.

long-term strategic outlooks of the United States and Western Europe.[197] As a NSC analysis in October 1981 rightly highlighted, the United States was anxious 'to cap or reduce the level of Western – or, at least, West European – trade with the Soviets. But a basic West European objective – to sustain or increase the level of that trade – is directly contradictory'.[198] The differences were stark indeed: by 1982, Western Europe's total trade with the Soviet Union amounted to $41 billion, compared to the US's relatively modest $2.5 billion.[199] These different structural pressures where now at the heart of the disunited and confused transatlantic response to the Polish crisis: whereas the Reagan administration reacted immediately by imposing far-reaching economic sanctions on both Poland and the Soviet Union, the West Europeans instead adhered to a policy of strict non-intervention, fearing that more drastic actions might compromise the state of East–West political and economic détente even further.[200]

The most contentious issue in the transatlantic disputes over Poland was the project of a proposed 5,000-kilometre gas pipeline from Siberia to Europe, designed to enable the Western Europeans to diversify their energy supplies whilst providing the Soviet Union with much-needed hard currency earnings.[201] Not only did the Europeans regard the project as a welcome opportunity to intensify East–West interlinkages and reduce their own reliance on Middle East oil, but they had also already invested significantly in the project, with FRG investments alone amounting to around $1.13 billion.[202] The United States, by contrast, feared that the project would enable the Soviet Union to

---

[197] W. Lippert, *The Economic Diplomacy of Ostpolitik: Origins of NATO's Energy Dilemma* (New York and Oxford: Berghahn, 2011).

[198] RRL/NSC, Executive Secretariat, Meeting Files, NSC00023, Political and Economic Costs of Allied and U.S. Oil and Gas Controls, 18 October 1981.

[199] A. Romano, 'The Main Task of European Political Cooperation: Fostering Détente in Europe', in Villaume and Westad, *Perforating the Iron Curtain*, 137.

[200] A. Chiampan, 'Those European Chicken Littles': Reagan, NATO, and the Polish Crisis, 1981–2', *The International History Review* 37/4 (2015), 682–99; G. F. Domber, 'Transatlantic Relations, Human Rights, and Power Politics', in P. Villaume and O. A. Westad (eds.), *Perforating the Iron Curtain: European Détente, Transatlantic Relations, and the Cold War, 1965–1985* (Copenhagen: Museum Tuscalanum, 2010), 197.

[201] For an overview of the episode, see K. Demidova, 'The Deal of the Century: The Reagan Administration and the Soviet Pipeline', in Patel and Weisbrode, *European Integration and the Atlantic Community*, 59–82; also Chiampan, 'European Chicken Littles', 682–99.

[202] Demidova, 'Deal of the Century', 62.

Reaganomics and Poland 201

blackmail Western Europe over energy supply; it also resented the further influx of hard currency into the Eastern bloc.[203] The declaration of martial law therefore seemed to offer an ideal pretext for the United States to block or delay the pipeline project, which is why initial US sanctions explicitly included export licences of oil and gas equipment such as pipe-layers.[204] Reagan, incensed by developments in Poland, clearly believed that he had morality on his side, and that it was time for the West Europeans to show their colours. 'Those "chicken littles" in Europe', he exclaimed in an NSC meeting on 23 December 1981, 'will they still be "chicken littles" if we lead and ask them to follow our lead? ... [I]f we really believe this is the last chance of a lifetime, that this is a revolution started against this "damned force," we should let our Allies know they, too, will pay a price if they don't go along; that we have long memories.'"[205]

Fearing US attempts to use the Poland crisis as a pretext to block the pipeline project, the West Europeans ganged up early in order to divert American calls for economic sanctions. Hesitation to follow the American lead was particularly pronounced in West Germany, with Schmidt bluntly telling Ambassador Burns that the FRG would under no circumstances 'stick its neck out first'.[206] While strong French support of this German position was of little surprise to anybody,[207] the British too voiced serious doubts about both the political effectiveness and the potential costs of economic sanctions from the very beginning. This was due not least to the fact that the Thatcher government had substantial stakes in the pipeline project as well, with $350 million governmental credits and an expected total of $385 million in contracts for equipment delivery in return.[208] Of particular concern to Thatcher was the significant involvement of John Brown Engineering, an already struggling company in an

---

[203] RRL/NSC, Executive Secretariat, Meeting Files, NSC00017, Record of Meeting, 9 July 1981.

[204] Chiampan, 'European Chicken Littles', 690.

[205] RRL, Executive Secretariat: National Security Council Meeting Files, NSC00035, Record of Meeting, 23 December 1981.

[206] RRL/NSC, Country File Box 14: Germany (FRG), Burns to State Department, 15 January 1982.

[207] For Franco–German cooperation over the issue, see, for example, AAPD 1982, Doc. Nr. 20 and Nr. 21, Gespräche des Bundeskanzlers Schmidt mit Staatspräsident Mitterrand in Paris, 13 January 1982.

[208] Demidova, 'Deal of the Century', 62.

economically deprived area of the UK which had over £104 million worth of contracts at stake.[209] This delicate combination of domestic pressures and genuine unease over US meddling in a European project turned Thatcher into an ardent proponent of West European positions in Washington. As early as 29 January 1982, for example, Haig reported how Thatcher had complained to him 'with unusual vehemence' how 'the cost of the sanctions imposed thus far are greater to Europe that to the U.S.', and had described 'the impact on Western Europe's economy of further financial and trading sanctions in the strongest of terms'.[210] The Americans would have 'to face the fact that the French and the Germans were never going to abandon the relevant contracts', Thatcher exclaimed, stressing that the proposed sanctions 'threatened $4 billion worth of European contracts' in total.[211] She followed this up with a personal letter to Reagan the same day, in which she stressed again the need to 'avoid measures which would do more harm to the West than to the Soviet Union' and warning him that 'the unity of the Western Alliance could be seriously damaged by the current differences'.[212] The 'French, Germans and Italians', Thatcher continued, simply 'cannot and will not give up the gas pipeline project', not failing to mention that Britain too had 'important contracts at stake'.[213]

Throughout the Poland crisis, Britain and Germany cooperated closely to foster a common West European position. At the British–German consultations in March 1982, Thatcher and Schmidt agreed to block any US attempts to extend sanctions retrospectively to already existing contacts, an idea discussed frequently at the time. '[I]f the Americans tried to undermine existing contracts', Schmidt asserted, 'they would get bloody noses. The equipment which European firms at present sought from the United States could be produced elsewhere, though this might delay things by a year or so'.[214] British policy-makers followed largely identical – though somewhat more diplomatic – lines in their subsequent conversations

[209] TNA/PREM19/943, John Brown Group to Thatcher, 8 June 1982.
[210] RRL/NSC, Head of State File Box 35: United Kingdom, Haig to President, 29 January 1982.
[211] TNA/PREM19/871, Record of Conversation between PM and US Secretary of State, 29 January 1982.
[212] TNA/PREM19/873, Thatcher to Reagan, 29 January 1982.   [213] Ibid.
[214] TNA/PREM19/764, Record of Conversation between PM and FRG Chancellor, 19 March 1982.

4.2 In spite of their regular fallouts over the European Community budget, Helmut Schmidt (left) and Margaret Thatcher (centre) cooperated closely in trying to mediate US Cold War policies under Jimmy Carter and Ronald Reagan, 11 May 1981. Source: Bettmann/Getty Images.

with the US, making clear that they 'won't buck the FRG and French on the pipeline'.[215] Thatcher too stressed these points repeatedly in her personal dealings with Reagan.[216] For the American President, however, the question had now become one of principle. 'We said there would be more punishments coming and here Walesa is still in jail and we are already talking about relaxing the sanctions', Reagan yelled during an NSC meeting on 24 May 1982, 'We will lose all credibility. We talk well, but the Europeans will always back off. The Soviet Union is economically on the ropes – they are selling rat meat on the market. This is the time to punish them. The Europeans should tell the Russians to ease up in Poland, relax martial law, release Lech Walesa. We are not able to afford politically to relax. The Europeans should have a bit of guts … Why don't we provide

[215] RRL/NSC, Executive Secretariat, Trip File Box 5: President's Trip to Europe 1982, Background Paper: East/West issues, 7 May 1982.
[216] See, for example, MTF, Thatcher to Reagan, 5 April 1982: www.margaretthatcher.org/document/122939 [accessed on 13 June 2018].

204 *Margaret Thatcher, 1979–1982*

the leadership and tell the Europeans who is the enemy – it is not us. We are willing to help the Russians if they straighten up and fly right. We want deeds and they can begin with Poland'.[217]

Tensions came to a head in June 1982, when the US indeed decided to unilaterally expand its export ban to US subsidiaries and licensees in Europe.[218] At dinner during the subsequent European Council in Brussels, the West Europeans were united in their dismay, proposing to simply ignore Reagan's sanctions. The assembled leaders were particularly annoyed by the fact that Reagan had announced these sanctions unilaterally and only after the G7 summit a few days earlier, which they regarded as a severe breach of trust.[219] In the *Bundestag*, Schmidt correspondingly declared that Reagan's decision implied 'an extraterritorial extension of US jurisdiction which . . . is contrary to the principles of international law', allowing German companies to undercut the effects of US sanctions. The UK Parliament too evoked the Protection of Trading Interests Act 1980 against compliance with the US embargo.[220] Thatcher was unwavering in her support of the European position. On 30 July, she wrote to Reagan that she had 'no option but to follow the provisions of our legislation to protect the interests of John Brown Engineering and other British companies with existing contracts';[221] a few weeks later, she even claimed publicly on BBC radio how she felt 'deeply wounded by a friend'.[222] In light of such complete European non-compliance, the Reagan administration finally lifted the sanctions on 13 November 1982. As a discussion paper for an NSC meeting ruefully admitted, the issue had indeed 'united our Allies as few other issues have in recent years'.[223] For once, the West

---

[217] RRL/NSC, Executive Secretariat, Meeting Files, NSC00050, Record of Meeting, 24 May 1982.

[218] Demidova, 'Deal of the Century', 76–7.

[219] PHSA, EG, Tagung Europäischer Rat, Band 2: 1979–82, Vermerk: Europäischer Rat 28/29. Juni 1982, 30 June 1982.

[220] Schmidt quoted in Lippert, *Economic Diplomacy of Ostpolitik*, 169; Chiapman, 'European Chicken Littles', 692, Demidova, 'Deal of the Century', 78.

[221] MTF, Thatcher to Reagan, 30 July 1982: www.margaretthatcher.org/document/122942 [accessed on 13 June 2018].

[222] MTV, Interview for BBC at Glasgow Airport, 1 September 1982: www.margaretthatcher.org/document/104815 [accessed on 13 June 2018].

[223] RRL/NSC, Executive Secretariat, Meeting Files, NSC00061, Discussion Paper, 16 September 1982.

Conclusions 205

Europeans had acted clearly and unequivocally together – and Britain and Germany had led the way.

By that time, however, Helmut Schmidt was no longer German Chancellor. The strains over economic policy had become untenable within the shaky SPD-FDP governing coalition; rifts that were intensified by strong internal divides of the SPD over the dual-track decision and tensions over the more general direction of Schmidt's foreign policy. On 17 September 1982, all FDP ministers resigned from their ministerial positions to negotiate a new governing coalition with the main opposition parties CDU/CSU. Two weeks later, Schmidt lost a vote of confidence in the *Bundestag*, triggering his replacement by the Christian Democrat Helmut Kohl who would govern the Federal Republic for the following sixteen years. Schmidt himself retired from active political life in 1986, finding a new role as editor of the German weekly *Die Zeit* and author of over thirty books before his passing on 10 November 2015.[224]

Conclusions

At first sight, the British–German relationship under Thatcher seems to have changed little from previous years under Wilson and Callaghan. Just like her Labour predecessors, Thatcher was faced with the unenviable task of having to reconcile the formidable structural and domestic obstacles against a more positive British role in the EC with growing external pressures for greater European cooperation triggered by the changing international environment of the late 1970s and early 1980s. Yet, Thatcher's political convictions, as well as her personal character and temperament, made her tackle these challenges in very different ways than her predecessors. Whereas Wilson had kept himself largely aloof from European questions and Callaghan had sought the closest possible relationships to mediate intra-EC differences as much as possible, Thatcher instead went about remedying Britain's comparatively weak standing within the EC through tough and confrontational bargaining, even at the danger of severely alienating her European counterparts. And this she did.

---

[224] T. Birkner, *Mann des gedruckten Wortes: Helmut Schmidt und die Medien* (Bremen: Edition Temmen, 2014).

Thatcher's strategy may well be seen to have paid off in the short term over the budget issue, both in terms of the size of the actual budget rebate and in temporarily appeasing growing domestic unease over EC membership. But the more long-term consequence of Thatcher's approach was that Britain remained largely marginalised in the foreign policies of its key European partners France and Germany. This applies in particular to the British–German relationship, where Schmidt's personal exasperation with Thatcher's budget crusade increasingly led him to question Britain's more general commitment to European cooperation and solidarity. By the end of Schmidt's chancellorship, the virulent intra-EC fights between Britain and Germany had thus come to overshadow the many other areas of strong bilateral collaboration, particularly within the transatlantic alliance, almost completely.

Behind Schmidt's and Thatcher's personal animosities, however, stood much wider differences in British and German attitudes towards European integration. Although Thatcher came to office with a firm commitment to British EC membership, this commitment was based essentially on a rational, cool-headed calculation of the potential advantages of membership, rather than on a more personal and emotive attachment to the principle of European integration. She therefore saw no contradiction between fighting for an improvement of Britain's position inside the EC, and at the same time working closely with her EC partners in many other areas and arenas. To Thatcher, the EC was only one of many possible frameworks for European cooperation, and not one she particularly liked, which is why she approached it with a rather transactional, 'zero-sum' mindset. Schmidt's views, by contrast, were very different. In spite of his personal dislike of certain EC institutions and mechanisms, he remained as attached as ever to his long-standing political conviction that a well-functioning EC was the crucial prerequisite for any successful West German foreign policy after 1945. The result was that he perceived Thatcher's fights over the EC budget or other areas of Community legislation as more general challenges against West European cohesion and solidarity on the international stage, which triggered an erosion of bilateral trust that eventually extended far beyond EC matters. Whatever the actual evidence of British support for West European positions within the wider transatlantic alliance, Thatcher's uncompromising pursuit of

Conclusions 207

the budget question therefore eroded Schmidt's trust in Britain's more general reliability and commitment towards its European partners – in spite of the almost unprecedented bilateral collaboration between the two countries taking place at the very same time. In this sense, British–German relations during Thatcher's first term exemplify the much bigger misunderstanding at the heart of British and German differences in post-war Europe.

Conclusions

When Britain voted to leave the EU on 23 June 2016, some German commentators were quick to depict the referendum outcome as merely one further episode of Britain's allegedly historic scepticism or hostility towards European integration since 1945. Already a few days prior to the vote, the weekly *Der Spiegel* had claimed that 'nothing' had changed in Britain's EU policies since the days of Margaret Thatcher. 'London has never viewed European integration as a project of overriding significance', it yelled; 'Britain has always tried to derive the maximum benefit for itself. The British weren't interested in any European added value'.[1] Once the British people had cast their vote, the *Zeit* editor Josef Joffe offered even more hyperbole in a hastily-arranged symposium by the online magazine *Politico*. 'The nation that masterminded Europe's fate for 400 years will slink off into an offshore Austria, a remnant of the once-mighty Habsburg Empire', he claimed; 'not since the Germans voted Hitler into power has a democratic electorate inflicted so much harm on its glorious history and its prospects ... History won't be kind to the 52 percent who bolted from greatness'.[2] It was only one of many examples where genuine regret over the British decision got mixed up with patronising and condescending remarks over Britain's alleged insularity and outdated nationalism. 'It seems hardly likely', the *Frankfurter Allgemeine Zeitung* wrote on 25 June 2016, 'that, in the conditions governing the 21st century, a state in splendid isolation can better serve the interests of its citizens, its young people and its economy than a community like the EU'.[3]

[1] *Der Spiegel*, 11 June 2016.
[2] *Politico*, 25 June 2016: www.politico.eu/article/britains-out-now-what-brexit-symposium-political-commentators-experts/ [accessed on 13 June 2018].
[3] *Frankfurter Allgemeine Zeitung*, 25 June 2016. Quoted in *Financial Times*, 'How Europe's press reacted to Brexit', 25 June 2016.

Conclusions   209

Such German commentary on the Brexit vote tied neatly into some bigger teleological and, at least on the German side, often self-congratulatory narratives of British–German relations since 1945; narratives in which post-war Germany had allegedly managed to reinvent itself as a liberal and democratic power by embracing the higher ideals of supranational European integration, whereas Britain had sunk into sustained political and economic decline coupled with imperial nostalgia and obsession with victory in the Second World War. These views had their heyday in the early 1990s, a period in which the intensification of European integration through the Maastricht Treaty coincided with public British unease over German reunification. In 1991, for example, the historian Lothar Kettenacker described the opposition to German reunification amongst parts of the British political elite as representative of a 'seemingly timeless, die-hard nationalist thinking', and similarly regarded the rise of Euroscepticism as reflective of 'how deeply Great Britain is stuck in the past'.[4] Günther Heydemann agreed, claiming that Britain's 'traditional, sometimes almost instinctive rejection of Europe' was due to its realisation 'that Britain lags behind the majority of EC-states in many political, economic and social areas'.[5] Such notions have sometimes also been mirrored in the internal British debate, where political commentators and historians alike have tended to contrast Britain's allegedly 'abnormal' attitudes towards European integration with the allegedly 'normal' development of attitudes amongst the EC founding member-states – a *Sonderweg* of a rather different kind.[6] As Wolfram Kaiser put it in 1996, the task of historians working on British European policy at the time almost seemed to resemble 'that of a pathologist concerned with identifying the

---

[4] L Kettenacker, 'Großbritannien: Furcht vor deutscher Hegemonie', in G. Trautmann (ed.), *Die häßlichen Deutschen? Deutschland im Spiegel der westlichen und östlichen Nachbarn* (Darmstadt: Wissenschaftliche Buchgesellschaft, 1991), 205–7. A few years later, however, Kettenacker admitted that he had given 'too much prominence' to the British rhetoric over German reunification. See L. Kettenacker, 'Britain and German Unification, 1989/1990', in Larres and Meehan, *Uneasy Allies*, 122.

[5] G. Heydemann, 'Partner or Rival? The British Perception of Germany During the Process of Unification 1989–1991' in H. Husemann (ed.), *As Others See Us: Anglo–German Perceptions* (Frankfurt am Main: Lang, 1994), 145–6.

[6] Just like the German *Sonderweg*, the notion of British exceptionalism is of course severely contested and frequently dismissed, particularly amongst knowledgeable historians specialising on Britain and European integration. For a particularly powerful rebuttal, see Young, *Britain and European Unity*, 184–202.

syndromes responsible for Britain's dysfunctional behaviour'.[7] Even the German journalist Thomas Kielinger's otherwise overwhelmingly positive work on British–German relations, jointly commissioned by the British and German foreign offices, could not resist taking a snipe at British European policy. 'Whether we take BSE or the "Euro", mad cows or complex monetary issues', Kielinger wrote, 'it all comes down to the same thing: Britain's fundamental reservations about Europe'.[8]

At first sight, then, the pattern of British–German relations during Helmut Schmidt's chancellorship seems to fit well into such cliché-laden narratives over Britain's allegedly eternal Euroscepticism. Contrary to widespread expectations, Britain did not assume its self-assigned leadership role once it had eventually joined the EC in 1973, but instead remained largely aloof from key developments in the integration process during the 1970s, such as the EMS. At times, it even seemed to question some of the EC's basic political principles and mechanisms, most famously during Wilson's renegotiations in 1974–5 and the budget question under Thatcher. As outlined above, the few specialised works on the bilateral relationship during the 1970s have therefore tended to look primarily at Britain's alleged 'problems' with the EC as the main explanation for the lack of improvement in the bilateral relationship after Britain's accession to the EC,[9] and the few available studies on British European policy in the 1970s have similarly often set out explicitly to explain Britain's continuing 'reluctance' or 'awkwardness' within the Community.[10] It is, of course, an interpretation that Schmidt himself had been keen to foster after his time in office. As he asserted in one of his last major television interviews in August 2012, Thatcher and Wilson 'were the two people who convinced me that I had been wrong in the 1960s when I thought we had to admit the English in any case, even against de Gaulle's will. Subsequently, I have come to agree with de Gaulle'.[11] Schmidt's

[7] W. Kaiser, *Using Europe, Abusing the Europeans: Britain and European Integration, 1945–63* (Basingstoke: Macmillan, 1996), xvi.

[8] T. Kielinger, *Crossroads and Roundabouts: Junctions in German–British Relations* (Bonn: Bouvier, 1996), 222.

[9] Larres, 'Uneasy Allies or Genuine Partners', 16; Smith and Edwards, 'British–West German Relations', 61–2; Wallace, *Britain's Bilateral Links with Western Europe*, 29–30.

[10] George, *Awkward Partner*; Gowland and Turner, *Reluctant Europeans*.

[11] ARD, *Menschen bei Maischberger*, 12 August 2012.

Conclusions 211

views can therefore be seen to represent a rather typical German view of Britain's allegedly eternally destructive role in the building of post-war Europe.

This book has sought to step back from such contemporary narratives whilst at the same time treating them seriously as in themselves part of the history of 1970s British–German relations. Through the prism of Schmidt's high-level encounters with his British counterparts, it has shown that what tore these different British and German leaders so continuously apart in intra-EC politics was not simply one-sided British obstructionism, but instead a deeper clash of different national strategies and perceptions that were the result of Britain's and Germany's very different historical experiences of the European integration process since 1945. This is evident in the views as well as in the actions of Schmidt and his British counterparts during the 1970s, which were shaped primarily by their very different perceptions of post-war European integration. Schmidt's story shows how, for West Germany, the European integration process had been key to the country's post-war economic recovery and international rehabilitation since the 1950s. For somebody of Schmidt's generation, who had witnessed at first hand the violence and atrocities of the Third Reich, it also contained a deeply moral dimension adding significant further weight to such strategic calculations. By the 1970s, the FRG's political elites – like Schmidt – had therefore come to regard the preservation and furthering of the European integration process more generally as a key and self-evident part of its national strategy. For 1970s Britain, by contrast, the European experience had at that stage hardly been a positive one. Lacking Germany's overarching strategic imperative for EC membership and having joined only belatedly amidst a global economic recession, Britain had to come to terms with rules and mechanisms that were already established and not necessarily suited to its interests, whilst also having to confront the political reality of the seeming impenetrability of the Franco–German relationship at the EC's core. These wider dynamics put the two countries almost inevitably at odds in intra-EC matters, and both the mindsets and actions of Schmidt and his British opposites during the 1970s and early 1980s reflect this.

Yet, the book has also shown that these tensions over EC issues, so prominently emphasised in both the literature and in Schmidt's own recollections, do not tell the whole story. Throughout Schmidt's time in office, Britain and Germany cooperated extraordinarily closely in key areas of non-EC cooperation, particularly as regards the fostering of joint European positions within the transatlantic alliance amidst the resurgence of Cold War tensions from the late 1970s. Over the major international issues of the day – such as NATO's dual-track decision, Afghanistan, or Poland – Britain and Germany extensively coordinated their responses, and eventually adopted remarkably similar positions in many instances. The reasons why such bilateral dynamics have become overshadowed by simultaneous intra-EC tensions so completely, however, again point to the very different importance attached to the European integration process in the two countries: for Germany, the political and indeed moral importance attached to European integration was such that bilateral cooperation within the looser framework of the transatlantic alliance seemed like a poor substitute for Britain's allegedly destructive behaviour inside the EC. British policy-makers, by contrast, did not prioritise the EC over the many other institutions for European cooperation at the time, and as such could not understand why British unease over the EC seemed to translate almost automatically into a more general British 'aversion' to Europe in German eyes. These were the key dynamics at the heart of the 'European misunderstanding' between 1970s Britain and Germany.

While the book has focused primarily on Helmut Schmidt's experiences of the British–German relationship before and during his chancellorship from 1974 to 1982, his story nonetheless illustrates some wider patterns of the post-war bilateral relationship. In fact, the deeper origins of many bilateral dynamics in the 1970s can be traced back to the immediate post-war years. As the first chapter has shown, Schmidt's political socialisation in the 1950s and 1960s coincided with profound changes in the European political landscape. For West Germany, the period saw the war-torn country's economic revitalisation and international rehabilitation based largely on its persistent pursuit of Franco–German reconciliation within the nascent EC and firm backing by the transatlantic alliance. For Britain, by contrast, the period signified the country's ultimate reduction to a post-imperial medium-sized European power, even if some characteristics of great power status remained. This lasting shift in the power balance between Britain and Germany shaped Schmidt's changing attitudes towards Britain prior to his assumption of office: although he remained sympathetic towards Britain, France, and the United States had by the mid-1960s come to occupy much greater importance in Schmidt's own

Conclusions 213

geostrategic thought, and in post-war German foreign policy more generally. Schmidt's reluctant attitude towards Britain's second EC application is particularly telling in this regard, showing how hesitant the future Chancellor proved to jeopardize the Franco–German relationship for the sake of British membership as early as 1967.

Quite apart from shaping the mindsets of British and German leaders in different ways, the divergent historical experiences of the 1950s and 1960s also meant that British and German European policies where operating in radically different domestic environments even after Britain had eventually joined the EC in January 1973. Whereas the European integration process had come to enjoy widespread cross-party support in the Federal Republic, it had not acquired any comparable degree of domestic consensus in Britain. These different domestic set-ups were exposed starkly by the British attempt to renegotiate its terms of EC membership at the very beginning of Schmidt's chancellorship in 1974–5, the focus of the second chapter. Whereas Harold Wilson's renegotiation strategy was determined first and foremost by his attempt to hold party and public together over the domestically highly controversial EC membership question, Schmidt's unresponsive attitude in turn reflected a more general German political instinct to protect and preserve the substance and cohesion of both the Franco–German relationship and the EC more generally. The episode therefore contributed heavily to the Franco–German rapprochement under Schmidt and Valéry Giscard d'Estaing, as the two leaders mended forces to protect both their own relationship and the wider cohesion of the EC against a potential intra-EC fallout over British demands. For Britain, by contrast, the result was a certain self-marginalization in its triangular relationship with France and Germany, as not least their subsequent differences over European representation at the proposed consumer-producer conference show.

While many of these aspects constitute powerful long-term dynamics driving Schmidt apart from his respective British counterparts, the ways in which these dynamics could play out rather differently in the concrete day-to-day diplomacy of British–German relations can be witnessed in the period of James Callaghan's premiership from 1976 to 1979. Callaghan, who was equipped with a more realistic picture of Britain's post-imperial power and whose stint at the FCO had illustrated to him the pivotal importance of high-level personal diplomacy in the multilateral environment of the 1970s, cleverly utilised his

214   *Conclusions*

relationship with Schmidt in order to improve both the climate and the substance of British–German relations. Apart from the successful solving of some long-standing second-rank bilateral disputes, Callaghan's adept handling of Schmidt also ensured that the more serious British and German differences over EC matters did not overshadow other aspects of bilateral collaboration, particularly within the transatlantic alliance. In this regard, British–German relations under Callaghan also benefitted heavily from the deterioration in the US–German relationship after the election of Jimmy Carter as US President in late 1976: Schmidt's troubled personal relationship with the new US President, as well as the FRG's continuing dependence on its Western allies for its security, elevated Callaghan to the role of a key transatlantic arbiter and mediator between Western Europe and Washington. Within the EC, however, Britain and Germany remained as far apart as ever, as not least Schmidt's and Giscard's joint pursuit of the EMS against Callaghan's reluctance shows. It highlights yet again the strategic gap that continuously separated British and German leaders over European integration, even though Callaghan proved much more skilful than his predecessor Wilson in explaining his domestic preoccupations and personal reasoning to Schmidt.

Yet, it was Thatcher's first term in office that most clearly brought to the fore the key paradox of British–German relations under Schmidt: while there were manifold structural pressures driving 1970s Britain and Germany closely together, the historically different attitudes towards the EC meant that such British–German communalities of interest never resulted in a corresponding strengthening of the bilateral relationship. Within the transatlantic alliance, for example, Schmidt and Thatcher cooperated unprecedentedly closely to pursue joint interests, not least over the dual-track decision and the Polish crisis; yet, such collaboration was overshadowed almost completely by their simultaneous tensions over the EC budget question. Again, the different perceptions and mindsets of the two leaders form key of the explanation: whereas Thatcher regarded the EC's rules of financing as genuinely unjust and therefore saw no problem in pursuing British interests aggressively, Schmidt by contrast regarded Thatcher's noncompromising and confrontational approach as a more general threat against the stability and cohesion of the EC, an institution he considered the very foundation of West German foreign policy after 1945. As a result, Schmidt yet again stuck to his political instinct to prioritise

Conclusions 215

the protection of the EC and the Franco–German relationship at its heart, even if this meant potentially forsaking some short-term economic benefits or risking a prolong diplomatic crisis with Britain. The budget controversy therefore also illustrates how high-level diplomacy could exacerbate rather than diminish tensions at times: clouded by his previous experiences of British European policy and his generally fatalistic outlook on the world situation at the time, Schmidt eventually came to regard Thatcher's aggressive pursuit of the budget question as merely one symptom of a much more general British reluctance against cooperation with its European partners – even though their simultaneous dealings within the transatlantic alliance offered much evidence to the contrary.

What, then, might Schmidt's interactions with his British counterparts during the 1970s reveal about some of the more general patterns of the post-war bilateral relationship? Although Schmidt's experience of the British–German relationship is obviously not wholly representative of the highly complex and multifaceted relations between the two countries after 1945, there are nonetheless some more general conclusions that can be drawn from his personal story. At first sight, of course, it clearly confirms the comparative lack of centrality of the British–German relationship compared to both countries' other relationships with the United States and, in the case of Germany, France.[12] But they also show that the lack of improvement in the British–German relationship after Britain's EC accession in 1973 was by no means inevitable, given the rather different bilateral climate under the premierships of Wilson, Callaghan, and Thatcher. Part of the explanation clearly stems from the three British PMs' very different approaches to personal diplomacy. In the context of the intensification of bilateral and multilateral summitry in the 1970s, personal communication on the highest level mattered a lot in shaping the bilateral relationship: at best, it served as a potential bridge to reconcile and perhaps overcome bilateral difficulties and misunderstandings, such as under Callaghan; at worst, it aggravated differences and personal animosities.[13] For much of the 1970s, the latter option proved to be the case. Both Wilson and Thatcher repeatedly

[12] Lee, *Victory in Europe*; Noakes et al., *Britain and Germany in Europe*; Larres and Meehan, *Uneasy Allies*; Morgan and Bray, *Partners and Rivals in Western Europe*.
[13] For an excellent discussion of the potentials as well as pitfalls of high-level summitry, see also J. W. Young, *Twentieth-Century Diplomacy: A Case Study*

216   *Conclusions*

used their high-level dealings with Schmidt in order to bolster their domestic images as doughty and determined fighters for British interests, rather than seeing them as genuine opportunities to strike up consensual and mutually beneficial compromises with their German opposite. Callaghan, by contrast, proved much more adept at playing the game of high-level summitry, the result being that intra-EC troubles rarely spilt over into other areas of British–German relations during his premiership.

At the same time, however, the very fact that Schmidt and his respective British counterparts clashed so frequently and persistently during the 1970s and early 1980s also points to some bigger and more general differences in British and German outlooks on post-war European cooperation that were relatively independent of the person-alities in charge. Again, the very different historical experience of European integration in the immediate post-war years lies at their heart. On the British side, all three British leaders – Wilson, Callaghan, and Thatcher – essentially regarded the EC as only one of many possible frameworks for European cooperation, and one that did not suit Britain particularly well. This resulted in a largely transactional relationship between Britain and its EC partners, in which all three PMs were quite happy to negotiate toughly and resiliently to secure or improve Britain's standing inside the EC, even if this meant questioning some of its core foundations and principles. Schmidt's views, by con-trast, show how the EC had by the 1970s already come to constitute a key and indispensable part of West Germany's post-war DNA. Although critical of some of the EC's institutions and mechanisms, Schmidt nonetheless regarded the EC as the FRG's main vehicle to rehabilitate itself and exercise influence on the international stage, an agenda that also had a strong moral dimension. As a result, Schmidt frequently perceived Britain's aggressive and often antagonistic hag-gling over key EC rules and mechanisms as a more general threat against the very foundations of post-war European cooperation, how-ever well-founded some British objections and demands might have seemed to him on paper and whatever the evidence of close cooperation in other areas of the bilateral relationship. This was a logic that the British never understood completely; and part of the reason why Wilson and his successors were ultimately all unable to see eye to eye

of British Practice, 1963–1976 (Cambridge: Cambridge University Press, 2008), 117.

Conclusions 217

with their German counterpart over European integration. But it is a story of mutual misperceptions and misunderstandings, rather than simply one-sided British obstructionism.

These bigger differences in the British and German approaches towards European integration, as evident in the interactions of Schmidt and his respective British opposites, also help explain why the often unprecedentedly close British–German collaboration in many non-EC areas during the 1970s has remained so much in the background in our perceptions of the bilateral relationship, and why historians still tend to describe it as the 'hidden dimension' or 'silent alliance' of post-war international politics.[14] Yet again, the comparison between Schmidt's outlook and that of his British counterparts offers some clues. Although British PMs like Callaghan or Thatcher clearly felt the structural pressures driving Britain and Germany closer together inside European frameworks, they also remained deeply attached to both the Anglo–American relationship and potential fora of European collaboration other than the EC; there was also little political mileage to be gained domestically from staging closer European cooperation to their parties and public. Schmidt, by contrast, not only benefited domestically from playing up his European credentials, but he also genuinely regarded the EC as an integral part of a wider German strategy to better protect West European interests against the uncertainties caused by what he regarded as a lack of American leadership. In Schmidt's mindset, Britain's controversial role in intra-EC politics thus eventually spilt over into other areas of European cooperation, whatever the actual hard evidence of constructive and proactive bilateral collaboration in non-EC matters. Schmidt's damning verdict on the post-war British–German relationship, then, was clearly unfair to the actual British contribution to West European cooperation during his chancellorship. But in international diplomacy, perceptions often 'matter as much as realities'.[15]

The ways in which the different British and German outlooks on post-war European cooperation went far beyond the particular personalities and diplomatic styles of those in office can be seen particularly clearly when compared to the Franco–German relationship under

---

[14] Kaiser and Roper, *Die Stille Allianz*; Heuser, 'Britain and the Federal Republic of Germany in NATO'.

[15] Reynolds, *Britannia Overruled*, 238.

Schmidt and Giscard during the same period. In theory, British and German objectives in the 1970s should have been much more compatible than Franco–German ones – given Britain's and Germany's more compatible industrial structures, their largely similar outlook on global trade, and their more general attitudes towards the transatlantic alliance. What held the Franco–German alliance together under Schmidt and Giscard, however, was a unique combination of short-term political congruences and longer-term strategic interests.[16] Schmidt and Giscard may have shared similar personal outlooks, but much more important was the fact that both regarded the protection of the EC and the Franco–German relationship as the key and overarching long-standing objectives of their European policies.[17] It mirrored the more general Franco–German consensus which had been set in motion under Adenauer and de Gaulle in the 1950s, and which was preserved and strengthened by manifold institutional as well as informal networks and interactions.[18] By contrast, Britain lacked a similar overarching strategic framework for EC membership, and its unfortunate standing in the triangular relationship between Britain, France, and Germany can thus ultimately be seen as the result of powerful path dependencies dating back to the 1950s. Indeed, many British politicians and officials were keenly aware of these dynamics, yet all too often seemed powerless to do anything about them. As the former British diplomat Sir Frank Roberts reflected grudgingly in 1999, 'We are always hoping that public opinion [in France and Germany] will somehow overrule their Governments and it never does; and we are always hoping that we can establish good relations with either France or Germany or both, which will somehow prevent them going ahead together'.[19] Successful personal diplomacy by skilled British leaders such as Callaghan may have eased the pain about some of these realities of post-war European politics, or even improved Britain's respective standing in the short-term; but it ultimately proved insufficient to overcome the long-term

---

[16] For an excellent comparative studies of the triangular relationship, see Morgan and Bray, *Partners and Rivals in Western Europe*; Wallace, *Britain's Bilateral Links with Western Europe*.

[17] Miard-Delacroix, *Partenaires de Choix*; Waechter, *Schmidt und Giscard d'Estaing*.

[18] U. Krotz and J. Schild, *Shaping Europe: France, Germany, and Embedded Bilateralism from the Elysée Treaty to Twenty-First Century Politics* (Oxford: University Press, 2013).

[19] British Diplomatic Oral History Project, Sir Frank Roberts, 3 July 1996.

Conclusions 219

dynamics of European cooperation set in motion during the 1950s. This is the real story of British–German relations during Helmut Schmidt's chancellorship, and part of the reason why intra-EC tensions have clouded his personal as well as more general perceptions of the bilateral relationship to such a large extent.

Whilst Schmidt's personal verdict on British–German relations during his time in office was therefore subject to significant distortions, his story can also be seen to offer some more general clues as to why notions of 'British un-Europeanness' have remained such dominant features in our perceptions of post-war British–German relations. Although essentially a study of Schmidt's high-level interactions with his British counterparts, the book has also developed and built upon two more general trends in the historiography of 1970s European integration. First, its attempt to connect the intra-EC and extra-EC dimensions of the bilateral relationship followed recent attempts by historians of European integration to widen their analytical scope from the narrow field of European *integration* to incorporate the much bigger field of European *cooperation*. Over the past few years, these approaches have changed our perceptions of 1970s EC politics significantly, painting the picture of a period in which the EC transformed itself into a capable political actor on the global stage and thereby planted the seeds for many subsequent developments in the 1980s.[20] Applying such an approach to 1970s British–German relations, this book not only adds further empirical substance to such findings, but it also forces us to reconsider Britain's role in 1970s European cooperation more generally. Whatever the significant intra-EC tensions at the time, Britain and Germany continued to cooperate closely in many other extra-EC areas, and Britain in fact frequently played a leading role in the fostering of an identifiable European position within the transatlantic alliance during the so-called 'second' Cold War from the late 1970s onwards.[21] The book thus changes not only the way we think about the bilateral relationship between Britain and Germany

---

[20] Romero, 'European Integration in the Long 1970s'; Migani and Varsori, *Europe in the International Arena*; J. Laursen, 'Introduction: Wilderness Years of European Integration, 1973–83?', in J. Laursen (ed.), *The Institutions and Dynamics of the European Community, 1973–83* (Baden-Baden: Nomos, 2014), 11–29.; C. Hiepel, 'Introduction', in C. Hiepel (ed.), *Europe in a Globalising World: Global Challenges and European Responses in the 'long' 1970s* (Baden-Baden: Nomos, 2014), 13.

[21] J. W. Young, 'Western Europe and the End of the Cold War, 1979–1989', in Leffler and Westad, *CHCW, Vol. III: Endings*, 289–310; N. P. Ludlow,

220   *Conclusions*

at the time, but also how we think about the nature of 1970s European cooperation more generally.

By putting the 'mental maps' and worldviews of Schmidt and his respective British counterparts at the centre of its study, the book further speaks to the second major trend in European integration historiography, namely the increased focus on the role of political and cultural narratives in the integration process. As has been shown, Schmidt's damning verdict on Britain's role in post-war Europe ties into a more general and highly teleological popular Euro-narrative of European integration as a gradual, progressive, and seemingly irreversible process; a process that centres overwhelmingly on the EC and in which Britain is frequently seen to have missed a boat or bus.[22] Yet, it is a narrative that clearly does not reflect the real nature of 1970s British–German relations, because it pays disproportionate attention to the intra-EC aspects of the bilateral relationship and prioritises certain areas of post-war European cooperation over others.[23] Through an analysis of how such abstract narratives frequently affected the high-level diplomacy between Schmidt and his respective British counterparts, the book has thus highlighted the need to historicise such competing British and German narratives of European integration, and to uncover their effects on both the actual course and the subsequent representations of the bilateral relationship – because, ultimately, Schmidt's self-proclaimed 'disillusionment' with Britain signifies a much bigger clash of competing British and German narratives of post-war European cooperation; a clash that was the result of the two countries' very different historical experiences of the integration process since 1945.

Taking a more long-term view, the recurrent misunderstandings that shaped British–German relations under Schmidt can also be found in the subsequent history of the bilateral relationship. Around the period of German reunification in particular, they could be witnessed again in the profound disagreements over how to best deal with the new geostrategic situation in Europe after the end of the Cold War: whereas the German Chancellor Helmut Kohl instinctively sought to allay fears

'The new Cold War and the Expansion of the European Community – A Nexus?', in Laursen, *Institutions and Dynamics*, 131–49.

[22] An excellent critique of this narrative is offered by Gilbert, 'Narrating the Process', 641–62.

[23] Ibid.; Laursen, 'Wilderness Years', 23.

Conclusions 221

over a resurgent Germany by embedding the newly unified country firmly into a resurgent European integration process through the Maastricht Treaty, his British opposite Margaret Thatcher instead regarded the intensification of the European integration as a potential route to European federalism and German domination.[24] During the 1990s, these dynamics eventually played out far beyond the realm of high politics, culminating in the virulent bilateral disputes surrounding Britain's Black Wednesday on 16 September 1992. They also contributed heavily to the irresistible rise of Euroscepticism within the British Conservatives since the late 1980s, a dynamic that eventually triggered PM David Cameron's singularly unsuccessful attempt to imitate Wilson's 1974–5 ploy by calling for a renegotiation of Britain's terms of EU membership followed by a nationwide referendum. Indeed, the German response to Cameron's demands was strikingly familiar to Schmidt's response to Wilson forty years earlier: offering some limited concessions whilst strictly rejecting anything that might go against the established rules and mechanisms of the now European Union. Once again, British policy was seen to question and potentially undermine some of the key principles and cornerstones of European integration – and once again, Germany's political instinct to preserve the EU's coherence and unity kicked in. The European integration process has, of course, changed profoundly since the period of Schmidt's chancellorship, as have Britain and Germany themselves. Yet, the evident similarities in the bilateral dynamics between the 1970s and contemporary politics suggest that the history of British–German relations under Schmidt might also offer some valuable background to the long-term patterns and rhetorical tropes underlying many of the British and German debates over Brexit today.

---

[24] Young, *Blessed Plot*, 306–74.

Bibliography

Unpublished Primary Sources

Archives

Germany

> Bundesarchiv (Koblenz).
> Politisches Archiv des Auswärtigen Amts (Berlin).
> Politisches Helmut-Schmidt-Archiv, Friedrich-Ebert-Stiftung (Bonn).
> Privates Helmut-Schmidt-Archiv (Hamburg).

United Kingdom

> Margaret Thatcher Foundation (Churchill College, Cambridge).
> The National Archives, Public Record Office (Kew).

United States

> Gerald R. Ford Presidential Library (Ann Arbor, MI). Accessed at www
> .fordlibrarymuseum.gov/collections-library.aspx [accessed 13 June 2018].
> Jimmy Carter Presidential Library (Atlanta, GA).
> Library of Congress (Washington, DC).
> Ronald Reagan Presidential Library (Simi Valley, CA).

Interviews

> British Diplomatic Oral History Project, Churchill College Cambridge, Sir
> Frank Roberts, 3 July 1996.
> British Diplomatic Oral History Project, Churchill College Cambridge, Sir
> Nicholas Henderson, 24 September 1998.
> Helmut Schmidt, Hamburg, 23 September 2013.

Bibliography 223

Published Primary Sources

Official Documents and Document Collections

Auswärtiges Amt (ed.), *Akten der Auswärtigen Politik der Bundesrepublik Deutschland [AAPD], 1974–82* (Munich: De Gruyter Oldenbourg, 2005–13).

Bundespresseamt [BPA], *Bulletin*, 1974–82.

Bundestag, *Protokolle des Deutschen Bundestages*, 1974–82.

Commission of the European Communities, *Euro-Barometre: Public Opinion in the European Community* 3 (June–July 1975), 23. Accessed at http://ec.europa.eu/commfrontoffice/publicopinion/archive s/eb/eb3/eb3_en.pdf [accessed 13 June 2018].

Fielding, S. (ed.), *The Labour Party: 'Socialism' and Society Since 1951* (Manchester: Manchester University Press, 1997).

Hansard, *House of Common Debates*, various volumes 1974–82. Accessed at http://hansard.millbanksystems.com/ [accessed on 13 June 2018].

Her Majesty's Stationary Office (ed.), *Documents on British Policy Overseas, Series III Vol. VII: German Unification 1989–90* (London: Routledge, 2010).

Labour Party, *Let Us Work Together – Labour's Way out of the Crisis* (London: The Labour Party, 1974).

Labour Party, *Report of the Seventy-Third Annual Conference of the Labour Party* (London: The Labour Party, 1974).

Labour Party, *Report of the Seventy-Fifth Annual Conference of the Labour Party* (London: The Labour Party, 1976).

US Department of State (eds.), *Foreign Relations of the United States*, various volumes.

Newspapers and Journals

Abendzeitung, Daily Express, Daily Telegraph, Der Spiegel, Die Welt, Die Zeit, Echo, The Economist, Europäische Gemeinschaft, Guardian, Financial Times, Frankfurter Allgemeine Zeitung, Fränkische Landeszeitung, Hamburger Sonntagsblatt, Le Monde, Manchester Evening Chronicle, New York Times, Newsweek, Observer, Politico, The Spectator, Stuttgarter Zeitung, Süddeutsche Zeitung, Sun, Sunday Express, The Times, US News & World Report, Vorwärts, Washington Post, Welt am Sonntag.

224 *Bibliography*

Secondary Sources

Unpublished PhD Dissertations

An, P. E., 'Anglo–German Relations in the EC/EU 1979–97' (Cambridge: University of Cambridge, 2006).

Aqui, L., 'Britain and the European Community, 1 January 1973–5 June 1975: Policy, Party Politics and Public Opinion' (London: Queen Mary University of London, 2018).

Cotton, C., 'The Labour Party and European Integration, 1961–83' (Cambridge: University of Cambridge, 2010).

Furby, D. E., 'The Revival and Success of Britain's Second Application for Membership of the European Community, 1968–71' (London: Queen Mary University of London, 2010).

Gijswijt T., 'Uniting the West: The Bilderberg Group, the Cold War and European Integration, 1952–66' (Heidelberg: Ruprecht-Karls-Universität, 2007).

Knowles, C., 'Winning the peace: The British in Occupied Germany, 1945–8' (London: King's College London, 2014).

Okamoto, Y., 'Britain, European Security and the Cold War, 1976–9' (London: Queen Mary University of London, 2014).

Rosenfeld, F., 'The Anglo–German Encounter in Occupied Hamburg, 1945–50' (New York, NY: Columbia University, 2006).

Zetsche, A., 'The Quest for Atlanticism: German–American Elite Networking, the Atlantik-Brücke and the American Council on Germany, 1952–74' (Newcastle upon Tyne: Northumbria University, 2016).

Film and Television

ARD, *Menschen bei Maischberger*, 12 August 2012.

NRD, *Ein Mann und seine Stadt: Der Hanseat über seine Heimat Hamburg*, 1986.

Books and Articles

Abelshauser, W., *Deutsche Wirtschaftsgeschichte seit 1945* (Munich: Beck, 2004).

Ahrens, M., *Die Briten in Hamburg: Besatzerleben 1945–58* (Munich and Hamburg: Dölling und Galitz, 2011).

Aldous, R., *Reagan and Thatcher: The Difficult Relationship* (London: W.W. Norton & Company, 2012).

Bibliography

Alt, J. E., *The politics of Economic Decline: Economic Management and Political Behaviour in Britain Since 1964* (Cambridge: Cambridge University Press, 1979).

Alt, J. E., 'The Politics of Economic Decline in the 1970s', in L. Black, H. Pemberton, and P. Thane (eds.), *Reassessing 1970s Britain* (Manchester: Manchester University Press, 2013), 25–40.

Aubourg, V., 'Organizing Atlanticism: The Bilderberg Group and the Atlantic Institute, 1952–63', *Intelligence and National Security* 18/2 (2003), 92–105.

Aust, S., *Der Baader Meinhof Komplex* (Hamburg: Hoffmann und Campe, 1986).

Auten, B. J., *Carter's Conversion: The Hardening of American Defense Policy* (Columbia, MI: University of Missouri Press, 2009).

Bache, I. and A. Jordan (eds.), *The Europeanization of British Politics* (Basingstoke: Macmillan, 2006).

Bange, O., *The EEC Crisis of 1963 – Kennedy, Macmillan, De Gaulle and Adenauer in Conflict* (Basingstoke: Macmillan, 2000).

Bange, O., '"Keeping Détente Alive": Inner-German Relations Under Helmut Schmidt and Erich Honecker, 1974–82', in L. Nuti (ed.), *The Crisis of Détente in Europe: From Helsinki to Gorbachev, 1975–85* (London: Routledge, 2008), 230–43.

Barnett, C., *The Audit of War: The Illusion and Reality of Britain as a Great Nation* (Basingstoke: Macmillan, 1986).

Basosi, D., 'The European Community and International Reaganomics, 1981–5', in K. K. Patel and K. Weisbrode (eds.), *European Integration and the Atlantic Community in the 1980s* (Cambridge: Cambridge University Press, 2014), 133–53.

Beckett, A., *When the Lights Went Out: Britain in the Seventies* (London: Faber, 2009).

Beloff, M., *Britain and the European Union: Dialogue of the Deaf* (Basingstoke: Macmillan, 1996).

Benn, T., *Against the Tide: Diaries 1973–6* (London: Hutchinson, 1989).

Berger, S., *The British Labour Party and the German Social Democrats, 1900–31* (Oxford: Oxford University Press, 1994).

Berstein, S. and J. P. Rioux, *The Pompidou Years, 1969–74* (Cambridge: Cambridge University Press, 2000).

Birkner, T., *Comrades for Europe?: Die 'Europarede' Helmut Schmidts 1974* (Bremen: Edition Temmen, 2005).

Birkner, T., *Mann des gedruckten Wortes: Helmut Schmidt und die Medien* (Bremen: Edition Temmen, 2014).

Black, L., H. Pemberton, and P. Thane (eds.), *Reassessing 1970s Britain* (Manchester: Manchester University Press, 2013).

Bluth, C., *Britain, Germany, and Western Nuclear Strategy* (Oxford: Clarendon Press, 1995).

Böhmer, K., '"We Too Mean Business": Germany and the Second British Application to the EEC, 1966–7', in O. Daddow (ed.), *Harold Wilson and European Integration: Britain's Second Application to Join the EEC* (London: Frank Cass, 2003), 211–26.

Bozo, F., 'France, "Gaullism," and the Cold War', in M. P. Leffler and O. A. Westad (eds.), *The Cambridge History of the Cold War, Vol. II: Crises and Détente* (Cambridge: Cambridge University Press, 2010), 158–78.

Bresselau von Bressensdorf, A., *Frieden durch Kommunikation: Das System Genscher und die Entspannungspolitik im Zweiten Kalten Krieg 1979–82/83* (Munich: De Gruyter Oldenbourg, 2015).

Brivati, B. and H. Jones (eds.), *From Reconstruction to Integration: Britain and Europe Since 1945* (Leicester: Leicester University Press, 1993).

Broad, R., *Labour's European Dilemmas Since 1945: From Bevin to Blair* (Basingstoke: Macmillan, 2001).

Brown, A., *The Myth of the Strong Leader: Political Leadership in the Modern Age* (London: Bodley Head, 2014).

Brunet, L. A., *Forging Europe: Industrial Organisation in France, 1940–52* (Basingstoke: Macmillan, 2017).

Brzezinski, Z., *Power and Principle: Memoirs of the National Security Adviser 1977–81* (New York: Farrar, Straus and Giroux, 1983).

Bullard, J., 'Great Britain and German Unification', in J. Noakes, P. Wende, and J. Wright (eds.), *Britain and Germany in Europe, 1949–90* (Oxford: Oxford University Press, 2002), 219–30.

Burk, K., 'The Americans, the Germans, and the British: The 1976 IMF Crisis', *Twentieth Century British History* 5/3 (1994), 351–69.

Burk, K. and A. Cairncross, *Goodbye, Great Britain: The 1976 IMF Crisis* (New Haven, CT and London: Yale University Press, 1992).

Burr, W. and D. A. Rosenberg, 'Nuclear Competition in an Era of Stalemate, 1963–75', in M. P. Leffler and O. A. Westad (eds.), *The Cambridge History of the Cold War, Vol. II: Crises and Détente* (Cambridge: Cambridge University Press, 2010), 88–111.

Butler, D. and U. Kitzinger, *The 1975 Referendum* (Basingstoke: Macmillan, 1976).

Callaghan, J., *Time and Chance* (London: Collins, 1987).

Carrington, P., *Reflecting on Things Past: The Memoirs of Lord Carrington* (London: Collins, 1988).

Carter, J., *White House Diary* (New York: Farrar, Straus and Grioux, 2010).

Casey, S. and J. Wright (eds.), *Mental Maps in the Early Cold War Era, 1945–68* (London: Macmillan, 2011).

Bibliography

Casey, S. and J. Wright (eds.), *Mental Maps in the Era of Détente and the End of the Cold War 1968–91* (London: Macmillan, 2015).

Catterall, P. (ed.), *The Macmillan Diaries, Vol. II: Prime Minister and After, 1957–66* (London: Macmillan, 2011).

Charlton, M., *The Price of Victory* (London: BBC Publications, 1983).

Chiampan, A., 'Those European Chicken Littles': Reagan, NATO, and the Polish Crisis, 1981–2', *The International History Review* 37/4 (2015), 682–99.

Christier, H., *Sozialdemokratie und Kommunismus: Die Politik der SPD und der KPD in Hamburg 1945–59* (Hamburg: Leibniz-Verlag, 1975).

Clemens, G., 'Der Beitritt Großbritanniens zu den Europäischen Gemeinschaften', in F. Knipping and M. Schönwald (eds.), *Aufbruch zum Europa der zweiten Generation: Die europäische Einigung 1969–84* (Trier: Wissenschaftlicher Verlag, 2006), 306–28.

Clemens, G. and A. Reinfeldt (eds.), *The Quest for Europeanization: Interdisciplinary Perspectives on a Multiple Process* (Stuttgart: Steiner, 2017).

Collins, A., 'The Cabinet Office, Tony Benn and the Renegotiation of Britain's Terms of Entry into the European Community, 1974–75', *Contemporary British History* 24/4 (2010), 471–91.

Conze, E., 'Staatsräson und nationale Interessen: Die "Atlantiker-Gaullisten"-Debatte in der westdeutschen Politik- und Gesellschaftsgeschichte der 1960er Jahre', in C. A. Wurm, U. Lehmkuhl, and H. Zimmerman (eds.), *Deutschland, Großbritannien, Amerika: Politik, Gesellschaft und Internationale Geschichte im 20. Jahrhundert, Festschrift für Gustav Schmidt zum 65. Geburtstag* (Stuttgart: Steiner, 2003), 197–226.

Conze, E., *Die Suche nach Sicherheit: Eine Geschichte der Bundesrepublik Deutschland von 1949 bis in die Gegenwart* (Munich: Siedler, 2009).

Conze, V., *Das Europa der Deutschen: Ideen von Europa in Deutschland zwischen Reichstradition und Westorientierung* (Munich: De Gruyter, 2005).

Corthorn, P., 'The Cold War and British Debates over the Boycott of the 1980 Moscow Olympics', *Cold War History*, 13/1 (2013), 43–66.

Daddow, O. J. (ed.), *Harold Wilson and European Integration: Britain's Second Application to Join the EEC* (London: Cass, 2003).

Daddow, O. J., *Britain and Europe Since 1945: Historiographical Perspectives on Integration* (Manchester: Manchester University Press, 2004).

Daddow, O. and T. Oliver, 'A not so awkward partner: the UK has been champion of many causes in the EU', *LSE Brexit Blog*, 15 April 2016: http://blogs.lse.ac.uk/brexit/2016/04/15/a-not-so-awkward-partner-the-uk-has-been-a-champion-of-many-causes-in-the-eu/ [accessed on 13 June 2018].

Deighton, A., *The Impossible Peace: Britain, the Division of Germany and the Origins of the Cold War* (Oxford: Oxford University Press, 1990).

Deighton, A., 'The Last Piece of the Jigsaw: Britain and the Creation of the Western European Union, 1954', *Contemporary European History* 7/2 (July 1998), 181–96.

Deighton, A., 'British–West German Relations, 1945–72', in K. Larres and E. Meehan (eds.), *Uneasy Allies: British–German Relations and European Integration Since 1945* (Oxford: Oxford University Press, 2000), 27–44.

Deighton, A., 'Britain and the Cold War, 1945–55', in M. P. Leffler and O. A. Westad (eds.), *The Cambridge History of the Cold War, Vol. I: Origins* (Cambridge: Cambridge University Press, 2010), 112–32.

Deighton, A. and N. P. Ludlow, 'A Conditional Application: British Management of the First Attempt to Seek Membership of the EEC, 1961–3', in A. Deighton and A. S. Milward (eds.), *Building Postwar Europe: National Decision-Makers and European Institutions, 1948–63* (Basingstoke: Macmillan, 1995), 107–122.

Deighton, A. and A. S. Milward (eds.), *Building Postwar Europe: National Decision-Makers and European Institutions, 1948–63* (Basingstoke: Macmillan, 1995).

Dell, E., *The Schuman Plan and the British Abdication of Leadership in Europe* (Oxford: Oxford University Press, 1995).

Demidova, K., 'The Deal of the Century: The Reagan Administration and the Soviet Pipeline', in K. K. Patel and K. Weisbrode (eds.), *European Integration and the Atlantic Community in the 1980s* (Cambridge: Cambridge University Press, 2014), 59–82.

Denman R., *Missed Chances: Britain and Europe in the Twentieth Century* (London: Cassell, 1996).

Deveney, P. J., *Callaghan's Journey to Downing Street* (Basingstoke: Macmillan, 2010).

Dinan, D., *Ever Closer Union: An Introduction to European Integration* (Basingstoke: Macmillan, 1999).

Dinan, D., *Europe Recast: A History of European Union*, 2nd Edition (Basingstoke: Macmillan, 2014).

van Dijk, R., '"A Mass Psychosis": The Netherlands and NATO's Dual-track Decision, 1978–9', *Cold War History* 12/3 (2012), 381–405.

Drössel, T., *Die Engländer in Hamburg 1914 bis 1945* (Göttingen: Cuvillier, 2008).

Dockrill, S., *Britain's Policy for West German Rearmament, 1950–5* (Cambridge: Cambridge University Press, 1991).

Domber, G. F., 'Transatlantic Relations, Human Rights, and Power Politics', in P. Villaume and O. A. Westad (eds.), *Perforating the*

Bibliography

Iron Curtain: European Détente, Transatlantic Relations, and the Cold War, 1965–85 (Copenhagen: Museum Tusculanum, 2010), 195–214.

Donoughue, B., *Prime Minister: The Conduct of Policy Under Harold Wilson and James Callaghan* (London: Jonathan Cape, 1987).

Donoughue, B., 'Harold Wilson and the Renegotiation of the EEC Terms of Membership, 1974–5: A Witness Account', in B. Brivati and H. Jones (eds.), *From Reconstruction to Integration: Britain and Europe Since 1945* (Leicester: Leicester University Press, 1993), 191–206.

Dülffer, J. and W. Loth (eds.), *Dimensionen Internationaler Geschichte* (Munich: De Gruyter, 2012).

Elli, M., 'Callaghan, the British Government and the N-Bomb Controversy', *Cold War History* 15/3 (2015), 321–39.

Ellison, J., *Threatening Europe: Britain and the Creation of the European Community, 1955–8* (Basingstoke: Macmillan, 2000).

Ellison, J., 'Accepting the Inevitable: Britain and European integration', in W. Kaiser and G. Staerck (eds.), *British Foreign Policy, 1955–64: Contracting Options* (Basingstoke: Macmillan, 2000), 171–89.

Ellison, J., 'Britain and Europe', in P. Addison and H. Jones (eds.), *A Companion to Contemporary Britain 1939–2000* (Oxford: Blackwell, 2007), 517–38.

Ellison, J., 'Stabilising the West and Looking to the East: Anglo-American Relations, Europe and détente, 1965 to 1967', in N. P. Ludlow (ed.), *European Integration and the Cold War: Ostpolitik-Westpolitik, 1965–73* (Abingdon: Routledge, 2007), 105–27.

Elvert, J., *Die europäische Integration* (Darmstadt: Wissenschaftliche Buchgesellschaft, 2006).

English, R. and M. Kenny (eds.), *Rethinking British Decline* (Basingstoke: Macmillan, 1999).

Faulenbach, B., *Geschichte der SPD: Von den Anfängen bis zur Gegenwart* (Munich: Beck, 2012),

Ferguson, N., C. S. Maier, E. Manela, and D. J. Sargent (eds.), *The Shock of the Global: The 1970s in Perspective* (Cambridge, MA: Belknap of Harvard University Press, 2010).

Forster, A., *Euroscepticism in Contemporary British Politics: Opposition to Europe in the British Conservative and Labour Parties Since 1945* (London: Routledge, 2002).

Gamble, A., 'Europe and America', in B. Jackson and R. Saunders (eds.), *Making Thatcher's Britain* (Cambridge: Cambridge University Press, 2012), 218–33.

Garrard, P., 'Cognitive Archaeology: Uses, Methods and Results', *Journal of Neurolinguistics* 20 (2008), 9–13.

Gartoff, R. L., *Détente and Confrontation: American-Soviet Relations from Nixon to Reagan*, Revised Edition (Washington DC: Brookings Institution, 1994).

Garton Ash, T., *History of the Present* (London: Penguin, 2001).

Gassert, P., 'Did Transatlantic Drift Help European Integration? The Euromissiles Crisis, the Strategic Defense Initiative, and the Quest for Political Cooperation', in K. K. Patel and K. Weisbrode (eds.), *European Integration and the Atlantic Community in the 1980s* (Cambridge: Cambridge University Press, 2014), 154–76.

Gehler, M., 'Internationale Geschichte und ihre europäischen Zugänge', in B. Haider-Wilson, W. D. Godsey, and W. Mueller (eds.), *Internationale Geschichte in Theorie und Praxis / International History in Theory and Practice* (Vienna: Verlag der österreichischen Akademie der Wissenschaften, 2017), 165–206.

Geiger, T., *Atlantiker gegen Gaullisten: Außenpolitischer Konflikt und innerparteilicher Machtkampf in der CDU/CSU 1958–69* (Munich: Oldenbourg, 2008).

Geiger, T., 'Die "Landshut" in Mogadischu: Das außenpolitische Krisenmanagement der Bundesregierung angesichts der terroristischen Herausforderung 1977', *Vierteljahreshefte für Zeitgeschichte* 57/3 (2009), 413–56.

George, S., *An Awkward Partner: Britain in the European Community* (Oxford: Oxford University Press, 1990).

Gfeller, A. E., *Building a European Identity: France, the United States, and the Oil Shock, 1973–4* (New York and Oxford: Berghahn, 2012).

Graf, R., *Öl und Souveränität. Petroknowledge und Energiepolitik in den USA und Westeuropa in den 1970er Jahren* (Munich: De Gruyter Oldenbourg, 2014).

Gray, W. G., 'Floating the System: Germany, the United States, and the Breakdown of Bretton Woods, 1969–73', *Diplomatic History* 31/2 (2007), 295–323.

Gray, W. G., 'Toward a "Community of Stability"? The Deutsche Mark Between European and Atlantic Priorities, 1968–73', in M. Schulz and T. A. Schwartz (eds.), *The Strained Alliance: US-European Relations from Nixon to Carter* (Cambridge: Cambridge University Press, 2010), 145–68.

Greenwood, S., *Britain and European Integration Since the Second World War* (Manchester: Manchester University Press, 1996).

Greenwood, S., *Britain and the Cold War 1945–91* (Basingstoke: Macmillan, 2000).

Bibliography

Greiner, F., 'Introduction: Writing the Contemporary History of European Solidarity', *European Review of History: Revue européenne d'histoire* 24/6 (2017), 837–53.

Grob-Fitzgibbon, B., *Continental Drift: Britain and Europe from the End of Empire to the Rise of Euroscepticism* (Cambridge: Cambridge University Press, 2016).

Gilbert, M., 'Narrating the Process: Questioning the Progressive Story of European Integration', *Journal of Common Market Studies* 46/3 (2008), 641–62.

Gilbert, M., *European Integration: A Concise History* (Lanham, MD: Rowman & Littlefield Publishers, 2012).

Gilmour, I., *Dancing with Dogma: Britain Under Thatcherism* (London: Simon and Schuster, 1992).

Gowland, D. and A. Turner, *Reluctant Europeans: Britain and European Integration, 1945–98* (Harlow: Longman, 2000).

Haase, C., 'The Hidden Hand of British Foreign Policy? The British–German Koenigswinter Conferences in the Cold War', in C. Haase (ed.), *Debating Foreign Affairs: The Public and British Foreign Policy Since 1867* (Berlin: Philo, 2003), 96–133.

Haase, C. (ed.), *Debating Foreign Affairs: The Public and British Foreign Policy Since 1867* (Berlin: Philo, 2003).

Haase, C., *Pragmatic Peacemakers: Institutes of International Affairs and the Liberalization of West Germany, 1945–73* (Augsburg: Wissner, 2007).

Haeussler, M., 'A "Cold War European"? Helmut Schmidt and European Integration, c. 1945–82', *Cold War History* 15/4 (2015), 427–47.

Haeussler, M., 'A Pyrrhic Victory: Harold Wilson, Helmut Schmidt, and the British Renegotiation of EC Membership, 1974–5', *The International History Review* 37/4 (2015), 768–89.

Haeussler, M., 'A "Converted European"? James Callaghan and the "Europeanization" of British Foreign Policy in the 1970s', in G. Clemens and A. Reinfeldt (eds.), *The Quest for Europeanization: Interdisciplinary Perspectives on a Multiple Process* (Stuttgart: Steiner, 2017), 153–66.

Haeussler, M., 'The Convictions of a Realist: Concepts of "Solidarity" in Helmut Schmidt's European Thought, 1945–82', *European Review of History: Revue Européenne d'histoire* 24/6 (2017), 955–72.

Haftendorn, H., 'Das doppelte Mißverständnis: zur Vorgeschichte des NATO-Doppelbeschlusses', *Vierteljahreshefte für Zeitgeschichte* 33 (1985), 244–87.

Haftendorn, H., *Deutsche Außenpolitik zwischen Selbstbeschränkung und Selbstbehauptung, 1945–2000* (Stuttgart: DVA, 2001).

Hanimäki, J. M., *The Rise and Fall of Détente: American Foreign Policy and the Transformation of the Cold War* (Washington, DC: Pontomac Books, 2013).

Hannay, D. (ed.), *Britain's Entry into the European Community. Report on the Negotiations of 1970–2 by Sir Con O'Neill* (London: Cass, 2000).

Hansen, J., *Abschied vom Kalten Krieg? Die Sozialdemokraten und der Nachrüstungsstreit (1977–87)* (Berlin and Boston: De Gruyter Oldenbourg, 2016).

Hanshew, K., *Terror and Democracy in West Germany* (Cambridge: Cambridge University Press, 2012)

Healey, D., 'NATO, Britain and Soviet Military Policy', *Orbis* 13/1 (1969), 48–58.

Healey, D., *The Time of My Life* (London: Michael Joseph, 1989).

Henderson, N., *The Private Office: A Personal View of Five Foreign Secretaries and of Government from the Inside* (London: Weidenfeld and Nicolson, 1984).

Henderson, N., *Mandarin: The Diaries of an Ambassador, 1969–82* (London: Weidenfeld and Nicolson, 1994).

Hennessy, P., *The Prime Minister: The Office and Its Holders Since 1945* (London: Allen Lane, 2000).

Heuser, B., 'Britain and the Federal Republic of Germany in NATO, 1955–90', in J. Noakes, P. Wende, and J. Wright (eds.), *Britain and Germany in Europe 1949–90* (Oxford: Oxford University Press, 2002), 141–62.

Heydemann, G., 'Partner or Rival? The British Perception of Germany During the Process of Unification 1989–91', in H. Husemann (ed.), *As others see us: Anglo–German perceptions* (Frankfurt am Main: Lang, 1994), 123–48.

Hickson, K., *The IMF Crisis of 1976 and British Politics* (London: Tauris Academic Studies, 2005).

Hiepel, C., 'Willy Brandt, Georges Pompidou und Europa. Das deutsch-französische Tandem in den Jahren 1969–74', in F. Knipping and M. Schönwald (eds.), *Aufbruch zum Europa der zweiten Generation: Die europäische Einigung 1969–84* (Trier: Wissenschaftlicher Verlag, 2006), 28–46.

Hiepel, C., 'The Hague Summit of the European Community, Britain's Entry, and the New Atlantic Partnership, 1969–70', in M. Schulz and T. A. Schwartz (eds.), *The Strained Alliance: U.S.-European Relations from Nixon to Carter* (Cambridge: Cambridge University Press, 2010), 105–24.

Bibliography

Hiepel, C., *Willy Brandt und Georges Pompidou: deutsch-französische Europapolitik zwischen Aufbruch und Krise* (Munich: Oldenbourg, 2012).

Hiepel, C. (ed.), *Europe in a Globalising World: Global Challenges and European Responses in the 'long' 1970s* (Baden-Baden: Nomos, 2014).

Hiepel, C., 'Introduction', in C. Hiepel (ed.), *Europe in a Globalising World: Global Challenges and European Responses in the 'long' 1970s* (Baden-Baden: Nomos, 2014), 9–26.

Hitchcock, W., 'France, the Western Alliance and the Origins of the Schuman Plan 1948–50', *Diplomatic History* 21/4 (1997), 603–30.

Hughes, R. G., *Britain, Germany and the Cold War: The Search for a European Détente 1949–67* (London: Routledge, 2007).

Ikonomou, H. A., A. Andry, and R. Byberg (eds.), *European Enlargement Across Rounds and Beyond Borders* (London: Routledge, 2017).

Jackson, B. and R. Saunders, 'Introduction: Varieties of Thatcherism', in B. Jackson and R. Saunders (eds.), *Making Thatcher's Britain* (Cambridge: Cambridge University Press, 2012), 1–22.

Jackson, B. and R. Saunders (eds.), *Making Thatcher's Britain* (Cambridge: Cambridge University Press, 2012).

James, H., *International Monetary Cooperation Since Bretton Woods* (New York/Oxford: University Press, 1996).

James, H., *Making the European Monetary Union* (Cambridge, MA: Harvard University Press, 2012).

Jenkins, R., *European Diary 1977–81* (London: Collins, 1989).

Jenkins, R., 'Wilson, (James) Harold, Baron Wilson of Rievaulx (1916–95)', in *Oxford Dictionary of National Biography* (Oxford: Oxford University Press, 2004).

Jouan, Q., 'Narratives of European Integration in Times of Crisis: Images of Europe in the 1970s', *Journal of European Integration History*, 22/1 (2016), 11–28.

Kaiser, K. and J. Roper (eds.), *Die Stille Allianz. Deutsch-Britische Sicherheitskooperation* (Bonn: Europa Union, 1987).

Kaiser, W., *Using Europe, Abusing the Europeans: Britain and European Integration, 1945–63* (Basingstoke: Macmillan, 1996).

Kaiser, W. and G. Staerck (eds.), *British Foreign Policy, 1955–64: Contracting Options* (Basingstoke: Macmillan, 2000).

Kandiah, M. et al., '"At the Top Table": British Elites' Perceptions of the UK's International Position, 1950–91', in J. W. Young, E. G. H. Pedaliu, and M. Kandiah (eds.), *Britain in Global Politics Volume 2: From Churchill to Blair* (Basingstoke: Macmillan, 2013) 179–97.

234 *Bibliography*

Karamouzi, E., *Greece, the EEC and the Cold War, 1974–79. The Second Enlargement* (Basingstoke: Macmillan, 2014).

von Karczewski, J., *Weltwirtschaft ist unser Schicksal: Helmut Schmidt und die Schaffung der Weltwirtschaftsgipfel* (Bonn: Dietz, 2008).

Keegan, W., D. Marsh, and R. Roberts, *Six Days in September: Black Wednesday, Brexit and the making of Europe* (London: OMFIF Press, 2017).

Kettenacker, L., 'Großbritannien: Furcht vor deutscher Hegemonie', in G. Trautmann (ed.), *Die häßlichen Deutschen? Deutschland im Spiegel der westlichen und östlichen Nachbarn* (Darmstadt: Wissenschaftliche Buchgesellschaft, 1991), 194–208.

Kettenacker, L., 'Britain and German Unification, 1989/90', in K. Larres and E. Meehan (eds.), *Uneasy Allies: British–German Relations and European Integration Since 1945* (Oxford: Oxford University Press, 2000), 99–126.

Kielinger, T., *Crossroads and Roundabouts: Junctions in German–British Relations* (Bonn: Bouvier, 1996).

Kieninger, S., *Dynamic Détente: The United States and Europe, 1964–75* (Lanham, MD: Lexington Books, 2016).

Kissinger, H. A., *White House Years* (Boston: Little, Brown, 1979).

Krause, S. H., 'Neue Westpolitik: The Clandestine Campaign to Westernize the SPD in Cold War Berlin, 1948–58', *Central European History* 48 (2015), 79–99.

Kreutzfeldt, J., *'Point of Return': Großbritannien und die Politische Union Europas 1969–75* (Stuttgart: Steiner, 2010).

Krotz, U. and J. Schild, *Shaping Europe: France, Germany, and Embedded Bilateralism from the Elysée Treaty to Twenty-First Century Politics* (Oxford: Oxford University Press, 2013).

Lahey, D. J., 'The Thatcher Government's Response to the Soviet Invasion of Afghanistan, 1979–80', *Cold War History* 13 (2013), 21–42.

Larres, K., 'Introduction: Uneasy Allies or Genuine Partners? Britain, Germany, and European Integration', in K. Larres and E. Meehan (eds.), *Uneasy Allies: British–German Relations and European Integration Since 1945* (Oxford: Oxford University Press, 2000), 1–26.

Lappenküper, U. and G. Thiemeyer (eds.), *Europäische Einigung im 19. und 20. Jahrhundert: Akteure und Antriebskräfte* (Paderborn: F. Schöningh, 2013).

Laursen, J. (ed.), *The Institutions and Dynamics of the European Community, 1973–83* (Baden-Baden: Nomos, 2014).

Laursen, J., 'Introduction: Wilderness Years of European Integration, 1973–83?', in J. Laursen (ed.), *The Institutions and Dynamics of the*

Bibliography

European Community, 1973–83 (Baden-Baden: Nomos, 2014), 11–29.

Lee, S., *An Uneasy Partnership: British–German Relations Between 1955 and 1961* (Bochum: Brockmeyer, 1996).

Lee, S., *Victory in Europe: Britain and Germany Since 1945* (Harlow: Longman, 2001).

Leffler, M. P. and O. A. Westad (eds.), *The Cambridge History of the Cold War, Vol. I: Origins* (Cambridge: University Press, 2010).

Leffler, M. P. and O. A. Westad (eds.), *The Cambridge History of the Cold War, Vol. II: Crises and Détente* (Cambridge: Cambridge University Press, 2010).

Leffler, M. P. and O. A. Westad (eds.), *The Cambridge History of the Cold War, Vol. III: Endings* (Cambridge: Cambridge University Press, 2010).

Lieber, R., *The Oil Decade: Conflict and Cooperation in the West* (New York: Praeger, 1983).

Lippert, W. D., *The Economic Diplomacy of Ostpolitik: Origins of NATO's Energy Dilemma* (New York and Oxford: Berghahn, 2011).

Lord, C., *British Entry to the European Community Under the Heath Government of 1970–4* (Aldershot: Dartmouth, 1993).

Lord, C., *Absent at the Creation: Britain and the Formation of the European Community, 1950–2* (Aldershot: Dartmouth, 1996).

Loth, W., 'Konrad Adenauer und die europäische Einigung', in M. König and M. Schulz (eds.), *Die Bundesrepublik Deutschland und die europäische Einigung 1949–2000: Politische Akteure, gesellschaftliche Kräfte und internationale Erfahrungen* (Stuttgart: Steiner, 2004), 39–60.

Loth, W., *Building Europe: A History of European Unification* (Berlin and Boston: De Gruyter Oldenbourg, 2015).

Lucas, H. D., 'Politik der kleinen Schritte – Genscher und die deutsche Europapolitik 1974–83', in H. D. Lucas (ed.), *Genscher, Deutschland und Europa* (Baden-Baden: Nomos, 2002), 87–114.

Ludlow, N. P., *The Making of the European Monetary System: A Case Study in the Politics of the European Community* (London: Butterworths, 1982).

Ludlow, N. P., *Dealing with Britain: the Six and the First UK Application to the EEC* (Cambridge: Cambridge University Press, 1997).

Ludlow, N. P., 'Constancy and Flirtation: Germany, Britain, and the EEC, 1956–72', in J. Noakes, P. Wende, and J. Wright (eds.), *Britain and Germany in Europe 1949–90* (Oxford: Oxford University Press, 2002), 95–112.

Ludlow, N. P. (ed.), *European Integration and the Cold War: Ostpolitik-Westpolitik, 1965–73* (Abingdon: Routledge, 2007).

Ludlow, N. P., 'European integration and the Cold War', in M. P. Leffler and O. A. Westad (eds.), *The Cambridge History of the Cold War, Vol. II: Crises and Détente* (Cambridge: Cambridge University Press, 2010), 179–97.

Ludlow, N. P., 'The Real Years of Europe? US-West European Relations During the Ford Administration', *Journal of Cold War Studies* 15/3 (2013), 142–3.

Ludlow, N. P., 'The new Cold War and the Expansion of the European Community – A Nexus?', in J. Laursen (ed.), *The Institutions and Dynamics of the European Community, 1973–83* (Baden-Baden: Nomos, 2014), 131–49.

Ludlow, N. P., '"The Unnoticed Apogee of Atlanticism? US-Western European Relations During the Early Reagan Era', in K. K. Patel and K. Weisbrode (eds.), *European Integration and the Atlantic Community in the 1980s* (Cambridge: Cambridge University Press, 2014), 17–38.

Ludlow, N. P., 'Safeguarding British Identity or Betraying It? The Role of British "Tradition" in the Parliamentary Great Debate on EC Membership, October 1971', *Journal of Common Market Studies* 53/ 1 (2015), 18–34.

Ludlow, N. P., *Roy Jenkins and the European Commission Presidency, 1976–80: At the Heart of Europe* (Basingstoke: Macmillan, 2016).

Macintyre, T., *Anglo–German Relations During the Labour Governments 1964–70: NATO Strategy, Détente and European Integration* (Manchester: Manchester University Press, 2007).

Mawby, S., *Containing Germany: Britain and the Arming of the Federal Republic* (Basingstoke: Macmillan, 1999).

Merseburger, P., *Der Schwierige Deutsche: Kurt Schumacher* (Stuttgart: DVA, 1995).

Miard-Delacroix, H., *Partenaires de choix? Le chancelier Helmut Schmidt et la France, 1974–82* (Frankfurt am Main: Lang, 1993).

Miard-Delacroix, H., 'Ungebrochene Kontinuität. François Mitterrand und die deutschen Kanzler Helmut Schmidt und Helmut Kohl, 1981–84', *Vierteljahrshefte für Zeitgeschichte*, 47/4 (October 1999), 539–58.

Migani, G. and A. Varsori (eds.), *Europe in the International Arena During the 1970s: Entering a Different World* (Brussels: Lang, 2011).

Milward, A. S., *The United Kingdom and the European Community, Vol. I: The Rise and Fall of a National Strategy, 1945–63* (London: Cass, 2002).

Möckli, D., *European Foreign Policy During the Cold War: Heath, Brandt, Pompidou and the Dream of Political Unity* (London: I.B. Tauris, 2009).

Bibliography

Möckli, D., 'Asserting Europe's Distinct Identity: The EC Nine and Kissinger's Year of Europe', in M. Schulz and T. A. Schwartz (eds.), *The Strained Alliance: US-European Relations from Nixon to Carter* (Cambridge: Cambridge University Press, 2010), 195–220.

Moore, C., *Margaret Thatcher: The Authorised Biography, Vol. I: Not for Turning* (London: Penguin, 2013).

Moore, C., *Margaret Thatcher: The Authorised Biography, Vol. II: Everything She Wants* (London: Penguin, 2015).

Morgan, G., *The Idea of a European Superstate: Public Justification and European Integration* (Princeton, NJ: University Press, 2005).

Morgan, K., *Callaghan: A Life* (Oxford: Oxford University Press, 1997).

Morgan, R., 'Willy Brandt's "Neue Ostpolitik": British Perceptions and Positions, 1969–75', in A. M. Birke, M. Brechtken, and A. Searle (eds.), *An Anglo–German Dialogue: The Munich Lectures on the History of International Relations* (Munich: Saur, 2000), 179–202.

Morgan, R. and C. Bray (eds.), *Partners and Rivals in Western Europe: Britain, France and Germany* (Aldershot: Gower, 1987).

Mourlon-Druol, E., 'Filling the EEC Leadership Vacuum? The Creation of the European Council at the December 1974 Paris Summit', *Cold War History* 10/3 (2010), 315–39.

Mourlon-Druol, E., *A Europe Made of Money: The Emergence of the European Monetary System* (Ithaca, NY and London: Cornell University Press, 2012).

Mourlon-Druol, E. and F. Romero (eds.), *International Summitry and Global Governance: The Rise of the G7 and the European Council, 1974–91* (London and New York: Routledge, 2014).

Mullen, A., *The British Left's Great Debate on Europe* (London: Continuum, 2007).

Nehring, H. and Ziemann, B., 'Do All Paths Lead to Moscow?', *Cold War History*, 12/1 (2012), 1–24.

Nichter, L., *Richard Nixon and Europe: The Reshaping of the Postwar Atlantic World* (New York and Cambridge: Cambridge University Press, 2015).

Niedhart G., 'The British Reaction Towards Ostpolitik: Anglo-West German Relations in the Era of Détente', in C. Haase (ed.), *Debating Foreign Affairs: The Public and British Foreign Policy Since 1867* (Berlin: Philo, 2003), 130–52.

Niedhart G., 'Peaceful Change of Frontiers as a Crucial Element in the West German Strategy of Transformation', in O. Bange and G. Niedhart (eds.), *Helsinki 1975 and the Transformation of Europe* (New York and Oxford: Berghahn, 2008), 23–38.

Niedhart G., 'Ostpolitik: Transformation Through Communication and the Quest for Peaceful Change', *Journal of Cold War Studies* 18/3 (2016), 14–59.

Njølstad, O., 'The Carter Legacy: Entering the Second Era of the Cold War', in O. Njølstad (ed.), *The Last Decade of the Cold War: From Conflict Escalation to Conflict Transformation* (London and New York: Cass, 2004), 196–225.

Njølstad, O., 'The Collapse of Superpower Détente, 1975–80,' in M. P. Leffler and O. A. Westad (eds.), *The Cambridge History of the Cold War, Vol. III: Endings* (Cambridge: Cambridge University Press, 2010), 135–55.

Noakes, J., P. Wende, and J. Wright (eds.), *Britain and Germany in Europe 1949–90* (Oxford: Oxford University Press, 2002).

Nuti, L., 'The Origins of the 1979 Dual Track Decision – A Survey', in L. Nuti (ed.), *The Crisis of Détente in Europe: From Helsinki to Gorbachev, 1975–85* (London and New York: Routledge, 2009), 57–71.

Nuti, L. (ed.), *The Crisis of Détente in Europe: From Helsinki to Gorbachev, 1975–85* (London and New York: Routledge, 2009).

Oberloskamp, E., 'Die Europäisierung der Terrorismusbekämpfung in den 1970er Jahren: Bundesdeutsche Akteure und Positionen', in J. Hürter (ed.), *Terrorismusbekämpfung in Westeuropa: Demokratie und Sicherheit in den 1970er und 1980er Jahren* (Berlin: De Gruyter Oldenbourg, 2015), 219–38.

Oliver, T. and D. Allen, 'Foreign Policy', in I. Bache and A. Jordan (eds.), *The Europeanization of British Politics* (Basingstoke: Macmillan, 2006), 187–200.

Oppelland, T., 'Gerhard Schröder: Protagonist des atlantischen Europas', in M. König and M. Schulz (eds.), *Die Bundesrepublik Deutschland und die europäische Einigung 1949–2000: Politische Akteure, gesellschaftliche Kräfte und internationale Erfahrungen* (Stuttgart: Steiner, 2004), 129–46.

Parr, H., *Britain's Policy Towards the European Community: Harold Wilson and Britain's World Role, 1964–67* (London: Routledge, 2006).

Patel, K. K. (ed.), *Fertile Ground for Europe?: The History of European Integration and the Common Agricultural Policy Since 1945* (Baden-Baden: Nomos, 2009).

Patel, K. K., 'Europäische Integration', in J. Dülffer and W. Loth (eds.), *Dimensionen Internationaler Geschichte* (Munich: De Gruyter, 2012), 353–72.

Bibliography

Patel, K. K., 'Provincialising European Union: Co-operation and Integration in Europe in a Historical Perspective', *Contemporary European History* 22/4 (2013), 649–73.

Patel, K. K. and K. Weisbrode (eds.), *European Integration and the Atlantic Community in the 1980s* (Cambridge: Cambridge University Press, 2014).

Peters, B., *Tödlicher Irrtum: Die Geschichte der RAF* (Berlin: Argon, 2004).

Petersen, A. D., *Die Engländer in Hamburg, 1814 bis 1914: ein Beitrag zur hamburgischen Geschichte* (Hamburg: Bockel, 1993).

Philippe, H., *'The Germans Hold the Key': Anglo–German Relations and the Second British Approach to Europe* (Augsburg: Wissner, 2007).

Pick, D., *Brücken nach Osten: Helmut Schmidt und Polen* (Bremen: Edition Temmen, 2011).

Pimlott, B., *Harold Wilson* (London: HarperCollins, 1993).

Pine, M., *Harold Wilson and Europe: Pursuing Britain's Membership of the European Community* (London: Tauris Academic Studies, 2007).

Putnam, R. D. and N. Bayne, *Hanging Together. Cooperation and Conflict in the Seven-Power Summits* (London: Sage, 1987).

Raphael, L. and A. Doering-Manteuffel, *Nach dem Boom: Perspektiven auf die Zeitgeschichte seit 1970* (Göttingen: Vandenhoeck & Ruprecht, 2008).

Ratti, L., 'Britain, the German Question and the Transformation of Europe: From *Ostpolitik* to the Helsinki Conference, 1963–75', in O. Bange and G. Niedhart (eds.), *Helsinki 1975 and the Transformation of Europe* (New York and Oxford: Berghahn, 2008), 83–97.

Reynolds, D. J. (ed.), *The Origins of the Cold War in Europe: International Perspectives* (New Haven, CT and London: Yale University Press, 1994).

Reynolds, D. J., *Britannia Overruled: British Policy and World Power in the Twentieth Century* (Harlow: Longman, 2000).

Reynolds, D. J. and K. Spohr (eds.), *Transcending the Cold War: Summits, Statecraft, and the Dissolution of Bipolarity in Europe, 1970–90* (Oxford: Oxford University Press, 2016).

Rhodes, R. A. W. and P. Hart (eds.), *The Oxford Handbook of Political Leadership* (Oxford: Oxford University Press, 2014).

Robb, T., 'The Power of Oil: Edward Heath, the "Year of Europe" and the Anglo-American "Special Relationship"', *Contemporary British History* 26/1 (2012), 73–96.

Rödder, A., *Die Bundesrepublik Deutschland 1969–90* (Munich: Oldenbourg, 2004).

Romano, A., *From Détente in Europe to European Détente. How the West Shaped the Helsinki CSCE* (Brussels: Peter Lang, 2009).

Romano, A., 'The Main Task of European Political Cooperation: Fostering Détente in Europe', in P. Villaume and O. A. Westad (eds.), *Perforating the Iron Curtain: European Détente, Transatlantic Relations, and the Cold War, 1965–85* (Copenhagen: Museum Tusculanum, 2010), 123–42.

Romano, A., 'Untying Cold War Knots: The European Community and Eastern Europe in the Long 1970s', *Cold War History* 14/2 (2014), 153–73.

Romero, F. (ed.), 'The International History of European Integration in the Long 1970s: A Roundtable Discussion on Research Issues, Methodologies, and Directions', *Journal of European Integration History* 17/2 (2011), 331–60.

Romero, F., 'Cold War Historiography at the Crossroads', *Cold War History* 14/4 (2014), 685–703.

Romero, F., 'Refashioning the West to Dispel Its Fears: The Early G7 Summits', in E. Mourlon-Druol and F. Romero (eds.), *International Summitry and Global Governance: The Rise of the G7 and the European Council, 1974–91* (London and New York: Routledge, 2014), 117–37.

Roseman, M., 'Generation Conflict and German History, 1770–1968', in M. Roseman (ed.), *Generations in Conflict: Youth Revolt and Generation Formation in Germany 1770–1968* (Cambridge: Cambridge University Press, 1995), 1–46.

Rossbach, N. H., *Heath, Nixon and the Rebirth of the Special Relationship: Britain, the US and the EC, 1969–74* (Basingstoke: Macmillan, 2009).

Ruane, K. and J. Ellison, 'Managing the Americans: Anthony Eden, Harold Macmillan and the Pursuit of "Power-by-Proxy" in the 1950s', *Contemporary British History* 18/3 (2004), 147–67.

Sandbrook, D., *Seasons in the Sun: The Battle for Britain, 1974–9* (London: Penguin, 2013).

Sargent, D., *A Superpower Transformed: The Remaking of American Foreign Relations in the 1970s* (New York and Oxford: Oxford University Press, 2015).

Saunders, R., 'A Tale of Two Referendums: 1975 and 2016', *The Political Quarterly* 87/3 (2016), 318–22.

Saunders, R., *Yes to Europe! The 1975 Referendum and Seventies Britain* (Cambridge: Cambridge University Press, 2018).

Saunders, R., '"Crisis? What Crisis?" Thatcherism and the seventies', in B. Jackson and R. Saunders (eds.), *Making Thatcher's Britain* (Cambridge: Cambridge University Press, 2012), 25–42.

Schaad, M. P. C., *Bullying Bonn: Anglo–German Diplomacy on European Integration, 1955–61* (Basingstoke: Macmillan, 2000).

Bibliography

Sarantakes, N. E., *Dropping the Torch: Jimmy Carter, the Olympic Boycott and the Cold War* (New York and Cambridge: Cambridge University Press, 2011).

Schmale, W., *Geschichte und Zukunft der Europäischen Identität* (Stuttgart: Kohlhammer, 2008).

Schmidt, H., *Defence or Retaliation: A German Contribution to the Consideration of Nato's Strategic Problem* (Edinburgh: Oliver and Boyd, 1962).

Schmidt, H., 'Deutschland und das europäische Sicherheitssystem der Zukunft', *Wehrkunde* XVI/3 (March 1967), 118–24.

Schmidt, H., 'The Shaping of Europe and the Role of Nations', in Deutsch-Englische Gesellschaft e.V. (ed.), *Europe's Role in a Changing World: Deutsch-Englisches Gespräch, Königswinter, 10.–12. März 1967* (Düsseldorf, 1967), 18–24.

Schmidt, H., 'The 1977 Alastair Buchan Memorial Lecture', *Survival* 20/1 (1978), 2–10.

Schmidt, H., *A Grand Strategy for the West: The Anachronism of National Strategies in an Interdependent World* (New Haven, CT: Yale University Press, 1985).

Schmidt, H., *Die Deutschen und ihre Nachbarn: Menschen und Mächte II* (Berlin: Siedler, 1990).

Schmidt, H., 'Politischer Rückblick auf eine unpolitische Jugend', in H. Schmidt and L. Schmidt (eds.), *Kindheit und Jugend unter Hitler* (Berlin: Siedler, 1992), 213–54.

Schmidt, H., *Verteidigung oder Vergeltung: Ein deutscher Beitrag zum strategischen Problem der Nato* (Stuttgart: Seewald, 1961).

Schönwald, M., 'Der Falkland-Konflikt und die Europäische Gemeinschaft', in F. Knipping and M. Schönwald (eds.), *Aufbruch zum Europa der zweiten Generation: Die europäische Einigung 1969–84* (Trier: Wissenschaftlicher Verlag, 2004), 165–86.

Schulz, M. and T. A. Schwartz (eds.), *The Strained Alliance: US-European Relations from Nixon to Carter* (Cambridge: Cambridge University Press, 2010).

Schwarz, H. P., 'Adenauer und Europa', *Vierteljahreshefte für Zeitgeschichte* 27 (1979), 471–523.

Schwarz, H. P., 'The Division of Germany, 1945–9', in M. P. Leffler and O. A. Westad (eds.), *The Cambridge History of the Cold War, Vol. I: Origins* (Cambridge: Cambridge University Press, 2010), 133–53.

Schwartz, T., *Lyndon Johnson and Europe: In the Shadow of Vietnam* (Cambridge, MA: Harvard University Press, 2003).

Scott, A., *Allies Apart: Heath, Nixon and the Anglo–American Relationship* (Basingstoke: Macmillan, 2011).

242   Bibliography

Seldon, A. and K. Hickson (eds.), *New Labour, Old Labour: The Wilson and Callaghan Governments, 1974–9* (London: Routledge, 2004).

Self, R., *British Foreign and Defence Policy Since 1945: Challenges and Dilemmas in a Changing World* (Basingstoke: Macmillan, 2010).

Sharp, P., *Thatcher's Diplomacy: The Revival of British Foreign Policy* (Basingstoke: Macmillan, 1997).

Simonian, H., *The Privileged Partnership: Franco–German Relations in the European Community 1969–84* (Oxford: Clarendon, 1985).

Sjursen, H., *The United States, Western Europe and the Polish Crisis: International Relations in the Second Cold War* (Basingstoke: Macmillan, 2003).

Sloman, P., 'Appendix 2: Statistical Tables', in B. Jackson and R. Saunders (eds.), *Making Thatcher's Britain* (Cambridge: Cambridge University Press, 2012), 253–77.

Smith, J. and G. Edwards, 'British–West German Relations, 1973–89', in K. Larres and E. Meehan (eds.), *Uneasy Allies: British–German Relations and European Integration Since 1945* (Oxford: Oxford University Press, 2000), 45–62.

Soell, H., *Helmut Schmidt: Vernunft und Leidenschaft – 1918–69* (Munich: DVA, 2003).

Soell, H., *Helmut Schmidt: 1969 bis heute: Macht und Verantwortung* (Munich: DVA, 2008).

Soutou, G. H., 'The Linkage Between European Integration and Détente: The Contrasting Approaches of de Gaulle and Pompidou, 1965 to 1974', N. P. Ludlow (ed.), *European Integration and the Cold War: Ostpolitik-Westpolitik, 1965–73* (Abingdon: Routledge, 2007), 11–36.

Spohr, K., 'Conflict and Cooperation in Intra-Alliance Nuclear Politics: Western Europe, the United States, and the Genesis of NATO's Dual-Track Decision, 1977–9', *Journal of Cold War Studies* 13/2 (2011), 39–89.

Spohr, K., 'Helmut Schmidt and the Shaping of Western Security in the Late 1970s: the Guadeloupe Summit of 1979', *The International History Review* 37/1 (2015), 167–92.

Spohr, K., *The Global Chancellor: Helmut Schmidt and the Reshaping of the International Order* (Oxford: Oxford University Press, 2016).

Steinnes, K., *The British Labour Party: Transnational Influences and European Community Membership, 1960–73* (Stuttgart: Steiner, 2014).

Tauer, S., *Störfall für die gute Nachbarschaft? Deutsche und Franzosen auf der Suche nach einer gemeinsamen Energiepolitik (1973–80)* (Göttingen: Vandenhoeck & Ruprecht, 2012).

Bibliography 243

Thatcher, M., *Statecraft: Strategies for a Changing World* (London: William Collins, 2002).

Thiemeyer, G., 'Helmut Schmidt und die Gründung des Europäischen Währungssystems 1973–9', in F. Knipping and M. Schönwald (eds.), *Aufbruch zum Europa der zweiten Generation: Die europäische Einigung 1969–84* (Trier: Wissenschaftlicher Verlag, 2004), 245–68.

Thiemeyer, G., 'The European Currency System and the European Policies of Helmut Schmidt', in J. Laursen (ed.), *The Institutions and Dynamics of the European Community, 1973–83* (Baden-Baden: Nomos, 2014), 172–201.

Tomlinson, J., *The Politics of Decline: Understanding Post-War Britain* (Harlow: Longman, 2000).

Tomlinson, J., 'Economic Policy', in A. Seldon and K. Hickson (eds.), *New Labour, Old Labour: The Wilson and Callaghan Governments, 1974–79* (London: Routledge, 2004), 55–69.

Tomlinson, J., 'The politics of Declinism', in L. Black, H. Pemberton, and P. Thane (eds.), *Reassessing 1970s Britain* (Manchester: Manchester University Press, 2013), 41–60.

Türk, H., 'The Oil Crisis of 1973 as a Challenge to Multilateral Energy Cooperation Among Western Industrialized Countries', *Historical Social Research* 39/4 (2014), 209–30.

Turner, A. W., *Crisis? What Crisis? Britain in the 1970s* (London: Aurum, 2009).

Turner, I. D. (ed.), *Reconstruction in Post-War Germany: British Occupation Policy and the Western Zones 1945–55* (Oxford: Berg, 1989).

Urban, G., *Diplomacy and Disillusion at the Court of Margaret Thatcher; An Insider's View* (London: Tauris, 1996).

Vaughan, P. G., 'Zbigniew Brzezinski and the Helsinki Final Act', in L. Nuti (ed.), *The Crisis of Détente in Europe: From Helsinki to Gorbachev, 1975–85* (London and New York: Routledge, 2009) 11–25.

Venn, F., *The Oil Crisis* (Harlow: Longman, 2002).

Vinen, R., 'Thatcherism and the Cold War', in B Jackson. and R. Saunders (eds.), *Making Thatcher's Britain* (Cambridge: Cambridge University Press, 2012), 199–217.

Viola, D. M. (ed.), *Routledge Handbook of European Elections* (Abingdon: Routledge, 2016).

Waechter, M., *Helmut Schmidt und Valéry Giscard d'Estaing. Auf der Suche nach Stabilität in der Krise der 70er Jahre* (Bremen: Edition Temmen, 2011).

Wall, S., *A Stranger in Europe: Britain and the EU from Thatcher to Blair* (Oxford: Oxford University Press, 2008).

244   *Bibliography*

Wall, S., *The Official History of Britain and the European Community, vol. 2: From Rejection to Referendum, 1963–75* (Abingdon: Routledge, 2012).

Wallace, H., 'Bilateral, Trilateral and Multilateral Negotiations in the European Community', in R. Morgan and C. Bray (eds.), *Partners and Rivals in Western Europe: Britain, France and Germany* (Aldershot: Gower, 1986), 156–74.

Wallace, H., 'The Conduct of Bilateral Relationships by Governments', in R. Morgan and C. Bray (eds.), *Partners and Rivals in Western Europe: Britain, France and Germany* (Aldershot: Gower, 1986), 136–55.

Wallace, W., *Britain's Bilateral Links with Western Europe* (London: Routledge, 1984).

Wiegrefe, K., *Das Zerwürfnis: Helmut Schmidt, Jimmy Carter und die Krise der deutsch-amerikanischen Beziehungen* (Berlin: Propyläen, 2005).

Wilkens, A., 'Willy Brandt und die europäische Einigung', in M. Köni and M. Schulz (eds.), *Die Bundesrepublik Deutschland und die europäische Einigung 1949–2000: Politische Akteure, gesellschaftliche Kräfte und internationale Erfahrungen* (Stuttgart: Steiner, 2004), 167–84.

Wilkens, A., 'New Ostpolitik and European Integration: Concepts and Policies in the Brandt Era', in N. P. Ludlow (ed.), *European Integration and the Cold War: Ostpolitik-Westpolitik, 1965–73* (Abingdon: Routledge, 2007), 67–80.

Wilson, H., *Final Term: The Labour Government, 1974–6* (London: Weidenfeld and Nicolson, 1979).

Wilson, H., *This Blessed Plot: Britain and Europe from Churchill to Blair* (London: Macmillan, 1999).

Young, J. W., *Britain, France and the Unity of Europe 1945–51* (Leicester: University Press, 1984).

Young, J. W., 'German Rearmament and the European Defence Community', in J. W. Young and M. Dockrill (eds.), *The Foreign Policy of Churchill's Peacetime Administration, 1951–5* (Leicester: Leicester University Press, 1988), 81–109.

Young, J. W., *Britain and European Unity, 1945–99* (Basingstoke: Macmillan, 2000).

Young, J. W., 'Killing the MLF? The Wilson Government and Nuclear Sharing in Europe, 1964–6', *Diplomacy & Statecraft* 14/2 (2003), 295–324.

Young, J. W., 'Europe', in A. Seldon and K. Hickson (eds.), *New Labour, Old Labour: The Wilson and Callaghan Governments, 1974–9* (London: Routledge, 2004), 139–53.

Young, J. W., *Twentieth-Century Diplomacy: A Case Study of British Practice, 1963–76* (Cambridge: Cambridge University Press, 2008).

Bibliography

Young, J. W., 'Western Europe and the End of the Cold War, 1979–89', in M. P. Leffler and O. A. Westad (eds.), *The Cambridge History of the Cold War, Vol. III: Endings* (Cambridge: Cambridge University Press, 2010), 289–310.

Zimmermann, H., 'Unravelling the Ties That Really Bind: The Dissolution of the Transatlantic Monetary Order and the European Monetary Cooperation, 1965–73', in M. Schulz and T. A. Schwartz (eds.), *The Strained Alliance: US-European Relations from Nixon to Carter* (Cambridge: Cambridge University Press, 2010), 125–44.

Index

Aaron, David 170
Adenauer, Konrad 32, 33, 40, 86, 218
Afghanistan 19, 151, 162–73, 182, 212
Agt, Dries van 159
Allen, Richard 187
Apel, Hans 81, 83, 113, 136
Argentina 195
Armstrong, Robert 79, 181
Atlantikbrücke 34
Attlee, Clement 26, 30
Australia 21
Austria 208
Auswärtiges Amt 16, 81, 122, 152, 210

Bahr, Egon 185
Bake, Mrs. 24
Basic Treaty 41
Bavaria 114, 115, 116, 156
Bundesverband der Deutschen Industrie (BDI) 136
Benelux 30
Benn, Tony 62, 67, 80, 87, 106, 111, 114, 115, 127
Berlin 28, 34, 39, 131
Berry, Sir Vaughan 25, 26
Brandon, Henry 17
Brandt, Willy 28, 40, 41, 42, 52, 86, 185, 188
Bretton Woods system 45, 46, 47, 55, 90, 95
Brexit 1, 2, 3, 20, 221
Brezhnev, Leonid 144
Britain
    and détente 132, 168–9, 199, 201
    and Empire 21, 22
    and EPC 171
    and European Community See also European Community
    and IMF loan 105–12, 113, 136

and occupation of Germany 3, 24, 26, 29
    and referendum on EC membership 18, 68, 75, 85, 87, 98, 119, 152
    and the European Monetary System 123–9
    attitudes towards European integration 2, 4, 5, 6–7, 10–12, 15, 20, 30–1, 96, 120, 121–2, 126, 127, 165, 170, 177, 188, 193, 205, 206, 208, 209, 210, 211, 212, 213, 214, 216–17, 218, 219–20
    Black Wednesday of (1992) 221
    economic situation of 22, 48, 93, 105–12, 134, 189
    first EC membership application 2, 31, 32, 39, 53, 57
    relationship with United States 1, 3, 12, 29, 50, 51, 91, 132, 143, 147, 170, 171, 215
    second EC membership application 2, 39–40, 53, 57, 213
    winter of discontent 100, 128, 146
British Army of the Rhine 4, 29, 113, 165
British budget contributions 2, 19, 149, 151–61, 164, 167, 173–82, 188, 190–2, 195, 206, 210, 214
    in 1974–5 renegotiations 77–8, 80
    in accession negotiations 56, 154
British Special Air Service [SAS] 117
Brzezinski, Zbigniew 130, 132, 133, 134, 170
Buchan, Alastair 35, 67
Bullock Committee 103
Bundesbank 106, 110, 126, 129, 137, 138
    Schmidt's appearance at Council 129
Bundeskanzleramt 16, 81, 109, 169

Index

247

Bundestag 1, 32, 35, 103, 134, 143, 204, 205
Burns, Arthur 110, 190, 197, 201
Butler, Michael 84

Callaghan, James 17, 26, 100–48, 193, 205, 213–14
  and dual-track decision 145–6
  and economic policy 102–4, 128
  and European Monetary System 123–9
  and Five-Point plan 136, 139, 140
  and G7 summit at Bonn (1978) 134–41
  and German terrorism 116–18
  and 'grey area' problem 144
  and Guadeloupe 145–6, 183
  and IMF loan 105–12
  and JET 114–16
  and Jimmy Carter 132, 133, 137–9, 143, 214
  and North-South conference 95
  and Offset 112–14
  and Schmidt's speech to Labour Party conference (1974) 68, 69
  and Theater Nuclear Forces (TNF) 144
  and United States 19, 89, 132, 134, 139, 147, 214, 217
  and winter of discontent 100, 128, 146
  as foreign secretary 60–1, 62–3, 68, 70, 72, 73, 74, 75, 82, 95, 102, 119, 213
  attitudes towards EC membership 58, 60–1, 62–3, 67, 68, 70, 72, 73, 74, 75, 77, 88, 152, 216–17
  attitudes towards European integration 19, 58, 119–20, 126, 147–8, 216–17
  diplomatic style of 9, 18, 71, 73, 99, 101, 102, 104, 107, 110, 112, 114, 116, 128, 129, 136, 147, 205, 213, 214, 215–16, 218
  personal relationship with Schmidt 19, 122, 129, 136, 144, 146, 214
Cameron, David 221
Carrington, Lord 44, 152, 161, 163, 165, 166, 167, 169, 170, 172, 175, 176, 177, 178, 179, 180, 193, 194

Carstens, Karl 165
Carter, Jimmy 17, 19, 100, 101, 124, 129, 130, 131, 132, 133, 134, 135, 137–9, 140, 143, 145, 162, 163, 164, 166, 167, 169, 170, 171, 182, 183, 214
Castle, Barbara 69
Chequers 73, 74, 75, 79, 108, 193
Christian Democratic Union of Germany (CDU) 86, 115, 136, 205
Christian Social Union of Germany (CSU) 86, 115, 136, 189, 205
Clappier, Bernard 126
COCOM 170
Cold War 6, 8, 14, 20, 22, 23, 28, 29, 32, 35, 40–5, 52, 130, 131, 132, 141–6, 151, 162, 164, 165, 167, 182–8, 195, 199–205, 212, 219, 220
Colombo, Emilio 179
Common Agricultural Policy 59, 154, 155, 156, 173, 175, 176, 195
Commonwealth 3, 21, 57, 59, 72, 73, 74, 76, 84
Conference on Security and Cooperation in Europe 90
Conservative Party, The 44, 129, 150, 151, 153, 161, 174, 190, 221
consumer-producer conference *See also* North-South conference
Cossiga, Francesco 177
Couzens, Ken 125, 126, 127
Crosland, Anthony 106, 111
Cuban Missile crisis 37

Dalton, Hugh 25, 26
Danzig 145
Day, Robin 122
Denman, Roy 97, 118
Denmark 164
Deutschmark 64, 114, 180, 190, 195
Dohnanyi, Klaus von 131, 175, 179
dollar 46, 47, 124, 137, 138, 139, 196
Donoughue, Bernard 72
dual-track decision 145–6, 151, 182–8, 196, 205, 212, 214
Durbin, Evan 26

248 *Index*

EC Commission 65, 78, 83, 84, 95, 127, 154, 160, 166, 167, 174, 179, 190
Economic and Monetary Union 48, 59, 62, 79
economic crisis 64, 86, 94–8, 147, 211
Emminger, Otmar 138
energy crisis 18, 44, 49–51, 92, 94–8, 140
European Political Cooperation (EPC) 4, 169, 171, 172, 173, 194
Eppler, Erhard 185
Ertl, Josef 115, 156
Eurogroup 44
European Coal and Steel Community 2, 30
European Community 1, 2, 21, 30, 31, 32, 35, 37, 38, 39, 49, 118, 119–20, 122, 147
  and British budget contributions *See* British budget contributions
  British membership of 2, 8, 11, 18, 22, 41, 54, 55, 56, 65, 87, 121, 177, 210, 213
  British renegotiation of membership terms 2, 18, 55–85, 98, 128, 154, 210, 213
  Common Fisheries Policy 121, 173
  enlargement of 41
  Franco-German cooperation in 5, 6, 18, 32, 33, 38, 40, 46–7, 49, 52, 54, 66, 75–6, 82–4, 85, 88–9, 93, 127, 160, 171, 177, 181, 191, 192, 193, 211, 212, 213, 215, 217–19
  green currencies 121
  institutional reform of 18, 64, 65–6, 76
  scholarship on 12–15, 219–20
  The Hague summit of (1969) 41
European Council 16, 78, 79, 86, 133
  Bremen (1978) 127
  Brussels (1975) 88, 89
  Brussels (1978) 128
  Brussels (1982) 204
  Copenhagen (1978) 124, 125
  creation of 9, 123
  Dublin (1975) 80–5
  Dublin (1979) 3, 149, 159, 161, 177
  Luxembourg (1976) 124
  Luxembourg (1980) 176, 177, 178
  Luxembourg (1981) 185

  Maastricht (1981) 188
  Rome (1975) 95–8
  Strasbourg (1979) 157
  The Hague (1976) 111
European Defence Community 63
European Economic Community *See* European Community
European Free Trade Area [FTA] 31
European Monetary System 2, 11, 101, 123–9, 136, 147, 166, 167, 173, 210, 214
European Parliament 35, 64, 76, 78, 85, 87, 89, 120
European Regional Fund 56
European Union 1, 2, 62, 208, 221

Falklands War 194–6
Finanzministerium 110, 155
First World War 24, 29, 166
Fischer, Per 79
Foot, Michael 106, 190
Ford, Gerald 17, 85, 90, 91, 93, 94, 101, 110, 111, 112, 130, 132
Foreign Office 16, 61, 86, 102, 119, 210
France 2, 22, 28, 29, 30, 32, 33, 35, 37, 38, 39, 40, 46, 48, 50, 51, 53, 54, 63–6, 75–6, 85, 88–9, 90, 91, 92, 96, 133, 142, 144, 163, 164, 169, 172, 173, 175, 177, 178, 181, 191, 202, 206, 212, 213, 215, 217–19
  See also European Community: Franco-German cooperation in
Franco–German Friendship Treaty 32
Free Democratic Party of Germany 80, 86, 110, 115, 136, 156, 180, 189, 205

G7 world economic summits
  Bonn (1978) 134–41, 147
  creation of 9, 90
  Rambouillet (1975) 90, 91
  Venice (1980) 171
  Versailles (1982) 198–9, 204
Gaulle, Charles de 1, 32, 37, 40, 57, 61, 63, 210, 218
Genscher, Hans-Dietrich 77, 83, 110, 115, 120, 122, 137, 165, 169, 170, 172, 175, 179, 180
German Democratic Republic (GDR) 41

Index

Germany
1976 elections 84, 87, 106, 109, 110, 115
1980 elections 180, 189
and détente 131, 133, 163, 167–8, 199
and economic policy 134, 135–6, 180
and France See European Community:Franco-German cooperation in
and German domestic terrorism 116–18
and transatlantic alliance 92, 142, 143, 185, 214, 218
and United States 37, 38, 52, 53, 133, 134, 138, 143, 163, 164, 171, 212, 215
attitudes towards British EC membership 2, 31–3, 81, 161, 164, 166, 172, 177, 189, 194
attitudes towards European integration 4, 6–7, 10–11, 15, 18, 20, 32, 52, 96, 120, 126, 127, 164, 180, 206, 209, 211, 212, 213, 214, 216–20, 221
contributions to EC budget 155, 178, 180, 190, 192
Ostpolitik of 40–5
rearmament of 29
reunification of 2, 149, 209, 220
situation in 1945, 21, 27, 28
Gilmour, Ian 165, 175, 179, 180
Giscard d'Estaing, Valéry 13, 18, 46–7, 52, 63–4, 65, 66, 71, 74, 79, 88, 89, 91, 92, 93, 100, 101, 125, 127, 145, 155, 156, 161, 172, 173, 174, 177, 178, 185, 187, 213, 214, 218
and Helmut Schmidt 5, 18, 46–7, 52, 63–6, 75–6, 82–4, 88–9, 90, 93, 99, 127, 153, 161, 172, 213, 214, 218
Gladstone, David 172
Godesberg Programme 28
Green Pound See also European Community: green currencies
Ground Launched Cruise Missiles (GLCMs) 183, 184
Guadeloupe summit 145–6
Callaghan's return from 100
Gymnich compromise 52

Habsburg Empire 208
Haig, Al 184, 187, 202
Hamburg 3, 16, 23, 24, 26
Hamburg University 26
Harmel Report 38, 141
Hart, Basil Liddell 35
Hattersley, Roy 66
Healey, Denis 35, 43, 44, 68, 102, 106, 111, 113, 125, 136
Heath, Edward 47, 50, 56, 58, 59, 65, 89, 112, 150, 151, 154
Helsinki Final Act See also Conference on Security and Cooperation in Europe
Henderson, Nicholas 60, 70, 82
High Level Group (HLG) 143
Hitler, Adolf 36, 208
Hong Kong 22
House of Commons 60, 79, 97, 109, 120, 121, 128, 143, 179, 204
Howe, Geoffrey 158, 176
Hunt, John 153

International Energy Agency 92
International Institute for Strategic Studies 34, 35, 142
International Monetary Fund 105–12, 113, 136
Ireland 48
Irish Republican Army 116
Italy 30, 48, 64, 133, 184, 197, 202

Japan 135
Jenkins, Roy 127, 160, 166, 167, 174
Jobert, Michel 50, 51, 92
John Brown Engineering 201, 204
Joint European Torus (JET) 101, 114–16, 118, 147
Jones, Jack 104
Jorgensen, Anker 160

Keynes, John Maynard 198
Kiesinger, Kurt Georg 40
Kissinger, Henry 35, 49, 52, 73, 89, 90, 91, 92, 94, 130, 132
Kohl, Helmut 120, 188, 192, 205, 220
Königswinter 34, 40

Labour Party 25, 26, 43, 57–8, 59, 61, 62–3, 65, 67, 68–70, 98, 100, 102,

103, 106, 109, 113, 120, 126, 127, 187, 189, 190, 213
Liberal Party, The 120
Lufthansa hijacking 116–18
Luxembourg 95

Maastricht Treaty 2, 209, 221
Macmillan, Harold 31, 33, 34, 57
Manchester 23
Martinique Summit (1974) 92
Matthöfer, Hans 114, 115, 125, 175, 180
Messina conference *See also* Treaties of Rome
Middle East 49, 50, 92, 169, 200
Miller, G. William 138
Mitbestimmung 102, 103
Mitterrand, François 185, 186, 191, 192, 193, 195, 196, 197
Mondale, Walter 133
Monnet, Jean 63
Morrison, Herbert 25
Moscow Olympics (1980) 163, 164, 167, 168, 170, 171
Mutual and Balanced Force Reductions (MBFR) 141, 194

NATO 21, 29, 37, 38, 43, 44, 141–6, 151, 165, 170, 182–8, 190, 194, 212
Netherlands, the 48, 164, 184
neutron bomb 137, 143, 144
New Zealand 74
Nitze, Paul 17
Nixon, Richard 49, 64, 90, 124
North-South conference 18, 92, 96, 213
    question of EC representation at 94–8
Nuclear Planning Group 38, 143

Offset 101, 112–14, 118, 147
oil crisis 55, 92, 93, 147, 180 *See also* North-South conference
Organisation for Economic Co-operation and Development (OECD) 92

Organisation of the Petroleum Exporting Countries (OPEC) 49, 50, 92, 93
Ortoli, François-Xavier 65, 95
Owen, David 121
Owen, Henry 140

Palestine Liberation Organization (PLO) 116
Paris 32
Paris summit (1974) 75–80, 86, 88
passport union 65
peace movement 184, 185, 187, 188
Pershing II 183, 188
Pétain, Philippe 33
Pinay, Antoine 63
Poland 19, 133, 151, 199–205, 212, 214
Pompidou, Georges 41, 42, 58, 63
Potsdam 28
Pound Sterling 21, 48, 64, 105, 106, 109, 126
Powell, Enoch 87

Qualified Majority Voting 76, 78
Queen, the 3

Reagan, Ronald 17, 182, 183, 184, 186, 187, 196, 197, 198, 199, 201, 202, 203, 204
Reaganomics 196–9
Rhodesia 168
Richardson, Elliot 17
Ridley, Nicholas 2
Roberts, Frank 218
Ruhrstatut 27

Salisbury, Lord 118
SALT II 141, 142
Salvation Army 69
Sauvagnargues, Jean 63
Schiller, Karl 46, 47
Schleyer, Hanns Martin 116
Schmidt, Helmut 81
    and 'balance of power' 43, 44, 142–6

Index

and Brexit 3
and Britain's first EC application 35, 36, 39
and Britain's second EC application 18, 39–40, 213
and British budget contributions 19, 157, 158–60, 164, 173–4, 178, 180, 206, 214
and détente 40–5, 131, 167–8, 181, 201
and domestic terrorism 116–18
and dual-track decision 145–6, 184, 185, 186
and economic and monetary union 48, 79, 123–4
and economic policy 46–52, 65, 102–4, 134, 139, 189, 190, 197
and European Monetary System 123–9
and France 17–18, 19, 37–9, 40, 42, 46–7, 50, 51, 52, 53, 63–6, 83, 93–4, 164, 191, 192, 212–13, 214, 217–19
and G7 summit at Bonn (1978) 134–41
and 'grey area' problem 142–6
and human rights 131
and IMF loan 105–12
and JET 114–16
and Jimmy Carter 131, 133, 134, 135, 137, 138, 139, 143, 147, 167, 170, 171, 214
and nuclear strategy 34–5, 36, 42–4, 142–6
and Offset 112–14
and Ostpolitik 40–5
and Reaganomics 196, 197, 198
and Ronald Reagan 183
and Siberian pipeline 201, 202
and Soviet invasion of Afghanistan 167–8, 170
and TNF 142–6
and Treaties of Rome 3
and United States 22, 36, 37–9, 50, 51, 53, 89, 92, 124, 125, 142–6, 147, 186, 187, 198, 212–13, 214, 217

and Year of Europe 50
as defence minister 18, 42–4
as finance minister 18, 46–52, 63, 139
as leader of Socialist Student Movement 27
attitudes towards Britain 1, 3, 6–7, 17–18, 20, 22–6, 33–40, 42–3, 53, 159–60, 166–7, 181–2, 189, 192, 194, 195, 206, 207, 210, 212–13, 217, 219–20
attitudes towards British EC membership 1, 3, 42–3, 53, 75, 78, 81–2, 152, 159–60, 165, 166–7, 181–2, 189, 191, 192, 194, 195, 206, 210, 212–13
attitudes towards British renegotiation of EC membership 60, 65, 67–8, 81–2, 213
attitudes towards European integration 1, 3, 6–7, 15, 17–18, 20, 26, 27–8, 33–40, 51, 52, 86, 87, 95, 96, 120, 126, 147–8, 164, 165, 180, 188, 206, 211, 212–13, 214, 216–20
death of 205
diplomatic style of 8, 9, 18, 102, 104, 107, 110, 112, 114, 116, 129, 136, 138, 171, 215–16
election as chancellor 18, 21, 51, 52, 54, 89
end of chancellorship 188
health of 166, 189
IISS speech (1977) 142
memoirs of 3, 23, 149
quest for European energy policy 93–4, 95–8
retirement of 205
school exchange to Manchester (1932) 23–6
speech to Labour Party conference (1974) 68–70
strategic thought of 17–18, 22–3, 27–8, 36, 37–9, 40–5, 53, 212–13, 217–19
Schmidt, Susanne 193
Schüler, Manfred 82
Schulman, Horst 126

Schumacher, Kurt 27
Schuman Plan 28, 30
Second World War 3, 21, 23, 28, 185, 190, 209, 211
Shakespeare, William 68
Shaw, George Bernhard 23
Shore, Peter 80, 179
Shultz, George 198
Siberian Gas Pipeline 200–5
Social Democratic Party of Germany (SPD) 26, 27, 28, 38, 40, 43, 86, 103, 131, 180, 181, 185, 187, 188, 189, 205
Sommer, Theo 2
Soviet Union 19, 28, 29, 35, 36, 37, 96, 130, 131, 132, 133, 141, 142, 144, 145, 151, 162, 165, 167, 182, 184, 186, 195, 200, 202, 203
SS-20s 141, 142, 183
Strauss, Franz-Josef 86, 189

Taylor, Jack 189, 195, 198
Thatcher, Margaret 3, 17, 84, 97, 146, 148, 149–207, 208, 210, 214–15
  and British budget contributions 19, 150, 154–5, 156, 158–9, 173–4, 176, 179, 214
  and détente 161, 162, 167–8
  and dual-track decision 183, 187
  and economic policy 151, 189, 197
  and German reunification 221
  and Reaganomics 197, 198, 199
  and Ronald Reagan 183, 198, 199, 202, 204
  and Siberian pipeline 201, 202, 204
  and Soviet invasion of Afghanistan 163, 167–8, 170
  and United States 161, 170, 202, 214, 217
  attitudes towards EC membership 13, 19, 149–50, 151–2, 155, 205, 206, 216–17
  attitudes towards European integration 2, 13, 19, 149–50, 151–2, 155, 188, 191, 205, 206, 214, 216–17, 221
  diplomatic style of 19, 158, 161, 180, 205, 215–16
  election of 150, 151, 162, 167
  handbag of 3

money of 149, 161
  resignation of 149
Theatre Nuclear Forces (TNF) 141, 142–6, 186, 187, 194
Thorn, Gaston 95, 190
Trade Union Congress 102, 104
transatlantic alliance *See also* NATO
Treaties of Rome 1, 3, 35, 52, 62
Treaty of Accession 62
Treaty of Rome 88
Treaty of Warsaw 41

Übersee-Club 119
UN Resolution 242 49
United States 1, 3, 7, 22, 23, 28, 29, 34, 36, 37, 38, 39, 46, 49, 50, 52, 53, 63, 92, 93, 96, 111, 112, 125, 130, 132, 135, 139, 140, 141, 142, 143, 162, 163, 164, 168, 185, 190, 197, 198, 199, 201, 202, 203, 204, 212, 215

Walesa, Lech 203
Washington Energy Conference 50, 51, 52, 89
Weimar Germany 27, 33
Weinberger, Caspar 188
Western European Union (WEU) 29
Wilde, Oscar 23
Wilson, Harold 3, 17, 18, 19, 54–99, 112, 119, 148, 205, 210, 213
  and agreement to differ 80
  and Britain's first EC application 57
  and Britain's second EC application 40
  and Commonwealth 57, 72, 74, 76, 84
  and EC institutional reforms 65, 66, 88, 120
  and renegotiation of EC membership terms 60, 62–3, 67, 70–5, 80, 85, 98–9, 221
  and United States 85, 89
  as prime minister (1964–1970) 57
  at G7 Rambouillet summit 91
  attitudes towards EC membership 13, 18, 56, 58, 62–3, 67, 68, 70–5, 78, 80, 82, 85, 96, 98–9, 216–17

Index 253

attitudes towards European
  integration 56–7, 58, 67, 70–5, 78,
  85, 88, 89, 96, 98–9
clashes with Schmidt over North-
  South conference 95–8
diplomatic style of 72, 73, 98–9, 101,
  107, 128, 205, 215–16
election as prime minister (1974) 59,
  89
health of 72

resignation of 97, 102
Wischnewski, Hans-Jürgen 82, 86
Wright, Oliver 118, 175, 178, 194

Yale University 1
Yalta 28
Year of Europe 49–51, 89
Yom Kippur War 45, 49

zero option 188